The Miracles of Our Lord. a Course of Schoolroom Lects. Ed. by a Member of the Congregation
by Edward Walker

Address:
HardPress
8345 NW 66TH ST #2561
MIAMI FL 33166-2626
USA
Email: info@hardpress.net

THE
MIRACLES OF OUR L

SCHOOL ROOM LECTU

EDWARD WALKER

THE MIRACLES OF OUR LORD.

THE

MIRACLES OF OUR LORD.

A COURSE OF

SCHOOLROOM LECTURES.

BY THE

REV. EDWARD WALKER, D.C.L.,
RECTOR OF CHELTENHAM.

" The Works that I do, they bear witness of ME."—St. John x. 25.

EDITED BY

A MEMBER OF THE CONGREGATION.

LONDON:
JAMES NISBET & CO., 21 BERNERS STREET.
1872.

PREFATORY NOTE.

The welcome accorded to "Notes of Open-Air Sermons" has induced the Editor to accede to the request of many friends, to publish these Notes of Lectures on the Miracles, most of which were delivered by the Rev. Dr. Walker during the winter of 1870–71, in the Parish Church Schoolroom, Cheltenham—and were intended chiefly for the working-classes and the very poor. Two or three of the Miracles were omitted in that Course, and these have been supplied, as far as possible, from Notes of Wednesday Evening Lectures in the Temporary (Parish) Church.

It must be remembered that these were not written discourses, each one being but a simple, extemporary exposition of the Gospel narrative, in the homeliest possible language—given after the arduous labours of the day, and in failing health.

It must also be remembered, that, in an audience such as that to which these Lectures were addressed, there would be many who needed ideas put before them in the very simplest way, and with much repetition. No attempt has been made to alter this, but the Lectures are given almost word for word as they were spoken.

The reader will notice that a few of the Lectures are given with less fulness than others, and also appear to lack the vigour which characterizes the rest. It is impossible in writing to give any equivalent for the solemn, pleading, earnest tones which rendered these, when delivered, some of the most impressive in the Course—and the very earnestness of which sometimes made the attempt to give a full literal report ineffectual. This will explain the want of connection apparent, here and there, in two or three of the Lectures.

It was manifest afterwards, that the effort on the part of the speaker—which rendered these Lectures so solemnly impressive, and so difficult to report adequately — was the premonitory sign of that illness against which, we now know, how he struggled through the winter, but which, only a few days after the last of these Lectures was delivered, assumed a serious form, and laid him aside for some months.

The Editor feels it is due to Dr. Walker that thus much should be said; and it is with heartfelt thanksgiving for his partial restoration to health, and the earnest hope that these words of his may be sown far and wide, that this volume is commended to the public.

CHELTENHAM, *November* 1871.

INDEX OF CONTENTS.

LECTURE I.

THE WATER MADE WINE.

ST. JOHN ii. 1—11.

NOVEMBER 1, 1870.

NOTES ON THE MIRACLES.

LECTURE I.

THE WATER MADE WINE.

" And the third day there was a marriage in Cana of Galilee; and the mother of Jesus was there. And both Jesus was called, and his disciples, to the marriage. And when they wanted wine, the mother of Jesus saith unto him, They have no wine. Jesus saith unto her, Woman, what have I to do with thee? mine hour is not yet come. His mother saith unto the servants, Whatsoever he saith unto you, do it. And there were set there six waterpots of stone, after the manner of the purifying of the Jews, containing two or three firkins apiece. Jesus saith unto them, Fill the waterpots with water. And they filled them up to the brim. And he saith unto them, Draw out now, and bear unto the governor of the feast. And they bare it. When the ruler of the feast had tasted the water that was made wine, and knew not whence it was; (but the servants which drew the water knew;) the governor of the feast called the bridegroom, and saith unto him, Every man at the beginning doth set forth good wine; and when men have well drunk, then that which is worse; but thou hast kept the good wine until now. This beginning of miracles did Jesus in Cana of Galilee, and manifested forth his glory; and his disciples believed on him."—ST. JOHN ii. 1–11.

THIS is the *first*, this is the *" beginning* of the miracles," that Jesus Christ wrought upon earth. You know there were those who said to Him in after days, "What sign shewest thou then, that we may see, and believe thee?" (St. John vi. 30).   They asked Him to do some great, wonderful thing, to convince them that He had a right and title to that claim which He set up—that He was the MESSIAH—that He had been "sent" of God.   They asked Him to show His supernatural power over material things—to prove that He had a rightful claim to the allegiance of the human soul. Here we find that Jesus, who had begun His ministry a few weeks before—(He had been baptized of John, He had been tempted of the devil, He had begun to teach in public, He had called five persons to be His disciples or followers)—now proceeds to take another step—to confirm His teaching by His *works*.   "This beginning of miracles did Jesus."

I need not stop to explain what a *miracle* is.   It appears to us to be the violation of the laws of nature; and indeed it is such an alteration, or interruption, of the course of nature, and is ever attended with the production of such results, as clearly prove the presence of superhuman power.   So now we find Jesus Christ doing mighty deeds, in order to show *who* and *what* He was. We find Him working miracles for this purpose—to "manifest," to set forth, "His glory."

Now, there is nothing in the world of such importance to us as to learn what Jesus Christ is, and to see how glorious is His exceeding excellency; because there is nothing else given us to save us and to bless us but only Jesus Christ.   And therefore we want to know who and what He *is*, and what He can *do*, what is in His heart, and what is the power of His arm. So, to manifest His glory, to show forth who and what He is, He did "*this*" great wonder.

"**And the third day there was a marriage in Cana of Galilee.**"

A little place is Cana of Galilee, in the tribe of Asher, in the northern part of the Holy Land; and, you know, it was said by Jacob, hundreds and hundreds of years before, of Asher in Genesis xlix., that he should "yield royal dainties." So these "royal dainties" are produced by Jesus, the Messiah, in this little, insignificant place called "Cana of Galilee." There are certain things to be noticed here. *First*, we find Jesus Christ and His disciples invited to a marriage, and they went. I scarcely need stop to point out what everybody has noticed, that this shows what an honourable estate matrimony is, instituted as it was in the time of man's innocence, and which Jesus Christ adorned and beautified with His presence, and with the working of His first miracle in Cana. It is Jesus Christ, you see, putting His hand on this holy estate, consecrating it, showing that it is holy. It was the *first* ordinance of God in Paradise; and here the *first* miracle of Jesus is performed at a marriage.

"**There was a marriage in Cana of Galilee, and the mother of Jesus was there. And both Jesus was called, and His disciples, to the marriage.**"

Now, all this shows another thing. It shows us that Christian people are not always to be going, as it were, to a funeral,—that they are not always to be shedding tears. I know it is a very hard thing to be both merry and wise at the same time ; yet this shows us that it is right and lawful, and that there is " a time to *rejoice*" as well as " a time to *weep*" (Eccles. iii. 4). Marriages are, proverbially, times of rejoicing. You may be quite sure that a marriage at which Jesus Christ was present, was conducted in a lawful, right, godly, pure, and holy way, from the beginning to the end,—you may be sure that there would be nothing foolish, nothing improper, nothing vain. Jesus Christ could not have been in any such scene, or have sanctioned any such doings. Thus we see this, that Christian people are not debarred from joyful, bright things ; that they are not to be always going about the world with a mournful, heavy heart, and that a marriage should be a time full of brightness, and of peaceful, happy enjoyment.

"This beginning of miracles" was wrought on a bright, joyful, happy occasion ; and it shows us this, too, that at the beginning of His ministry, Christ would give a little foretaste of what was to come, when it is said, " Blessed are they which are called unto *the marriage-supper of the Lamb*" (Rev. xix. 9). Those people who called Jesus Christ to *their* marriage will, no doubt, be called *by* Jesus Christ to *His* marriage-supper, when all the saints, the whole Church, shall appear together with Him, "in the day of His espousals, and in the day of the gladness of His heart" (Song iii. 11).

But people do not always, at a marriage, call Jesus Christ to it. You know there is (perhaps it is outside the subject—still, I think I ought to dwell on it—there is) such a thing as backsliding nationally, and there is such a thing as a nation forgetting what its duties are. And, when we see a nation celebrating marriages at which Jesus Christ is not to be named, surely there must be something wrong. Many people, now, get their marriages conducted, without even the pretence of asking the presence of Jesus Christ. And people, too, may even go to church, and be married by the best service, with the very best prayers; but, if it is not in their hearts to call Jesus Christ to be the Head of the feast, it is just as if they had not made the *pretence* of doing so. But this wedding festival was one to which Jesus Christ *was* invited with His disciples, and they came.

And then we find that something went wrong. There are few occasions in the world, where there is not something that goes wrong. So, even at *this* marriage, something went wrong.

"They wanted wine."

A Jewish marriage took a long time to get over. It took several days to transact all its affairs. There was something or other to keep up, and many things to be done; and there must be food and drink and amusement all provided for the guests—so that it was a serious matter (and it is a serious matter even now) amongst the Jews, to get married,—there is such a deal of form and ceremony. So here. Before the thing was well over, they had not enough of one of the principal elements of the feast—" they wanted *wine.*" There was no more wine.

Now, we must always remember this—that when Jesus Christ was here on earth, He was conversant amongst *poor* people. His reputed father was a "carpenter," and Jesus Himself wrought at the same trade, and was *called* "the carpenter." All His relations, though they were of royal and noble extraction, were very poor in Israel; so that their friends and relations would be in the same condition. And therefore, those people, who would ask Jesus and His mother to a wedding, would not be likely to have too much of this world's goods; so that it is not any wonder to us to find that the wine ran short. And when this was so, this circumstance happened——

"The mother of Jesus saith unto him, They have no wine."

It was a strange thing for her to say. Remember, she had never *seen* Him work a miracle before; and we do not know that she had got any idea *that He* COULD work miracles. This is a fact nevertheless,—though she had never seen Him work a miracle; and we ask, Why is this—that "when they wanted wine, the mother of Jesus saith unto *him*, They have no wine"? She does not say any more; she simply comes and says, "*They have no wine.*" Many have sought to find out the meaning of this, and have given various explanations of it. I cannot say that I see anything in it but this,—whatever may have been her thoughts, whatever her expectations might have been, I see no more than this—that she had found out in the years which she had passed with Him at Nazareth—when He had said,

"Wist ye not that I must be about my Father's business?"—and when He went down to Nazareth, and was "subject to" her, setting an example to all youth—in all those years He lived with her, whenever she was in a *difficulty*, she naturally went to Him,—whenever she was in *trouble*, she naturally went to Him; and so it had come to pass, gradually and imperceptibly, that when there was *any* trouble, *any* difficulty, *any* sorrow, *any* want, it was all carried to HIM. And she had found out, in course of time, that He had the right word for every sorrowful case, that He had a remedy for everything that went wrong; so that they naturally came to Him to get things set right in the whole house, in all the family relationship. This was very simple—very natural. Remember, He was now thirty years old; He had only just appeared in public; but He had lived those thirty years in His home at Nazareth, and, of course, they would find out that He was not a common man—that He was *more* than a man. They would find out that He never spake a wrong word, that He never did anything that was wrong. They had never seen a single instance of selfishness, they had never found a single flaw in anything He said or did; therefore, it was natural that when she was in difficulty or sorrow, His mother should come to Him straight away. Here there is a calamity, a misfortune in the house—the wine has run short. Mary is so accustomed to go to Him in any difficulty, that she runs *now* to Him, and says—" There is a difficulty, 'they have no wine.'"

That appears to me to be the natural meaning of her

words.   She had never found Him fail her, so she goes
to Him now.   He had always the right word for her;
He had sympathy, resources, tenderness, strength, and
compassion.   Whatever went amiss in all that family, no
doubt of it, all those thirty years, she carried to Him to
set it right.   It was a little thing apparently, but
whether they were little things or great things, if they
were troublesome or hard, she went to Him—just as
we ought to go to Him *now*,—just as every real Christian who has fellowship with Christ should go like John
and lean on His bosom,—go like Mary and sit at His
feet,—go like the Virgin with this trouble, and say
simply what it was—" they have no wine."   It was very
simply said; she just spread it before Him, just like
Mary and Martha when they sent to tell Jesus that
Lazarus was sick,—without making much ado about it.
   Now comes THE ANSWER OF JESUS.
   **"Jesus saith unto her, Woman, what have I to do
with thee ?   Mine hour is not yet come."**
   Now, I don't think there is any disrespect here.
Jesus Christ was never guilty of *any* disrespect.   Jesus
Christ was never *guilty of anything*.   But He was perfectly *incapable* of a hard word to His mother; He was
perfectly incapable of using any single word of disrespect to her in any way.   Therefore, I have no sympathy with people who seem to represent Jesus as
putting her down, as it were, because He says " *Woman*."
There is no more respectful word, in our English language, than the word *woman*.   It is the highest and
noblest word we have, and the most *respectful* word.

It is the very word our blessed Lord used on the cross, when he said to Mary, " *Woman*, behold thy son " (St. John xix. 26). I do not think there is anything but respectfulness and tenderness in this. But it is true that these words are very peculiar. You all know that Jesus Christ did not talk to His mother in the English language. I suppose you all know that,—little children know it; they do not talk English in the far East. When Jesus said, "Woman, what have I to do with thee?" the words in the Greek language are, literally, " *What to me and to thee?*" Now, you may make as much out of that as you can. In the ordinary translation it is, " What have I to do with thee?" But, literally, "What is it to me and to thee? What is there in common between me and thee—between thy thoughts and my thoughts—in this matter? Mine hour is not yet come."

No doubt, in this our blessed and Divine Lord was not giving her a rebuke; no, *not a rebuke*, but gentle instruction, to one who did not know very well what she was about on this occasion. She knew *one* thing,—she knew that her beloved Son could set all difficult things right. And oh! what a blessed thing it would be if we *all* knew that,—if we all felt that we have One who is *ours*, One to whom we are related and united, to whom we may go with any difficulty, and be sure that He will set it right. She knew *that*, but she did not know what was going to happen. She was not quite up to this; so He says, "What to me and to thee? Mine hour is not yet come. You cannot understand exactly what I am going to be about. *Mine hour is not yet come.*"

What does that mean? I will tell you what I think it means. It means simply this, she saw the wine was being drawn off; it was not quite exhausted, but she saw that very soon, before more could be got (and she did not know where from), it would all be gone. But Jesus said, "*It must* ALL *be gone first.* They must not only use it, but they must all find out that it is done. There must be no collusion, no deception, no excuse for fancying that there has been a deception. *Mine* hour is not yet come." Oh, let us never forget this— Jesus Christ has His own time for helping His people, and He will have them feel their want before He supplies it; He will have them feel their disease before He will cure it; He will have them find out their necessities and difficulties before He helps them. *His* "hour" is when nobody else can help; when the woman had spent all her living on many physicians, and was nothing better, but rather the worse, *then* was His time. It was not His time, so long as she had got any money left to pay any more fees; it was not His time, so long as she was not satisfied that the physicians could not cure her: but when her money was all gone, and the physicians were used up, *then* was *His* time: and His hour is "the time of love" (Ezek. xvi. 8). So here, when the wine was not quite used up, "Mine hour is *not yet* come," but it will come.

And what did she do? Look at this blessed woman, and remember that if anybody knew Him, *she* ought to have known Him. If anybody was likely to have a right thought about Him, *she* was ; and what does she do? She immediately takes His word, she has no reply to make to it, but she goes to the servants and says—

"**Whatsoever He saith unto you, do it.**"

Now, that was *Mary's* estimate of CHRIST. That was her preaching. She preached to these servants about Him. "Whatsoever He saith unto you, *do*." Oh, she was a grand preacher of Jesus Christ when she said that! It was a grand sermon for her to preach— "Whatsoever *He* saith unto you, do." Yes, she knew what He was; she knew what she was about—she knew what she meant when she said, "Whatsoever He saith." Oh, it was a good, faithful, happy discourse ! Short it was, but wonderfully powerful and suggestive.

My dear friends, what I say to you to-night, is just only this—"Whatsoever *He* saith unto you, do." Oh, what happy people we should all be if we did it ! How happy should we be in our hearts, in our lives, in our homes, if only we listened to that sermon of the Virgin Mary—" Whatsoever He saith unto you, do it." Yes— there can be no happiness really to us, there can be no turning of our water into wine, unless we hear in our inmost hearts, "Whatsoever He saith unto you, that do."—Everything was ready.

"**There were set there six waterpots of stone, after the manner of the purifying of the Jews, containing two or three firkins apiece. Jesus saith unto them, Fill the waterpots with water.**"

There was a reason for having these waterpots, because the Jews did nothing without washing. If they went only to the market, they would not go without washing. And there is a great deal in this. Somebody has said—"Cleanliness is next to godliness"—and I quite agree with him ; though *they* made a *superstitious* use of it. All these Jews would require a good deal of water for their purifying ablutions, and so forth. "There were (therefore) set there six waterpots of stone,"—holding, perhaps, say five-and-twenty gallons apiece—these six waterpots ; so that they were capable of holding a considerable quantity. And Jesus presently says to the servants—"Fill the waterpots with *water*." Nothing else but water was put there. Now the first miracle, you remember, that *Moses* wrought was *turning water* into BLOOD ; the first miracle of *Jesus Christ* is *turning water* into WINE.

I have little to say about this wine. I do not suppose it was the intoxicating drink made in this country, though it did intoxicate, and we have warnings against the over-use of it. But here it is clear, that much wine was used at this feast, and that it was consecrated by Jesus Christ. Many are not to be trusted with it, and many ought not to be trusted to touch it at all. But there was no danger at this feast, at any rate. And

"Jesus saith unto them, Draw out now, and bear unto the governor of the feast."

One person was chosen to preside at the feast, generally a near relative. Just as we choose a chairman at a public meeting to regulate affairs, so the Jews chose an honourable person, who took the chief place, and regulated all the proceedings at the marriage festival, and had the seat of honour; and Jesus says, "Bear unto the governor of the feast"—to the chief person—and let him taste it.

"**When the ruler of the feast had tasted the water that was made wine, and knew not whence it was.**" It was a new taste; it had not a taste like what he had had before, and he "knew not whence it was." The Lord's work was to speak for itself. He bore no witness to Himself. He did not lift up His voice to proclaim His glory. His works, which He did, bare witness of Him. And we, too—oh, how often—receive the gift, drink the good wine of His bounty, not knowing *whence* it is. Happy for us, if His servants who have done His bidding, and know "the secret of the Lord," are at hand to teach us who He is, who gives such superabundant and precious gifts. If temporal blessings, if spiritual blessings come to us, do we know *whence* they come? The gift should lead us on to the Giver; the good wine in our hands must be the witness to us of the love, and grace, and power of Him who, that we might drink the "new" wine of the kingdom, poured out His own most precious Blood. "He knew not whence it was, **but the servants which drew the water knew.**"

I have already said, that these were poorish people, and their wine would probably be of a poor, sickly flavour—perhaps a sort of make-shift. Now, the governor of the feast got *this*, and, not knowing where it came from, and because it was so wondrously different from what he had previously been drinking, he sent for the bridegroom, whose business it was to provide everything for the festive occasion, and saith unto him,

"Every man at the beginning doth set forth good wine; and when men have well drunk (so that they do not care much about the taste), **then that which is worse; but thou hast kept the good wine until now."**

He says, "This is the way at a marriage-feast: the bridegroom brings out his best first, and then gives the worst last; that's the way." Yes, that was the way at marriage-feasts, and elsewhere too. That's the way all the world over—the good first, and then the bad. "*Every one*, at the *beginning*, doth set forth *good* wine: and when men have well drunk, *then* that which is *worse*." Yes; just as the roguish man puts his good potatoes at the top of the sack, and the worst at the bottom. And the deceitful world does just the same: it gives people their good things first—it gives them the pleasures of sin, and its enjoyments and delights, and what will gratify the mind and heart, and carnal wishes and carnal tastes. It gives all that, and *then* it fails at length, and THEN, alas! comes, indeed, "that which is worse." We get our health and strength *first*, but pain and sorrow at *last*. "Every one at the beginning doth set forth good wine, . . . but *thou hast* KEPT the *good* wine until now."

Jesus Christ does just the other thing; whether He gives the worst or not, He always gives the best last. He gives first the cross, and at last He gives the crown. He gives trial and tribulation, it may be, in the world, but He gives rest, and peace, and glory at last. In his lifetime, the worldling has his "*good* things," and, in eternity, he gets his "*evil* things." But the believer has, in his lifetime, whatever evil things he will ever have, and then he gets life everlasting. Here we have all the sorrow we shall ever have, and then comes an "exceeding and eternal weight of glory." There may be a time of tears and trouble, of difficulty and sore pressure, to be passed through here, but the good wine is kept, and comes at last. Jesus Christ does here, what He does with regard to all His people, in His dealings with them—He keeps the good wine till the last. The world may try and delude you, and give you good things—things, at least, that you *think* good—things to please and satisfy you for a moment; and then, what more has it to give! Then, only what is *worse*, and *worse*, and *worse*. But they who come and seek for the right to go to the marriage-feast with Jesus Christ, will find that the *best* is LAST, and that the *last* is FOR EVER. "This beginning of miracles" showed what He was, this showed what He could do, how worthy He was to be obeyed. Therein, He **"manifested forth His glory."**

Now, let us just gather up two or three,—we cannot attempt to gather up all, but just two or three—of the chief thoughts, to carry away with us to-night. The *first* is, the necessity of being *related to Jesus Christ*. But, before we can become related to Him, we must have come to Him, and, as poor sinners, have been,

B

by the Holy Spirit, united to Him. We must be "married" to Him, as the apostle Paul says; yes, he uses that word, "*married*" to Him (Rom. vii. 4). We must come as sinners, just as we are, and ask to be made part of His Spouse, of His Bride. And when once we are related to Him, what then? Here we have a woman nearly related to Jesus Christ, and all who believe in Him are His "mother, and sisters, and brethren," and as much related to Him as the Virgin Mary, for even her true relationship with Him was really "by faith," as yours is. She called Him "God *my* SAVIOUR" (St. Luke i. 47); that was the true relationship. And what did *she* do? She brings (it came natural to her, as we say), she brings every one of her burdens and puts them on Him, and that is what He delights in. We do not find that the most part of mankind, when we throw our burden at their feet, care to share it. But He delights in it; that is what He is for. He is the burden-bearer of His people. "Cast thy burden upon the Lord, and He shall sustain thee" (Ps. lv. 22). And this good woman did this. She knew how kindly He would take it up, and how thoroughly He would bear it; so she casts all upon Him, her own and other people's burdens, too. "They will be in trouble and ashamed" (she says), "and I come and lay the burden on Thee." You will say, They might have done without, that it was not as if it had been bread, or some necessary thing. But this shows us that *everything* is to go to Him, and that it is our *privilege* to take everything to Him. Oh, what a friend, then, is Jesus Christ !

The next lesson is in the words of the Virgin Mary, —" Whatsoever He saith unto you, do it." Do we know what Jesus Christ has " said ?" Amongst other things He *said*, " Blessed are the poor in spirit ;" He *said*, " Blessed are the meek ;" He *said*, " Except ye repent, ye shall perish ;" He *said*, " Repent and believe the gospel ;" He *said*, " Except a man be born again, he cannot see the kingdom of God ;" He *said*, " Come unto me, all ye that labour and are heavy laden, and I will give you *rest*." " *Whatsoever* He saith unto you, DO." But first, before we can do it, we must find out what He has said. · The first thing we have to do, is to ask what Jesus Christ has *said*. Then, having found out what He has said from His own word, we have to *do* it. He *said* to these servants, " Fill the waterpots with water." They did not ask questions, whether it would be any good ? *Why* should they fill them up ? They were told to bear to the governor of the feast, and they did not say, Why should they bear *water* to him who expected *wine ?* They did not say, This is surely poor beverage, and we may get only rebuke. No ! at the word of Jesus they drew out, and bare it to the governor. They questioned not, because they had been told (and they believed the word), " *Whatsoever* He saith unto you, *do* it."

Now, if He says, Come to Me,—Believe on Me ; if He says, Repent ; if He says, Obey, DO IT—do *whatever* He *says*.

And there is another lesson. In any trouble, we may go to Him, as freely as she who spread before Him this small care, " they have no wine."

And last, but not least, there is the great Giver, the great Storehouse, the true Joseph, here set before us. Joseph, you know, laid up the corn of Egypt, that he might have abundance to give to the famine-stricken people; and all came to get their corn, their *good* things from him. So here, Jesus Christ is the great Storehouse. He can turn the *water* of earthly sorrow into the *wine* of heavenly joy; He can turn troubles into blessings; He can make homes of sorrow the abodes of peace and consolation; and, if not, if He sees not fit now to turn my water into wine,—if my wine is half-sour, if my wine is very poor, it will only be for a little while; He KEEPS the *good* wine, and, at last, He gives the good wine—joy and great gladness; and " blessed are they which are called unto the marriage-supper of the Lamb."

If even you carry home these three thoughts, we shall not have met in vain. I hope, please God, to be here next week, and then to go on to tell you about another of the wonderful things, which were wrought by Him whose Name is " Wonderful."

II.

THE HEALING OF THE NOBLEMAN'S SON.

"*Now, after two days he departed thence, and went into Galilee. For Jesus himself testified, that a prophet hath no honour in his own house. Then when he was come into Galilee, the Galilæans received him, having seen all the things that he did at Jerusalem at the feast: for they also went unto the feast. So Jesus came again into Cana of Galilee, where he made the water wine. And there was a certain nobleman, whose son was sick at Capernaum. When he heard that Jesus was come out of Judæa into Galilee, he went unto him, and besought him that he would come down, and heal his son; for he was at the point of death. Then said Jesus unto him, Except ye see signs and wonders, ye will not believe. The nobleman saith unto him, Sir, come down ere my child die. Jesus saith unto him, Go thy way; thy son liveth. And the man believed the word that Jesus had spoken unto him, and he went his way. And as he was now going down, his servants met him, and told him, saying, Thy son liveth. Then inquired he of them the hour when he began to amend. And they said unto him, Yesterday at the seventh hour the fever left him. So the father knew that it was at the same hour, in the which Jesus said unto him, Thy son liveth; and himself believed, and his whole house. This is again the second miracle that Jesus did, when he was come out of Judæa into Galilee.*"— ST. JOHN iv. 43–54.*

THERE had been a long time between the work which we read of last Tuesday night, and this wonder-

ful miracle.   The turning of water into wine was
accomplished by our blessed Lord, in the *first* year of
His ministry—about the month of February; and it
seems that the miracle we have now to consider, was
wrought at (what we should call) the end of our year
—late in December, or in the beginning of the January
after.   Therefore, there had been a long interval between the turning water into wine and this miracle,
which was wrought by Jesus again in Cana of Galilee.
You will say, What had the Lord been doing in all
that interval of time?   *One* thing we know, that He
went up to Jerusalem to the passover, and that when
He went up to Jerusalem to the passover, certain
strange things happened; and, amongst them, this was
the first thing—Jesus made a whip of small cords, and
drove the buyers and the sellers out of the temple.
Then, at the end of the second chapter of this Gospel,
we are told of many wonderful things that He did.
Many miracles were wrought by Him in Jerusalem, of
which no account is given, for "if all the works which
Jesus did . . . . should be written every one, I suppose
that even the world itself could not contain the books
that should be written" (St. John xxi. 25).   But He
did such things, and so many, that "many believed on
Him,"—they said He was a prophet.

Another thing happened there—a chief man among
the Pharisees, "a ruler of the Jews," Nicodemus by
name, was so struck by the works of Jesus, that, afraid
lest the rulers should excommunicate him, he actually
went, under cover of the night, to ask Jesus about these

miracles, and said, "Rabbi, we know that thou art a teacher come from God : for no man can do these miracles that thou doest, except God be with him." You remember all about it, and what Jesus said, and then how He told him the precious story, "God so loved the world, that He gave His only-begotten Son, that whosoever believeth in Him should not perish, but have everlasting life" (St. John iii. 2, 16). Very well. Then there were other things done in all this time ; and, at length, *Jesus went back again from Judæa into Galilee.* That was very much as if we were to travel from London up into Yorkshire, and, you know, that if you have got to travel from London to Yorkshire, you have to go through the Midland Counties. So it is said of Jesus, that " He must needs go through *Samaria,*" which was, so to speak, the midland county in the Holy Land. And, you remember, what happened when He was passing through it—He sat on a well, "wearied with his journey," and there came a woman, not at all a respectable character either, and Jesus asked her for water. And many of you, I daresay, remember the interesting conversation that took place, but it is necessary for me to dwell on one thing, because it forms a very striking contrast to something that we shall have to speak of presently. She said to many whom she came in contact with, " Come to Jacob's well, and see a man which told me all things that ever I did." Now that was very astonishing. Jesus had not done it *really.* He had only told her certain things about herself, and she says, " He told

me *this*, therefore He sees *all* that is in my heart—
come and see Him." And they went, and saw Jesus
sitting by Jacob's well, and then they said this, " Now
we believe, not because of *thy* saying, for we have
heard Him *ourselves*, and know that this is indeed the
Christ, the Saviour of the world." *What* convinced
them ? *What* convinced the woman of Samaria ? *Not*
the miracles, not the cure of her child, not the making
water into wine. Jesus did no miracle there. When
she said, " How can you draw without a vessel ? " He
might have done it ; but He did not. He just said a
few words, He told her a certain thing, and she said,
" I know it *must* be He, even the Christ—come and
see." And they came, and He *spoke* to them, and they,
too, believed—not because He wrought a miracle, but
because they heard Christ's word. And, you may depend upon this, when Christ's word comes, by the
Holy Ghost, into the heart, men are as much convinced, nay, more surely convinced, than if Christ
raised the very dead before their eyes.

Well now, this brings us up to our present subject.
The Samaritans believed on him. " They besought
Him that He would tarry with them." Strange that was !
Some didn't want Him, they asked Him to " *depart* out
of their coasts " (St. Matt. viii. 34) ; but these wanted
Him to *stop*, not because He multiplied their loaves,
not because He healed their sick, or opened their
graves, but because He had opened their hearts, and
they thus knew that Christ was able to save their
souls. He tarried there two days, and then went to

the northern part of the land, where He generally was.

There is one thing here, that is a little difficult. He went because **"a prophet hath no honour in his own country."** Galilee was His own country. True, He was born in Bethlehem, but He did not stop in Bethlehem. Nobody dreamed of Bethlehem's being His country. The place that is called "His own country" was *Nazareth*, and when He was going back to Galilee, it would have been natural for Him to go to Nazareth, where He had been brought up. But He didn't, He went somewhere else, because you remember what the Nazarenes had done. They had tried to kill Him. He had gone into the synagogue, and had said many precious things to them, but they "rose up, and thrust Him out of the city, and led Him unto the brow of the hill whereon their city was built, that they might cast Him down headlong" (St. Luke iv. 29). But they could not. He went away—and this was the "honour" He received in "His own country." So He went to another place, and thus the very place which He had left in February, is naturally the spot for Him to go to now. His mother evidently had relatives there. Nathanael was of "Cana in Galilee" (St. John xxi. 2), Nathanael, "an Israelite indeed, in whom was no guile" (i. 47), and he was likely to have a house and a home there open for the Lord.

"The Galilæans received Him."

What made the Galilæans receive Him? They received Him, not as the Samaritans, but for another reason, not for so good a reason by half,—for a *fair* reason, but not for so *good* a reason.   Jesus had done no miracle in *Samaria*, but He had made the Samaritans look at themselves; He had shown them what they were, He had shown them their need of a Saviour, and that is *the best thing*—and because He had done *that*, they asked Him to stop.   And that is the only thing which will, truly and infallibly, make us the friends and companions of Jesus Christ.   We might see the dead raised, and yet presently be ready enough, as the Jews, to cry, "Crucify Him."   The only safe thing is to be made to look ourselves in the face, to be shown our own hearts, and our own need, and then to learn how Jesus Himself came to supply that spiritual need.

Why then did the Galilæans receive Him?   Because they had

"seen all the things that He did at Jerusalem at the feast."

You remember that "when He was in Jerusalem at the passover, in the feast day, many believed in His name, when they saw the miracles which He did" (ii. 23).   We have no history of these miracles, but no doubt they were very striking.   Perhaps He healed the sick, cured the paralytic, cleansed the lepers, opened the eyes of blind men.   At any rate, He wrought *many* miracles, and the Galilæans had seen them.   *How* came they to see them?

"For they also went unto the feast."

Think for a moment of these Galilæans, away in the north; there were no railways, no stage-coaches then. It was hard work to travel.   There were *no roads* there even ; there are none yet—there are not fifty miles of good road in Palestine *now*, and certainly not *then.* The roads were impassable, there was no convenience, yet they go from the north of the country right away to Jerusalem. These men had gone in the month of February to the Feast of the Passover. The law commanded that all the men should go up to Jerusalem to the feasts three times a year. If they had not gone to the feast, they would not have seen Jesus ; if they had not seen Jesus, they would not have had the chance of seeing His miracles. People do not know what they *lose by not going* to the feast, not to a carnal feast, but to the Feast of the Passover. And what *was* the Feast of the Passover? It was the setting forth, in type, of Jesus as the "Lamb of God that taketh away the sin of the world." The Passover Feast was the great setting forth of Jesus Christ—the paschal lamb set Him forth before all, as the sacrifice for sin ; and Jesus Christ, as a *slain* Lamb, was the sum and substance of that feast. People do not know what they lose when they do not go up to the feast. Wherever Christ is preached, there is a kind of Passover Feast, and people who do not go to the feast, and have their eyes and their ears opened, do not know *what* they miss. They miss the seeing of Christ, and the seeing of the miracles of Christ, they miss seeing the wonders of the love of Christ. Let every one here lay this to heart ! "Has it been my custom to go to the feast? Has it been my custom to go where Christ is set forth—where His atoning death is set forth—to go Sabbath by Sabbath where Jesus Christ is evidently and truly set forth, crucified for us?" If you miss it, if you let things go on in this way, if week after week, month after month, year after year, you neglect the sacred ordinance, oh, how you miss seeing Jesus Christ! The Galilæans went up to the feast, and there they met Christ; and when Christ came back, though they had not advanced far in knowledge, they were ready to receive Him. We do not know what blessing we may get when we receive Jesus Christ into our hearts and homes.

Have *you* never seen a thing that Jesus Christ has done—a wonderful miracle? Have you never seen any one who has been really converted? Have you never seen a thorough worldling, a thoroughly ungodly man, as completely changed as if he had been raised to life again? If you go up to the feast, you will see many who can tell you that they have had this miracle wrought on them. The Galilæans received Christ now, because they had been at the altar of the slain Lamb, and Christ was there.

"So Jesus came again into Cana of Galilee, where He made the water wine. And there was a certain nobleman, whose son was sick at Capernaum."

Now, this was a good way off, we do not know *how* far,—but suppose Northleach, or Stow-on-the-Wold, or any place on yonder hills, to be "Cana of Galilee," and Cheltenham, where *we* are, to be "Capernaum;" Jesus is, as it were, at Stow-in-the-Wold, and in, (as it might be,) Cheltenham, there is a nobleman whose son is sick, and he hears of Jesus all that way off. There was no penny post, there was no telegraph in those days, and very little means of communication—yet Jesus Christ was in everybody's mouth, and this nobleman heard of Him. The people had been at the feast, and some had gone to Bethsaida, some to Capernaum, and some to the North, and all had something to say about the wonderful things they had seen. And, down in Capernaum, they heard that Jesus was in Galilee, and, no doubt, they wondered whether He would come to Capernaum, for it was a place of considerable importance. And then they find that He has gone to an insignificant place—to the village of Cana. "And there was *a certain nobleman*, whose son was sick."

Now, we do not know who this nobleman was, but some guess. They think that we read about his wife in the eighth chapter of St. Luke, "Joanna, the wife of Chuza, Herod's steward." However, he was a *nobleman*, a man in a high position, and, possibly, of considerable wealth, and his son was sick. We see that rich people, as well as poor people, have their troubles, and that in this world no door, however fast-barred, could keep out trouble. No, there is nothing that can shut out trouble and anxiety of all kinds, and suffering, from the house of the rich, any more than from that of the poor. No; sin brought utter ruin and misery into the world, and sorrow goes in the track of sin—it goes alike to the palace and to the cottage, and often the higher men are in the world, the more uneasy the head lies, and the more heavy the heart is; and the loftier the position, it is only the more manifest a target for the poisoned shaft, and the more easy of access to the sorrow of the world. Here is a nobleman, but he is not free from trouble, *his " son was sick."*

Then we see another thing. People are apt to think that if only they had such and such things, and were in such and such a position, trouble would not come ; and very often, people of a certain age think it will not come till they are very old. The young do not think they will sicken till they are old. Every young person —there is scarcely an exception,—I may say, *every* young person believes that he or she will grow up to manhood and womanhood, and then advance to old age ; and the last thing young persons think of is, that it is possible for them *to die young.* Yet you have only to go through the graveyards, and you will read there that the *bulk* of mankind die comparatively young. It is only when *trouble* comes that this thought comes—we cannot hinder sickness from coming, even sickness " unto *death.*"

Here we have two parables at once,—a man near to the king, a man of wealth and honour,—and a youth. All is in their favour, yet the child is " sick "—sick apparently unto death. *Riches* are no safety against trouble ; they often court trouble. *Youth* is no safety against death,—the little flower is often cut down before the strong, sturdy oak. Death may come early to the young whom I here address. You may never live even to be as old as I am. Then the first thing you are bound to ask yourselves is, Are you fit to die ? The next thought is, No human power can shut trouble out of your heart, no wealth or position can shut trouble out of your house. "There was a certain nobleman, whose son was sick." This must have been a very severe affliction, for,

"When he heard that Jesus was come out of Judæa into Galilee, he went unto Him, and besought Him that He would come down, and heal his son, for he was at the point of death."

Now, you see, this man needed a strong motive-power before he would come to Jesus Christ. Don't you think that first he tried all other means at his disposal? He had tried everything that wealth and interest could possibly afford, to effect the healing of this child of his; but all had been in vain. And so, at last, he is (I must use the word—he is) *driven* to Christ. He does not come, as it were, voluntarily. No. It is only when heavy affliction is crushing him down, that he is made willing to come to Christ. Do you think that Naaman, if he had not had a terrible disease, would have gone to Elisha the prophet? It was the terrible disease of leprosy that drove him to the prophet of Israel. And it is a great mercy to get to Jesus Christ *anyhow*. No matter what the motive-power is, no matter how heavy the affliction, if only it brings us there. Then we shall say, "It is *good* for me that I have been afflicted" (Ps. cxix. 71). This man must have sung that, many a time, after this day.

We see this now—few give a thought to Christ. We are but a little company here to-night, but look at the multitudes outside, full of joy and mirth—I say, there

are multitudes who will not give Christ a thought, so
long as they can get a sort of happiness in the world.
But, here, God lays hold of this man ; he shall be *driven*
to Jesus Christ—he shall be driven to see that there is
no power on earth to help him, but only *Christ.* It is a
great mercy to be brought to that. Till we know that,
we can never be saved. But then, we can look the
trouble and the sorrows that come on us in the face,
because we are willing to acknowledge our need, and to
come only for help to the Good Physician. God says, I
use trouble to draw you to Christ.

There are many, many parents who have gone to
Christ for their *children,* when nothing else would bring
them. It has, often, been pointed out, that in the Bible
we do not find children coming to Christ for their
parents ; but we ever find parents coming to Christ for
their children. Take, for instance, the father whose
son was " lunatic and sore vexed" with a devil—
" Lord, have mercy on *my son*" (St. Matt. xvii. 15).
And the woman of Canaan, whose daughter was
" grievously vexed with a devil"—she came to Jesus,
and " besought Him that He would cast forth the devil
out of *her daughter*" (St. Mark vii. 26). These parents
came to Christ *about their children*—so here the nobleman comes to Christ to " heal *his son.*" This man
comes to Christ for his child, and he not only gets a
blessing for his child, but he gets a blessing for himself
too, and for his " house" into the bargain. When we
are really brought to Christ, we little know what blessings we may carry away. This man comes for *one,* and

he carries away *many* that he never thought of. He goes to Christ for the cure of his child,—he gets that, and goes away with a cure for himself and his wife too, and with a blessing for his household.

When the world has nothing more to give, when nobody else can help, the father comes to Christ *at last*. And what does Christ say? His words, first of all, are very discouraging. Those are not always our worst friends, who are rather discouraging at first. Jesus Christ is often rather discouraging at first to people, in order that they may find out how much they have needed the blessing, and that they could not do without it. He says here, quietly—

"Except ye see signs and wonders, ye will not believe."

The Samaritans had believed *without* a sign, because Christ had shown them themselves, and that was sign enough. When, by the Spirit, a man gets turned inside out, and *sees himself*—sees himself down to the depth of his heart, I mean—he does not want a miracle. He has seen *enough*, and all a man wants, when he has seen himself, is to see CHRIST. But Jesus said to him, " Except ye see *signs* and wonders, ye will not believe." " Is that what you are looking for?" The nobleman says, " I know nothing about that ; I am come for one thing—

" Sir, come down ere my child die."

" Never mind (he says); I have only one thought, one idea, one wish—Come down ere my child die. I am come for *that*, I want *that*, I beg for *that*, I entreat

C

you for that—COME DOWN." It is a long way from
Stow-on-the-Wold to Cheltenham, so it was a long way
from Cana to Capernaum, and a bad journey; but "come
down—come down *ere my child die.*"

How little he knew about Jesus Christ! He
thought Christ must *travel* to effect a cure. He thought
that Christ was a great man, a great prophet; and
he thought He must "come down." How unlike he
is to another man, whom (if we are spared) we shall
have to consider! This man seems to say, " I know
that Jesus Christ has turned water into wine; but then
—*He was there.* I know He has wrought many miracles
in Judæa; but then—*He was there.* Come down, *ere*
my child die,—if my child *die*, all is over. If the child
is dead, Jesus Christ cannot do anything for him. He
cannot help us, if the child is dead."

How little he knew of the Lord—how *very* little!
He had a great deal to learn, even that He " quickeneth
the *dead*, and calleth those things which be not as
though they were" (Rom. iv. 17). He had to learn
that He who should go down into the grave, was the
same who said—" I have power to lay down my life,
and I have power to take it again" (St. John x. 18).
Jesus Christ is the *quickener of the dead.* We know, if
we are Christians at all, that we were "dead in tres-
passes and sins" when Christ spoke to us the word
" Live," and cast His garment over us (Ezek. xvi.).
This man says—" Come down *ere* my child die." Oh,
how little he knew! But look at the grace of Christ—
He says these few, simple words,——

"Go thy way ; thy son liveth."

Now, as Jesus spake those words, He gave the man faith, and tried the faith that He gave. If He had not given faith, the man would have stumbled at what was said. But Christ gave it, and then tried it to see if the man believed. " Let Me see if you will turn over a new leaf in your lesson, and think of Me differently—' Go thy way ; thy son liveth'—I will not go with you. If you have confidence in Me, you will go. If My words are not true, I do not deserve to be trusted."

"And the man. believed the word that Jesus had spoken unto him, and he went his way."

Yes—it was a greater miracle, that was being wrought in the man's *heart,* at that moment, than that which was being wrought, in Capernaum, on the man's *son.* There was a greater healing of the man's mind than of the body of the child—" The man *believed the word that Jesus had spoken to him,* and he went his way."

What an example, what a lesson is this ! It is a great lesson to us all. Multitudes think, that if only they saw Christ, that if only they heard Him with their bodily ears, that if only He were here, they would believe. Yes, then they would see. If He were here, He would be nearer, and abler to help them—then they could come, with some degree of hope, to get their sins healed. Why, He *is* here, as much as He was there at Capernaum, because He is " the mighty *God"* as well as "'the *man* Christ Jesus. And now, though He is in heaven, He is no farther from us than was Capernaum from Cana ; and when He says the word, it is as sure

as ever it was then—" Thy son liveth."   There He was
at Cana, and He knew what His virtue and power were
doing in Capernaum ; and He says to the father, " Thy
son *liveth.*"   And so He says now, in power, as He
speaks, to the anxious, seeking heart, words of heavenly
blessing—" Thy *son* liveth, thy *parent* liveth, thy *friend*
liveth, thy *soul* liveth."   " Go thy way, thy son liveth,"
—and he went.

**"And as he was going down, his servants met him,
and told him, saying, Thy son liveth."**

How startled he must have been !   How startled
he *must* have been, when he meets his servants, and
they give him no time to speak, but they,—who have
never been at Cana of Galilee,—say the very words
that Jesus had said—*the very words* that *Jesus* had used
—"THY SON LIVETH!"   The father goes back, and
meets his servants coming out, and *their* first words are,
" Thy son liveth "—and the man knew Who it was that
had *first* spoken these words to him—" Thy son liveth."
Yes,—Jesus Christ had been there in Capernaum in
spirit ; and the servants come and tell the father, " It is
done.   The word Christ spake is true "—though they
did not know that He had spoken thus.

**" Then enquired he of them the hour when he began
to amend."**

Poor man ! he had a great deal to learn *yet*.   He
thinks that Jesus Christ cures by degrees—that there
had been some little symptom of health, and that it
would go on, day by day, till the child was cured at last.
But the servants say—" No, he did not begin to *amend*

—no such thing! It was not a little symptom of amendment, but to our astonishment (they seem to say) the fever went away, and *left* him—left him *well*.

"Yesterday at the seventh hour the fever left him."

And the father says in his heart, That was *the very hour* in the which Jesus said, "Thy son liveth,"—right up in Cana of Galilee. And, even so, the moment that Jesus speaks the word in the higher country, in the house of His Father, it is done here.

If we would only bring our soul's sickness to the place where He sits on throne, to be healed, if we would but bring the sorrows that fall upon us, the troubles that sin brings into our hearts, if we would but bring our poor, guilty, lost souls to the feet of Jesus, and, like this man, ask Him to come and take possession, to heal our disease—He would speak the word, and it would be *done.* He said "Thy son liveth," and *that very hour* "the fever *left* him"—yes, at that moment.

"And himself believed, and his whole house."

He believed, and his wife believed. If it was Chuza, *he* believed, and if it was Joanna, *she* believed ; and, no doubt, this child believed, and their servants believed— for they found that Jesus was the great God who could "speak" in *one* place, and it was "done" in *another*—that He was the great God who could heal sickness, and that if He could thus heal sickness by His word, surely He could forgive sins also.

Now, we must remember these things—

1. Nobody can shut themselves in from sorrow, much less from death.

2. There is only one cure for the soul's disease, and that is in the hand of the Good Physician Himself.

3. He is just as near to us now, as if He were speaking to us in very words. He is just as able to speak the word, and as ready to bring the blessing, as if you saw Him with your bodily eyes. Therefore, let all lay themselves, with all their great spiritual disease, at Christ's feet, that He may speak the word; and they shall be healed.

4. And see what there is more in this. The man brings back a blessing with him, that fills the house, and finds that Jesus gives life to the soul, even as He gives healing to the body.

"This is again the second miracle that Jesus did, when He was come out of Judæa into Galilee."

Not the second *really*, because He had been in the south, and had done many wonderful things, but they are not recorded. This is the second recorded as done in *Cana*. They were privileged people in Cana of Galilee, and so all people are privileged, where Jesus Christ manifests His truth, manifests His name, and manifests Himself for salvation.

Next Tuesday, if God spare us, we will take up another of the miracles of Jesus.

III.

THE FIRST MIRACULOUS DRAUGHT OF FISHES.

" And it came to pass, that, as the people pressed upon him to hear the word of God, he stood by the lake of Gennesaret, and saw two ships standing by the lake: but the fishermen were gone out of them, and were washing their nets. And he entered into one of the ships, which was Simon's, and prayed him that he would thrust out a little from the land. And he sat down, and taught the people out of the ship. Now when he had left speaking, he said unto Simon, Launch out into the deep, and let down your nets for a draught. And Simon answering said unto him, Master, we have toiled all the night, and have taken nothing: nevertheless at thy word I will let down the net. And when they had this done, they inclosed a great multitude of fishes: and their net brake. And they beckoned unto their partners, which were in the other ship, that they should come and help them. And they came, and filled both the ships, so that they began to sink. When Simon Peter saw it, he fell down at Jesus' knees, saying, Depart from me; for I am a sinful man, O Lord. For he was astonished, and all that were with him, at the draught of the fishes which they had taken: and so was also James and John, the sons of Zebedee, which were partners with Simon. And Jesus said unto Simon, Fear not; from henceforth thou shalt catch men. And when they had brought their ships to land, they forsook all, and followed him."—St. Luke v. 1-11.

THIS, I suppose, is, most probably, the *third* miracle that is recorded of all those that were wrought by

Jesus.   Upon this occasion, He was on the borders of the lake, the Lake of Galilee,—that is, the Lake of Tiberias, sometimes called the *Sea* of Tiberias, because of its very great size.   It had all the dangers that are peculiar to a *lake*,—a lake is a famous place for upsetting a boat,—and it had also some of the peculiarities belonging to the great, wide *sea*.   It appears, now, that our blessed Lord had been passing the night in prayer to God, and that, in the morning, He had come forth from His place of seclusion in one of the hills, and was here at the dawn, as the fishermen were coming in, weary from their night of toil, and disappointed with their want of success.   He was there on the beach ; and, early as it was, and strange as was the place, multitudes already—as soon as they heard that Jesus was on the beach—gathered round Him.

Is there any reason to wonder at this ?   Surely, the inhabitants of *Capernaum* might well rush out of their houses, when they heard that Jesus was there.   Why ? Not many weeks since, He had said words right up in Cana of Galilee, which had taken effect right down in Capernaum.   He had said to the nobleman, " Go thy way, thy son liveth ;" and the nobleman had come down from the hills to Capernaum, and found, miles away, that it was just as Jesus had said.   Surely *that* must have made a great stir in Capernaum, even if Jesus had not wrought more miracles there, which are not recorded.   The ministry of Jesus was beginning to bear fruit.   Galilee was not only the northern part of the Holy Land, but, like the northern part of our own

country, it was the *manufacturing* part of the Holy
Land, and had a great manufacturing population.
There were, as we see in Lancashire and Yorkshire,
great tanneries, manufactories, and potteries, stretching
up northward to Tyre and Sidon. There were what
we call skilled artisans, in hundreds and thousands ; and
the ministry of Jesus was beginning to tell on them all.
They were beginning to feel that there was a great
power in their midst, and to ask, What word has this
prophet to say unto us ? They were beginning in their
heart to make inquiry. And, you may depend upon
this, it is *something* when men begin to ask questions, and to be unsettled in their minds—to ask the
question, Am I right? am I safe? Have I ground for
believing that, in the world to come, all will be well ?
Or, am I leaving it all hap-hazard, and am I willing to
leave it so ? I say, when men come to ask this, and
are evidently anxious to hear the word of God, then
there is hope. We must not take too much for granted,
and imagine, that, because great crowds come together
to hear the Word, all will come and seek the way of
life from Christ. But, when we see multitudes rushing
down to hear the words of Him who spake as "never
man spake," then, I say, there is some *hope;* and here
they "**pressed upon Him**," till they got down to the
sea-shore,—"to hear the Word of God."

You know, that, in that country the air is so light,
that sound travels a great way. The voice of Jesus—
that heavenly voice, that voice sweeter than any music
we have ever heard—would certainly travel a great

way; yet those, who were on the outside of the crowd, so pressed on those who were within, that our Lord was pushed down to the sea.   They " pressed upon Him." What for ?   *Not* for loaves and fishes, not for Him to cleanse their lepers, not to raise their dead, not to heal their sick, not for Him to give them anything for their *bodies*, not for any temporal purpose, but

"To hear the Word of God."

It was a grand motive—to hear the WORD OF GOD.   There is nothing so awful to an intelligent mind, as to realise the possibility of an eternal silence—to fancy that there is no voice to tell us of our great future, no voice to guide us in the darkness, no voice to still the tempest around us.   Oh ! if there were no Word of God, how miserable must we be !   The miseries in the world are deep enough, terrible enough, fearful enough, and so they have been for this six thousand years ; but what heart could ever dare to dwell on the miseries that have been endured on this earth, if there were no voice to tell us of the way to happiness, no voice to guide us out of misery into bliss, out of darkness into light?   Is there no Word of God?   How came the world into existence, with all its beautiful conveniences and suitabilities for every creature's need ?   Have these a Maker ?   *Who* made them ?   Is there no " voice nor any to answer?" (1 Kings xviii. 29).

Yes.   They pressed upon Him to hear the *Word of God*—to hear what was worth hearing, to hear what, above all other things, is worth hearing, to " hear the Word of God."   You see, at once, that there are many who are anxious to hear what such and such people say. Just take this, for instance. There is a great war going on now in Europe, a terrible war. Supposing one of the Queen's ministers, the Prime Minister, gets up in a public assembly, how anxious all are to hear what he has got to say. Why? Because they think a great man will say what is of great importance. See how people run to get a newspaper, if any of the contending parties, standing in high positions, have written a letter, or uttered a word, or issued a circular! But, what is all this compared with asking, "Has He who made me, and who will judge me, and judge the world —has HE spoken to me? Do I seek to hear, not the word of man, but the Word of *God?* Am I eager to hear what *God* has said?" Do you ever look at the Bible from this point of view—" I am but a child of dust, my life is 'but a vapour.' I know it may pass away as a breath of wind, and, when it goes, *what* shall I be, and *how* shall I be, and *where* shall I be?" And do you open your Bible and ask, "Has the God who made me thus, the God who ruleth over all, said any-thing about it? Can I get a sight of the words *here?*"

There are many in the world, multitudes, who do not want to hear that. Many are so determined not to hear, that they say there is no such Word, and never was. We hold up the Bible and confront them with overwhelming evidence, but they will not have it. They close their ears, and harden their hearts, and why? Why, because they love sin, because they love their own way, because they do not want to hear God's

Word.   They are like those naughty children who close their ears when the parent calls, and run away, though they are hearing all the while the parent's call to duty. " There are none so deaf as those who *will not* hear." There are none so blind as those who *will not* see. There are multitudes of such people in the world who *won't* hear, because they know that God condemns what they are and what they do, and calls them to submission to His authority, and obedience to His Word. But here the people pressed upon Him " to *hear* the Word of God."

Do not, I beseech you, let this pass away !   We are beings who must live for ever, and, unless we hear the Word of God, we cannot know or tell where we shall live.   These men came for a good purpose—they came to the right person, because Jesus *came from God to speak the Word of God;* yea, He was Himself the Word of God.   As I said before, there must have been a great crowd, and they were all crowding round and pressing upon Jesus, till He was close to the sea. Now, there are, even at this present moment, in this spot, a considerable number of what we call *creeks*, or little bays.   Travellers tell us so—that where Jesus must have been on that occasion, there are little bays, with the jutting rocks on either side, so that a little boat could easily ride between the two projections, and, from it, Jesus could conveniently address the congregation gathered on both sides, right and left, and in front too—as you are gathered before me here to-night.

Jesus **"saw two ships standing by the lake: but the fishermen were gone out of them, and were washing their nets."**

He knew these fishermen.   He had before called three, at least, of them to be His disciples, but they had gone on with their old occupation as fishermen, and earned their living in that way.   So Jesus got into one of the boats ; it happened to be Simon Peter's,— **"and prayed him that he would thrust out a little from the land. And He sat down, and taught the people out of the ship."**

Now we ask the question, *What* did He teach them ? As He sat there, in the still morning, with the fresh breezes from the mountain coming down, and the fresh breezes from the sea coming up, and this multitude gathered round the great Teacher,—what did He teach them ?   They *came for* the Word of God, and He *gave* them the Word of God.   We are not told what the sermon was ; we are left to conjecture, but we can gather much from what He had been saying to others. He would show them that they were sinners, and that He was the *sinner's* Friend,—that He was friendly to sinners, and that He had come to seek and to save them.   He would tell them, what we have been singing in the second hymn to-night,—

" Make me poor and keep me low."

He would tell them, " Blessed are the poor in spirit, for theirs is the kingdom of heaven " (St. Matt. v. 3). " Blessed is the lowly and contrite heart, for of such is the kingdom of heaven."   He would tell them, " Except ye be converted, and become as little children, ye shall not enter into the kingdom of heaven " (St. Matt. viii. 3). He would set before them, as, no doubt, He did over and over, and over again, the great facts of *sin* and *salvation*, the great facts of the *fall* of man in the first Adam, and of the *redemption* of man in the last Adam. He would deal with them honestly ; He would deal with their consciences. He would not make them think about their neighbours, but about themselves ; and, we know, He spake to them such words of grace and power as "never man spake."

Now, you must just bear this in mind—it is a good thing to come and *hear* the Word of God, and it is a blessed thing to *speak* the Word of God. And people cannot be gathered together more wisely and profitably, than as these people were, who pressed upon Jesus to hear from Him the Word of God.

" Now when He had left speaking, He said unto Simon, Launch out into the deep, and let down your nets for a draught."

So there was an end of the speaking. He told them the story of grace, and then left them to ponder on that story. And now, He says to Peter, " Launch out into the deep." Peter had stopped to listen to Christ's preaching ; and now Christ will go with Peter a-fishing. Peter had been hearing from Christ the Word of God, and now he carries Christ with him in the ship. *That is a good thing*—to come and hear the Word of God, and, then, to carry Christ away with you to your occupation, and to your home.

Then, Jesus says to Peter, " Launch out into the deep." Yes, He says, Go into the deep sea, where perhaps it is not only deep, but rough. Very sad must be the launching into the deep, unless we carry Christ with us, unless we carry Christ into the deep of sorrow, into the deep of affliction, and carry Him into the swellings of Jordan ! If Christ go not forth with us when we launch into the deep, then are we without peace, without safety, and without blessing.

Peter comes and sits at the feet of Christ, and now, Christ says, I go with Peter. THAT *should be the end of all preaching.* People should come and hear the Word of God, and then they should carry Christ away with them,—carry Christ to the deep, to the workshop, to the daily labour. People who come and hear the Word of Christ, ought to make up their minds that this is the end of preaching. If you go and make a purchase, you would make sure that you carry it away with you. Then let it be looked on as a lost occasion, if Christ is not carried back again.

Why, if Christ tells us to go "into the deep," we may well go, for then His power will protect us, and His presence will bless us. " Launch out into THE DEEP "—not into the shallows, not only where you go fishing, but right out into *the deep.* Let these people look on, and let down your nets for a draught." Why, this was strange work. People do not go fishing in the daytime. The night is the time to catch fish. They had been at it all night, but now the sun was shining, with its terrific violence, on the Sea of Galilee, and its glaring brilliance was enough to frighten all the fishes away. Yet Jesus says, Let down your nets, not for a chance, but for a *draw*.

"Simon answering said unto him, Master, we have toiled all the night, and have taken nothing."

These men, whom Jesus came to, were "diligent in their business," and now they "stand before" a great "King" (Prov. xxii. 29). He found them diligent in their business, and toiling hard, and toiling long, and yet not disheartened. They had had a great disappointment that night, yet they were willing, in the morning, to listen to the sermon of Christ. They felt, no doubt, that the sermon might bring peace into their hearts, and give them some recompense for their lost night of toil. "We have toiled *all the night*, and have taken nothing."

Now, let me ask, did it never strike you, that, if this was so, people may toil all their *lives* and take nothing? Did it never strike you that, unless some secret, hidden power works, and helps, and blesses, we might toil and toil for ever, and *never* take anything? Let us carry the seed into the field, and till the ground, and labour on ; but, though you can cast in the seed, can you make the seed *spring* up? Can you make the seed bear fruit? Have you any power in your possession to *compel* the seed to bring forth fruit? Can you compel the sun to shine? Can you compel the rain to fall? Can you make the light break forth? What can man do between barrenness and fruitfulness? "We have toiled all the night, and have taken nothing." And why not all the *week*, and all the *month*, and all the *year* ?

Why are there fishes in the sea? *Man* did not make them, man did not provide them. Somebody else provided them. Some people say, "There is no God." Oh, what a cure it would be for those people, if they could only be put on some little isolated spot, and there be told to provide for themselves, to make the sun shine, and the rain fall, and the fishes come! "*We* have toiled all the night, and have taken *nothing*." Ought we not to learn the lesson, then, that if we toil all the night and take *something*, there should be thanksgiving to some one who gives it—that the blessing comes from somewhere, and thanks are due for it? What does our Lord say? God "is kind to the *un*thankful and to the evil" (St. Luke vi. 35). "He maketh his sun to rise on the evil and on the good, and sendeth rain on the just and on the unjust" (St. Matt. v. 45). And yet, you see, He is forgotten, He is neglected, He is denied. People live as if there were no God at all. "Master, we have toiled all the night, and have taken nothing :"

"**Nevertheless** (says Peter), **at Thy word** (that, indeed, is the Word of *God*), **I will let down the net.**"

Yes, says Peter, "Lord, if *Thou* tell me anything, however unlikely—and there are few more unlikely things than letting down the net with the sun shining on it, and few more unlikely things to bring a favourable result than this—we have been scouring all the coast with nets, and see, we have taken *nothing;* and

D

for them to come now, at this unlikely time ! but if *Thou* tell me, if it be *Thy* word, *I will do it*." But Peter, in his heart, says, " This Master of mine never tells me or mine to do what is not to be fruitful, and to bring a blessing. If He says so, there *will* be a blessing at the end, no matter *what* He says. Didn't He turn the water into wine ? Didn't He send a message of health from Cana to Capernaum ? I know not what He is going to do, but, " nevertheless, *at Thy* word, I will let down the net." It is like Mary saying, " Whatsoever He saith unto you, do it " (St. John ii. 5).

Then, let us ask, What are the words of Jesus ? These men were in disappointment—they had been toiling, hard and long. They had gone seeking *much*, and had brought in *nothing;* and they were *poor* men, remember, and therefore they listen to the " word " of Jesus. The word of Jesus tells them what to do ; and there is no disappointment that we can have, no trouble that we can get into, but there is a " *nevertheless*" somewhere.

" **And when they had this done, they inclosed a great multitude of fishes: and their net brake.**"

It was breaking. The Greek word here means " break-*ing*," not that it actually broke. Now let us look at this. At the word of Jesus, they have put down the net. Did it ever strike you what David said, a thousand years before, about this Son of man ? David said, that, when He came, He would have wonderful authority—" Thou madest him to have dominion over the works of thy hands ; thou hast put *all* things under his feet : all sheep and oxen, yea, and the beasts of the field ; the fowl of the air, and *the fish of the sea*, and whatsoever passeth through the paths of the seas. O Lord our Lord, how excellent is Thy Name in all the earth" (Ps. viii. 6-9). That is what David said of Christ, a thousand years before He came—that He should have dominion over the fish of the sea; and here, we see Him saying, "Let down your nets for a draught," and all the fishes rush, in obedience to that authority, into the net, so that the net is giving way because of the great multitude of fishes.

Is it not a mercy to see this, to see One with power over all creatures, with power over all things? Some people would like the world to go on in its own way, and say that miracles are inconceivable. Some say that God made the world, but that He never interferes ; they like to speak of the world as rushing on independently, because of *its own* laws. I sometimes think, though it is only a small comparison—I sometimes think of the great steam-engine on the rails, what would be more terrible than to see one of those mighty pieces of machinery getting up steam, and going on at the rate of fifty miles an hour, with no intelligent being to guide it, no engineer to govern it, nobody to stop it —nobody to prevent its rushing madly on—what must be the end but *destruction ?*—because there is not a thinking, living, intelligent being to rule it and govern it. So with regard to the world, rushing on in its complicated way, turning round in a marvellous manner ; yet, dare we think of it without Him at the helm ? I like to see Jesus, able to govern the fishes of the sea,

and to make them go into the net ; and I like to think
of Him as guiding the stars in their courses, holding all
in His power throughout His vast dominion, and able
to say, " Hitherto shalt thou come, and no further."
When He says, " Let down your nets for a draught,"
they inclose "a great multitude of fishes." Nothing
can stay His hand.

And then what did they do ? " They *beckoned* unto
their partners." Now, I like to think of the little words
of the Gospel. I like that word "beckoned" amaz-
ingly. Remember, they were fishermen, they were
Palestine men, they were on the Sea of Galilee, and
used to a country where there were plenty of echoes,
where the human voice echoes far. Fishermen like to
hear the sound of their own voices. Have you ever
heard sailors coming into harbour, and unloading their
ship ? They will not be without a merry song all
the day through. So that, *naturally*, these men would
have *called* to their companions. It is one of the most
cheery things in the world to hear them shouting in
their ships. Why did not these ? They *did* not, they *could*
not. They were awe-stricken in the presence of Jesus,
and their voices were silent ; they only " beckoned."

**" They beckoned unto their partners, which were in
the other ship, that they should come and help them."**
The partners knew that something unusual was going
on ; they knew Jesus had said, " Launch out into the
deep," and they knew that something was amiss.

**" And they came and filled both the ships, so that
they began to sink."**

Tons of fishes came at the very word of Jesus.

We must now hasten to a close, and just draw the practical conclusion from the miracle. The Evangelist tells us of the words of Peter. Peter had thought Jesus a dear, kind, blessed, gracious man, speaking the Word of God—now, he sees something *more* than that. He had seen, before, much to be loved, much to be admired, much to be trusted—now he sees something more, and he **"fell down at Jesus' knees, saying, Depart from me; for I am a sinful man, O Lord."**

Peter has found out what he had not found out before; he had followed Jesus, and admired Jesus, and listened to Jesus; but his heart had never been opened up to see this before—the infinite distance there is between the sinner and the living God. Like Job, in olden time, " I have heard of thee by the hearing of the ear, but now mine eye seeth thee. Wherefore I abhor myself, and repent in dust and ashes" (Job xlii. 5, 6), so Peter says,—" Depart from me, for I am a sinful man, O Lord." And yet, he does not wish Him to go. He would not for the world have been taken at his word. His thought seems to be—" I do not want Thee to go, though I know I am not fit to be near Thee. Thou art the great God, and I am a sinful man." This was just what Isaiah and the angels did. The angels cover their faces and cover their feet, and cry—" Holy, Holy, Holy is the Lord of hosts." And so Isaiah says, he, too, is a sinful man, and feels his sinfulness—" Woe is me, for I am undone, because I am a man of unclean lips, ... for mine eyes have seen the King, the Lord of

hosts" (Isa. vi.).   And so was it with Peter.   As somebody has said, " God can never *do* anything with anybody, till He has *un*done them "—till He has made
them feel that they are undone, that they are sinful
men.   That is the right position—I am a sinful man,
and He is the living God.   Peter had got a glimpse of
Jesus; yet he did not know all that was in his own
heart.   He had learnt something from the miracle; but
miracles will not teach us everything.   Peter had more
to learn, not from seeing what Jesus *did*, but from the
look of Jesus—a look that went right into his inmost
heart—a look that went right *through* him, making him
weep " bitterly."   He had yet to find out some deeper
mysteries—" I am a sinful man;" but the Lord says,
" Thou *art* a sinful man, but thou shalt catch men."
Yes, he *was* " a sinful man;" but yet, he was to " catch
men."   God does not catch men by means of angels;
He does not gather sinners by the tongues of angels,
but by sinful men, by men like themselves.

This, remember, is what we come for.   This is *why*
we speak as ministers, that we may catch you if we can.
Some say, Catch us if you can; they are determined
that we shall *not* catch them; but if they are not caught
in the Gospel net—if they are not brought into the
vessel where Jesus is, what must be their end ?

Let us learn the lessons, then.   If we come to hear
the Word, let us see that we carry Jesus away with us
when we go.

And then, He will show us the wonders of His grace,
and love, and goodness, and supply all our need.

Let us take care to learn this——that we are sinful, and that He is the Holy One ; but let us take care to do, as Peter did. No doubt, he clung to His knees, and while he said, " Depart from me, for I am a sinful man, O Lord," he was taking care that Jesus should not depart, by clinging to Him with all his might; and feeling that he could not go into the deep of the sea again, unless Christ were with him to keep him in safety, and to give him good success.

IV.

THE STILLING OF THE TEMPEST.

" And the same day, when the even was come, he saith unto them, Let us pass over unto the other side. And when they had sent away the multitude, they took him even as he was in the ship. And there were also with him other little ships. And there arose a great storm of wind, and the waves beat into the ship, so that it was now full. And he was in the hinder part of the ship, asleep on a pillow: and they awake him, and say unto him, Master, carest thou not that we perish? And he arose, and rebuked the wind, and said unto the sea, Peace, be still. And the wind ceased, and there was a great calm. And he said unto them, Why are ye so fearful? how is it that ye have no faith? And they feared exceedingly, and said one to another, What manner of man is this, that even the wind and the sea obey him? "—ST. MARK iv. 35–41.

OUR subject, to-night, is a miracle which is recorded by St. Matthew, St. Mark, and St. Luke; but we will take the account given us by St. Mark. This is one of the miracles wrought by our Lord in Galilee, and its being recorded by all the three first Evangelists shows its exceeding great importance. This miracle occurred at the close of one of the most remarkable days in our Lord's ministry. It had been a very hard day—a very toilsome day. We will not inquire what He had done in the morning of the day, but there had been a regular set upon Him by His foes—by the Pharisees; and, as the day was wearing on, He came down from the city to the beach, where we saw Him last week, and when He had taken His place in a boat, He addressed the multitudes, and spake to them all the parables recorded in St. Matthew xiii. You remember how He begins :— A sower went out to sow, and some seed· fell by the wayside, and some on stony ground, some on thorny ground, and some on good ground. Then He went on to tell them of the tares among the wheat, and then about the leaven in three measures of meal; then about the mustard seed—then about the pearl—then about the treasure—then about the net cast into the sea. This last parable must have been very striking, spoken with the great sea before them. But they did not understand these things, and the disciples asked Him what He meant, and then He said a very solemn thing. He said, These things are spoken in parables, that these might find occasion to stumble, but "to you it is given to know the mysteries of the kingdom of God" (St. Luke viii. 10). Then He went back to the city, and gathered the disciples together, and expounded to them these parables—told them what the meaning of the parables was.

And then, as the evening was drawing on, He seems to have left the house where He was sitting, talking— and, as He was making His way down to the beach, three people met Him; the first who met Him said, "I will follow Thee whithersoever Thou goest," and Jesus

stopped and said, " You little know what you are talking about—' Foxes have holes, and birds of the air have
nests ; but the Son of man hath not where to lay His
head ' " (St. Matt. viii. 20).   He was going to " lay His
head," presently, on a pillow in the hinder part of the
ship, in that raging, tossing, tempestuous sea.   He had
to be content with even such a resting-place as that ; so
·He told the man that, if he would follow Christ, he
must be willing to take Christ just as He was—just as
these disciples " took Him, even as He was."   So you,
if you will follow Christ, must break with everything
behind, you must break with the old sins, with the old
entanglements, with the world you have loved so well ;
you must break with everything, and take Christ and
what Christ gives you, what Christ appoints you.   You
must do just what is said in earthly things—a man must
" break his bridges behind him ;" there must be no
turning back—no *looking* back.   " Remember Lot's
wife " (St. Luke xvii. 32).

And then, another came and said, " Suffer me first to
go and bury my father "—and Jesus spoke to him differently ; he did not need warning so much as he needed
a spur to urge him on—" Let the dead bury their dead ;
but go thou and preach the kingdom of God " (St Luke
ix. 60).

Then another met Him, and said certain things to
Him, but Jesus said—" No man, having put his hand
to the plough, and looking back, is fit for the kingdom
of God :" and He left him (perhaps the middle one
went on with Him), and came down to the seashore at

Capernaum. And *then* begins the history contained in our passage to-night.

"And the same day, when the even was come, He saith unto them, Let us pass over unto the other side."

He *knew* what was on the other side, and the disciples, probably, had some notion of what was on the other side—what sort of country it was, and what they were likely to meet with. "Let us pass over unto the other side." But they did not know what the Lord was going to do, they did not know what purpose He had in His mind, when He said, "Let us pass over unto the other side." Jesus often sends His people errands, when they do not know *why* He sends them. The hymn we have been singing, says, "like Abram of old" —God sent him, but He did not explain to him what for. Many things have happened to us, (if I am speaking to Christians to-night,) in life,—dark things, and we could not understand them—disappointments perhaps, a turn or twist in our journey; and, years after, we can go back to that twist in the journey, and see that *the Lord* was saying there, "Let us go over to the other side,"—see that *His* hand was guiding us. It is a blessed thing, depend on it, to be guided by the mind and word of Jesus Christ, to have Him cut and carve for us, to have Him appoint our lot, and when we have got our lot, believingly to take it; and though it may be very hard, and we may not know where it will lead, yet to be assured that it will be *right*. When Jesus Christ sends us on any errand, on any journey, when He gives us any particular work, how little we know what we shall meet with! He never promises His people a *smooth* journey, but He does promise *at the end* "a city which hath foundations," (Heb. xi. 10), and eternal life. He never promises an easy journey, but He says, there is a glorious "inheritance, incorruptible, and undefiled, reserved in heaven;" (1 Pet. i. 5), and He never undertakes what He does not make good. And He never says to any child of God, that he shall not have troubles on the journey, but He says, "Let us pass over unto the other side;" and if that child of God is wise, he will go.

"And when they had sent away the multitude, they took Him even as He was in the ship."

Peter, James, and John were all strong, stalwart, brave fishermen, accustomed to go in storms on the lake, accustomed to ride on the waves of the boisterous Sea of Galilee. They knew every shoal, every rock, every gorge in the mountains; they knew how to turn their sails to catch, or to avoid, the winds that came down the gorges in the mountains there. "*They* took Him, even as He was, in the ship." What does this suggest to you? It suggests this, that Jesus must have been very weary. He did not *go;* "they *took* Him." It must have been that, that day, He was thoroughly worn out. He had had to meet the Pharisees in controversy. His mother and brethren had that day been a great cause of anxiety to Him,—trouble had sprung up in His own house. Then He had been speaking, out of doors, a long sermon, with many great, glowing thoughts in it; and then, indoors, He gave a careful lecture, explaining it all to very dull people ; and then He had met the three men we just alluded to, and had spoken to the multitudes on the beach, and He was evidently worn out. The human frame of the " Man of sorrows" had borne all that it could bear ; "they *took* Him"—took Him just "as He was," without any provision, without any previous preparation. The *Master* says, " Let us go over to the other side ;" and *they* say, " We must take Him out of the multitude, out of the turmoil, and go on this placid lake ; it is all peace there." There it lay, glittering in the evening brightness, tempting by its stillness, quietude, and peace ; "and they took Him, even as He was, in the ship." But they could not go by themselves—

"There were also with Him other little ships."

We must not forget these many "little ships" around the ship in which He was. Many went hanging on to the skirts of His garment, as it were, not quite close, but hanging on ; and we shall see, by-and-bye, what happened to *them*. If people put off in little ships after Christ, they must share Christ's lot, they must suffer Christ's sufferings, they must go in the tempest with Christ. Christ said, " Let *us* pass over to the other side ;" and these in the little ships see, that if they do not go too, if they shrink from going into the ship after Him, if they decline to go on the journey *with Christ,* they may stop on the land, but Christ will not stop with them. *He* will be gone. The only way to get the blessing of Christ, is to go *with* Christ wherever He goes, whether it be into the sunshine or into the storm.   And so the little ships put off with the other one in which Christ was.

"And there arose a great storm of wind, and the waves beat into the ship, so that it was now full."

Now, you know that Sea of Galilee—which we were talking about so much last week, and of which we must speak a good deal again to-night—has mountains on both sides as well as on the north, and in these mountains there are great gorges; and, you know, how the wind gathers in a gorge causing a great draught, and these gorges act just like tunnels, gathering all the force into a little compass; consequently, these gorges brought the wind down to the lake with great violence.   (Illustration by map).   And *here*, from the western side, Jesus was going across the lake to the land of the Gergesenes, when down came the wind upon the lake, and stirred up the waves.   There is nothing so dangerous as a storm on a *lake.*   If I am to be in a storm, let me be on the open sea, rather than on an inland lake with its waters stirred by the winds.   " There arose a great storm of wind."   " The floods lifted up their voice, the floods lifted up their waves " (Ps. xciii. 3).

Now we see, that to go with Christ, though He is " mightier than the noise of many waters, yea, than the mighty waves of the sea " (Ps. xciii. 4), is not always to escape the storm.   If we choose Christ for our portion, we have Christ's portion for ours.   If *He* gets into the storm, if He gets into trouble, if He gets beaten on by the waves, *we* must come in for it, too.   So here—" the waves beat into the ship, so that it was now full."   Do

you say, " Surely Jesus Christ could keep out of trouble?
If He could turn water into wine, if He could heal the
nobleman's son, if. He could produce the miraculous
draught of fishes, surely He could have hindered the
storm from coming, surely He could have given them a
fair passage." Yes—*He could.* But then, would it have
been *right*, would it have been *good* for them ? When
God said He would give Jacob this and that, we imagine
that Jacob will have no trouble ; but he had to leave his
home, and run off into Syria, and be there. a poor outcast, for years, and labour and toil day and night, before
he came to his inheritance.

One of the ways God chooses to prepare us for rest, is
by leading us through trouble here, yes, through " the
needful time of trouble " (Ps. x. 1, P. B. V.)—the time of
trouble full of *needs.*   Look at the strong, sturdy oak of
the forest ; it would never have been a strong oak, if no
storm of wind had blown upon it ; it would not have
grown to its magnificent dimensions, if there had been
no " stormy wind and tempest " (Ps. lv. 8, P. B. V.) It
is the *storm* that has rooted it firmly into the earth, and
caused it to cling to, and entwine itself firmly around,
the rock.   It is the *storm* that has caused it thus mag-
nificently to grow.   So Christians, if they are never
weary and tempest-tossed, if they are put under a glass
case and do not weather the storm, will be poor, sickly
things, even if there be any life at all in them.   No.
Jesus Christ will have His people go through the storm,
and if they do not get it in *outside* things, they have it
within.   It does not follow that, because external storm

and tempest does not trouble them, they have not *any* trouble.   It does not follow, because we do not *see* a Christian's troubles, that he has not got them ; yes, he has them often underneath a very placid countenance, and calmly bears them with a very patient spirit.   Jesus does not hinder the waves from rising.   People say, " why *does* the Lord let trouble come ?   Why doesn't the Lord keep trouble off ?"   And then impatience is stirred within them.   No doubt, it was so with these disciples.

You remember a storm, recorded in the Old Testament, where the shipmen came and said to the sleeper, " Arise, call upon thy God " (Jonah i. 6).   But oh, how different was *this !*   It was a sound sleep in both cases. The storm did not wake Jonah, and the storm did not wake Jesus.   The one slept the fast sleep of guilt, when sin had hardened and deadened the conscience. The other slept the sleep of perfect, holy, pure repose. So we find the guilty conscience sleeping through the storm, because it is hard, cold—just as the dead man sleeps through it ; but the conscience that is at peace can sleep, but sleeps *otherwise*, through the storm.

"And He was in the hinder part of the ship, asleep on a pillow."

How great the exhaustion of that day must have been to the human frame of Jesus, when He slept that sound sleep !   But what a comfort it is to us to see Him sleep !   Let us look at the sleeping Jesus, and learn the lesson.   What *is* the lesson ?   While He was *the living God*, curing the nobleman's son when He was miles off,

—while He was the living God, producing the draught of fishes, yet He was, also, *the man*, with all the weaknesses, and all the wearinesses, and all the painfulnesses that belong to these human frames of ours. Jesus could be *exhausted*—Jesus could *sleep* the sound, peaceful sleep, which thorough exhaustion brings.on the human frame. While Jesus Christ was " perfect God," He was also " perfect man." And there is not a state of weakness, there is not a state of exhaustion, which the human mind or body can ever feel, but we can say, Jesus is " touched with the feeling of" my " infirmities " (Heb. iv. 15). He was completely, entirely exhausted; and " so " His heavenly Father gave " His beloved sleep " (Ps. cxxvii. 2).

This is the only time that we hear of Jesus as " asleep on a *pillow ;*" and just consider, what a place it was to sleep in ! The only time we hear of Jesus as being asleep on a pillow, is, when the waves were all tossing and surging. He had never a pillow but on the raging waves of the sea, and that Jesus of whom we sometimes sing,—

> " I will lay my head on Jesus,
> Pillow of the troubled soul "—

here Himself, on the troubled sea, rests on a pillow. All the waves and storms were going over Him (Ps. xlii. 9). And He does not seem ready to hear, ready to come to help, when the ship was nearly *full*. As many say, " My cup is full, I cannot bear any more," so these men say, " If another wave comes, the ship will be full." We say, it is the last ounce that breaks the camel's back,

E

—this is the last but one,—*one more* is sure to do it. " The waves beat into the ship, so that it was full."

"And He was in the hinder part of the ship, asleep on a pillow; and they awake Him, and say to Him, Master, carest thou not that we perish?"

" Master, master," another of them cried, " we perish." (St. Luke viii. 24). Now look at these men. When all was calm, when they could manage by labouring at the oars to get the vessel along, they let the Lord sleep; but when deep trouble comes, they go to Him. When they cannot help themselves, they cry, " Master, master, we perish." Many of us know this; we think we can get on when circumstances are all favourable, we think we can pull the vessel through, that we can do without the Lord, without His watchful eye; but when the trouble gets deeper and deeper, then we find that we *cannot do without Him.*

Let us lay this seriously to heart, not only with regard to converted persons, but to the unconverted. There are multitudes round about us who say, " I can get on very well without Christ; it is hard work, I know, but still I can pull the vessel along—I can do without Christ;" and they laugh, perhaps, at the poor soul who says, " Without Christ I dare not go, without Christ I dare not live, without Christ I dare not die." But only let deep trouble come ! It is said, you know, by the old prophet, " If thou hast run with the footmen, and they have wearied thee, then how canst thou contend with horses? And if in the land of peace, wherein thou trustedst, they wearied thee, then how

wilt thou do in the swellings of Jordan ? " (Jer. xii. 5).
And so, when the tempest comes, when the raging
waves and storm of the last conflict come, and death is
darkly setting over the soul, then it will be, " Master,
we perish ; "—" Master, carest thou not that we perish ?"
—when the Master may reply, " You have had ten,
twenty, seventy years, and you never asked *yourself*
whether you would perish or not, and now you
cry to Me, ' Master, carest *Thou* not that I perish ? ' "

You may depend upon this, there must, there will
be an hour (unless the conscience gets hard as the
granite rock), when the ship will be found to be nearly
full, and yourself sinking in the deep, and then you will
cry, " Master, master, we perish." I was reading, only
a few days ago, in the newspaper, of something that
happened a short time since, which will illustrate what
I am saying. There is, unfortunately, a man in this
country who writes many pernicious pamphlets, and
goes about giving lectures ; he calls himself a Secularist
—that means, I suppose, an Atheist—a man who says
he can do without God,—who says " in his heart, there
is no God" (Ps. xiv. 1) : and he goes about lecturing,
and does a great deal of mischief. It was in a colliery
district, that this man had delivered his lecture, to show
that there is no eternity, no Christ, no God, no soul, no
judgment ; and he said at the end, " I challenge any
man here to confute what I have said." And, in the
midst of the assembly, a collier got up and said, " Master,
I should like to make a statement. You have challenged
any one to speak, and I accept the challenge. Me and

my mate, Jim, we were Methodys and professed religion;
and one of your infidel fellows came lecturing, and they
made Jim turn infidel, and then there was no more
class-meetings and such-like for Jim.   But one day,
when we were at work together, me and Jim, a great
cob of coal fell on Jim's head, and Jim thought he was
struck for dead, and oh! how he did holloa! oh, *how
frightened he was to* DIE !   And how he did cry to the
Lord to have mercy on him!"   And then the, collier
added, emphatically, " There's nowt like cobs of coal
to knock infidel notions out of men's heads."

And so it is.   When they come to die, they cry,
" Master, master, carest thou not that I perish ? Where
am I going?   What is at the bottom of this great sea ?
Where will these waves wash me to ?   What shore will
they land me on ?   Master, master, I perish."

**"And He arose, and rebuked the wind, and said unto
the sea, Peace, be still. And the wind ceased, and
there was a great calm."**

There was peace, because He, who had been lying
there in the exhaustion of our weak, human frame, rose
up in the might of His Godhead, " mightier than those
mighty waves," and spake to the winds and the waves.
" And there was a great calm."

We see from this, how little we know, when we pray,
what things we are praying for, what is included in our
prayer.   When these men prayed Christ to save those
in their little fishing craft, perhaps they only meant
those in *this* craft ; yet their prayer reached far beyond
themselves, even to the other " little ships."   There were

many other little ships, tossing and creaking just as this one did ; they were in as much danger—apparently, in *more;* and the disciples cry, " Lord, save *us.*"   When any man comes to the feet of Christ, when he pleads for his own soul, when he cries " Lord, save *me,*" he little knows what may be the result of his salvation— just as these disciples little knew that, because of *their* prayer, all the little ships would come into peace. When a man is saved himself, and the Master speaks peace, he cannot tell what influence as a real Christian he may have, nor what work he may be called to do, whether as a preacher of God's Word, or as a teacher of the old or of the young, or as a Christian parent, relative, child, or friend ; there will be some " little ship" that is sure to come in for a share of the blessing.

" There was a great calm."

Jesus can, *with a word*, make a great calm, and cause the storm to cease.   And then, what does He say to them ?   He speaks to the feelings of their hearts ; He does not find fault with their words, but with their being frightened.   They *ought not* to have been frightened ; they ought to have looked at Jesus " asleep on a pillow," and said,

" With Christ in the vessel, I smile at the storm."

But they could not say that.   Jesus says, as St. Luke tells us, " Where is your faith?"

" Why are ye so fearful ?   How is it that ye have no faith ?"

" Where is your faith" (St. Luke viii. 25)?   Perhaps He turned to one and said, " *How* is it that ye have no faith"

(St. Mark iv. 40)? and then to another, " *Where* is your faith?" and to another, " O ye of *little* faith" (St. Matt. viii. 26)—and so forth. *Where* is your faith ?

We need to have our faith *ready at hand.* We ought not to be like a man with all his money in the bank ; when he has got some small account to pay, perhaps he goes and finds the bank shut—he ought to have some in his pocket, ready to meet the emergency. A Christian ought to take care, not only that he has Christ with him, but that his faith in Him is in lively exercise. *Where* is your faith ? These men are like many who (if we may descend to a lower sphere), when an accident happens, lose all their presence of mind ; we need their help, but they can only look on, and are perfectly stupefied and helpless.

" *Where* is your faith ?" Take care that you take Jesus with you at all times, and take care, too, that your faith is in exercise. We cannot tell what may be coming on us. We cannot tell what may happen within the next twenty-four hours. The storm may come down the gorges, and stir up the lake, stir up the waves beneath us. Then let us take care that Christ is with us in the ship, and that our faith is in vigorous exercise. These men ought to have remembered Cana of Galilee, they ought to have remembered the nobleman's son, they ought to have remembered the draught of fishes, and to have known that " with Christ in the vessel," they *could* not be lost. And so He says, *Where, where* is your faith ?—When they saw His mighty work,

" They feared exceedingly."

When a man is brought to trust in Jesus, as a little child trusts a good loving parent, it ought to be, and it will be, " with reverence and godly fear " (Hebrews xii. 28). Oh happy men riding in this vessel ! Happy to know this—that the winds and the waves, and everything in this great universe, have got a *Master*—a Master who can speak to them, and command them, and still them, and rule them. If there were wild beasts in this country, we should be glad to know that there were those who could hold them in check, that we might not perish. And, when we look on the raging elements, and the storm, and the tempest, and think what *might* be, and ask, " Have the winds a Master ? Have the waves a Lord ? Have these worlds a Ruler ? "—if we can say, They *have* a Ruler, a Ruler in human form—our Brother —our Brother who loved us and died for us—our Brother who feels *for* us, who feels *with* us—who could sleep, exhausted, on a pillow, and yet rise in the might of Godhead and rebuke the tempest, and say, " Peace, be still ;"—then, we have blessedness indeed in knowing, that there *is* " a Saviour, and a great one " (Isa. xix. 20) who is able to save to the very uttermost.

V.

THE RAISING OF JAIRUS'S DAUGHTER.

OUR subject to-night is in two parts. Let us read verses, Mark v. 22—24—

" And, behold, there cometh one of the rulers of the synagogue, Jairus by name ; and when he saw him, he fell at his feet, and be- sought him greatly, saying, My little daughter lieth at the point of death : I pray thee, come and lay thy hands on her, that she may be healed ; aud she shall live. And Jesus went with him ; and much people followed him, and thronged him."

Here an interruption takes place—a woman comes to Christ, who had had a grievous malady as many years as this child, the daughter of Jairus, had lived. That we must leave till another time, and go on now to the 35th verse.

" While he yet spake [to the woman], there came from the ruler of the synagogue's house certain which said, Thy daughter is dead ; why troublest thou the Master any further ? As soon as Jesus heard the word that was spoken, he saith unto the ruler of the synagogue, Be not afraid, only believe. And he suffered no man to follow him, save Peter, and James, and John the brother of James. And he cometh to the house of the ruler of the syna- gogue, and seeth the tumult, and them that wept and wailed greatly. And when he was come in, he saith unto them, Why make ye this ado, and weep ? the damsel is not dead, but sleep- eth. And they laughed him to scorn. But when he had put

*them all out, he taketh the father and the mother of the damsel,
and them that were with him, and entereth in where the damsel
was lying.   And he took the damsel by the hand, and said unto
her, Talitha cumi; which is, being interpreted, Damsel, I say unto
thee, Arise.   And straightway the damsel arose, and walked;
for she was of the age of twelve years.   And they were astonished
with a great astonishment.   And he charged them straitly that
no man should know it; and commanded that something should
be given her to eat."*—ST. MARK v. 22-24, and 35-43.

YOU will have noticed that I have passed by one
miracle.   You know that, last Tuesday night, we were
talking of the miracle of stilling the tempest, of the
passage of our Lord and of others over the Sea of
Galilee.   When they got over to the other side, there
met Him " two possessed with devils, coming out of the
tombs, exceeding fierce "—one possessed of a " legion "
of devils, and he " ware no clothes."   I pass this by,
because many of you heard me speak of it in Chapel
Street, some time ago ;* and, you remember, that the
people of the country, when they saw Jesus, though He
had cast the devils out of one of their fellow-country-
men, " besought Him that He would depart out of their
coasts."   And so He got into a ship, and passed back
again to the western side, where there must surely
have been those, who were anxious to know the fate of
the vessels, which had been so tossed in the tempest.
They knew, probably, that many whom they respected
and loved had gone on board; they knew that Peter
and James and John, all fishermen, had got into the
boats, and you remember, it is said there were many

* See " Notes of Open-Air Sermons," iii. p. 33.

other little ships that went with them ; therefore, there must have been a considerable number in all the vessels. And then the great hurricane arose. If you had a husband, or a mother, or a father, or a brother, or any other relative just gone on board ship, and a hurricane came up, so that the beams and timbers in your very house creaked, you would say, If the tempest is so violent on the land, how will they fare on the rough sea? No doubt, these people on the western shore were very anxious all night, and, in the morning, went down to the shore, and looked on the lake, and then saw that all was calm ; and, instead of all the boats being shipwrecked, they would see them on the other side,—for Jesus, the Mighty One, had said, " Peace, be still." Therefore, no wonder, they came down to meet Jesus, to ask how they had all outridden the storm ; they themselves had, perhaps, been nearly blown away on *land*, yet how was this?—Not a sail rent, not a mast destroyed,—no injury to the ships. How had this happened, that while the hurricane was great, and perhaps destructive, on the *shore*, no harm had been done, through its violence, at *sea ?*

The next day probably, when many were sitting in the house of a remarkable man, Matthew, a publican,— who had made a feast, and brought a number of other publicans to hear the words of Jesus—(which is just what people ought to do; Matthew had come and found Jesus precious to his soul, and he says, " I will bring men as bad, as hard as I was, to hear Jesus ")— many controversies were carried on, and many hard words said. And, while Jesus was sitting there with the " publicans and sinners," there came—who do you think ?

"Behold, there cometh one of the rulers of the synagogue."

That was a great thing indeed—even a ruler himself had come to seek help at the hands of Jesus. The Pharisees said, " Have any of the *rulers* or of the Pharisees believed on him ? " (St. John vii. 48). Yes. *One*, at any rate—a ruler of the synagogue in Capernaum, a great man, a man highly esteemed among the people. It must have been a hard thing for him to break loose from all the old traditions, and to go after Christ. He must have felt it to be a very low door by which he came to Christ. It is *always* through a low door that men come to Christ; a man of a lofty and high spirit is sure to knock his head against that low door. But there is no knowing what trouble, when sanctified, may bring a man to do. Look at Naaman. What brought Naaman the Syrian to come, and humble himself at the cottage-door of the prophet of Israel ? Why, because he had a great, sore affliction, that he could not get rid of in any other way.

This " ruler of the synagogue " comes right into the feast amongst the publicans. What a strange company was that into which he came ! Here was the chief person in the synagogue, the man who stood at the head of religious profession in Capernaum, the man most highly esteemed as the chief teacher, and ruler of the principal place of worship, in Capernaum—and *where* did he come ? Not into a company of religious folks at all, not into another synagogue, but into a company of *publicans*, whom every Pharisee (and this man, no doubt, was one) and every chief ruler looked upon as unclean. Why, they looked on the publicans, as being as utterly unclean, as the very swine. They looked on the publicans (and indeed they deserved it) as thoroughly outcast, as thoroughly unclean things ; and they wondered, when Jesus Christ came, that He should look at one, take notice of one, " eat with " one (St. Luke xv. 2), because they mistook His mission, for He came to " call " " *sinners* to repentance " (St. Matt. ix. 13) ; and, therefore, He took His people from among sinners,—acknowledged sinners.

"Sinners gathered round Him ;
Lepers (whom nobody would dare speak to) sought His face."

And here, amongst all these, the ruler of the synagogue, lofty as he was, came to Jesus ; and, in one Gospel, it is said, that he " worshipped him " (St. Matt. ix. 18) ; here it is said,

" When he saw Him, he fell at His feet."

What a happy thing it is when a man is brought down to the feet of Christ ! The happiest place, the highest place really,—for it is the place of safety, the place of salvation, the sure way to the crown of honour and glory. The ruler came to Jesus, and " when he saw Him, he fell at His feet." What was it that drove him there ? It was trouble, it was affliction ; sorrow came into his house, something that touched him far more nearly, than if he himself had been the actual sufferer. This it was, that *drove* him into the presence of Jesus Christ. He comes, and confesses Jesus Christ in the presence of these publicans of Capernaum. We cannot easily imagine what sort of an impression this must have given. This ruler was not unknown. Everybody knew him; he was set on a pinnacle, as it were, in Capernaum — he was the great religious teacher, and one whom everybody looked up to; yet *he* comes and says, "*Jesus Christ is what I want*," and he finds Him amongst publicans and sinners.

How very different is this to what we read in St. Luke xv., where some came—they were of the Pharisees, and said, " This man receiveth sinners, and eateth with them :" therefore (as they imply) He cannot be a good man. Why, that was what He came for—to *receive* SINNERS, to *save* SINNERS. It is a great mistake for a man to think he is not a sinner. It was a great mistake for the Pharisees to think that these publicans were sinners, and that they were not. It would have been a great mistake for Jairus to have thought, that, because he was a great man and a ruler of the synagogue, therefore he did not need Jesus. " Matthew may go to Him—other publicans may go to Him; but *I* do not need Him. I do my best, I do what is right : let the publicans and sinners go to Him." No. Jairus might be a man without a spot on his character, a man of devout bearing and sincere religion,—but he says, " I cannot do without Jesus Christ; trouble is come to my house." And he came to Jesus, and fell at His feet—

" And besought Him greatly."

Now I want you to remember that word—"*greatly.*" There are some people who pray, who ask, who say, "Lord, save me;" but this man besought Jesus "greatly." *Why* did he beseech Him greatly? Because he knew what he was after, he knew what he was about, he knew what he wanted. He knew he could not do without it. His heart was breaking within him, he knew what he had left at home—he knew what Christ could do, he knew what Christ had been doing in Capernaum, and he says, "Why not for *me?* Jesus has done great things for others; He can do great things for me." So he comes.

Now, let me ask every one here, to-night—you have got a great trouble, every one of you, unless you have been healed, unless you have been to the feet of Christ and got the cure—let me ask you, every one, Have you come to lay your trouble at the feet of Jesus Christ, and have you "besought"—no, not besought only, but "besought Him *greatly,*" for deliverance from that great woe? You have something worse in your heart, than this ruler had in his house. Have you brought your soul to Jesus Christ for salvation? It is of no use our complaining, and standing aside mourning over calamities, unless we come with them to the great Physician,—come as this man came; when *he* had trouble in his house, he left his house, he left his wife, his servants, and his child, saying in his heart, "I must go to Christ," and when he came to Christ, he "besought Him *greatly.*" Have you carried your soul's sore disease there? have you carried your temptations there? and have you carried your child there, and besought Him greatly? *That* is the way to pray, and that is the *only* way to pray. People come and say, as we did just now, that they are lost, "miserable sinners;" but, when we ask what they mean, they seem to have meant nothing at all. They say, " Be merciful to us, miserable sinners,"—but they don't think themselves that, at all; they are, in their own esteem, a very respectable sort of sinners, if sinners at all. But this man *meant* what he said, and therefore he besought the Lord greatly, and he was not going to take a denial.

"My little daughter lieth at the point of death."

The man loved his child; she was his only child, and he loved her greatly (St. Luke viii. 42). Very likely, she was a very lovely child, and, therefore, very loveable. " My little daughter lieth at the point of death,"—

"I pray thee, come and lay thy hands on her, that she may be healed; and she shall live."

Yes; he had *one* daughter, and how greatly he beseeches Jesus. You have but *one* soul; have you ever besought Jesus greatly, about that one soul of yours? Have you said, " My soul is lying at the point of the second death?" This man had but one little daughter, and because he had *but one*, he was so thoroughly in earnest about her. And oh! you have but one soul— *but one soul*—but one life to live, and if that soul is lost, what utter desolation will that be! There is not another life in which you can come to Jesus—not another life in which to work out your salvation. There is *only one.* This ruler prays greatly, and shows, by his attitude, that he is not going away, unless he has the Lord with him. He will not stir an inch, he stops there with the publicans and sinners, beseeching Jesus Christ greatly *till* He comes—" My little daughter (mine only one) lieth at the point of death ; I pray thee, come and lay thy hands on her, that she may be healed ; and she shall live." Is not an immortal soul as precious, as the life of a little daughter, however precious that might be? Is not a soul that can never cease to be, a soul at the point of death, worth going to Jesus Christ on behalf of? " Come, lay thy hands on this dying soul of mine, and I shall live—live for ever."

"**And Jesus went with him ; and much people followed Him, and thronged Him.**"

Jesus arose—rose up from the table of Matthew, and quietly followed Jairus. Yes, Jesus Christ knows what He will do. He *can* be moved to rise up and go, but He must be besought *greatly*.

We come now to the point, where a great trial arose. We do not know the size of Capernaum, nor how far Jesus had to go from Matthew's house, which was probably outside the town, to that of the ruler, which would be near the synagogue ; but it was, probably, some considerable distance. This had been a great gathering at Matthew's house, and, consequently, we find that many of the publicans followed Jesus ; they had heard what Jairus had said, and they had seen Jesus rise up, and they say, " We will go with Him, and see what He is going to do." They had heard His fame, they had listened to the words of the ruler, " Come and heal my child, and she shall live;" and these hard-faced, hard-handed tax-gatherers go and follow Jesus. It is a wonderful sight! And as He was going the crowd thickened, as crowds always do. When there is something to be seen, a great crowd soon gathers; so a great crowd gathered round Jesus. And, presently, He stopped suddenly, and said, " Who touched me?" You remember how Peter rebuked Him, and said, " Master, the multitude throng Thee and press Thee, and sayest Thou, Who touched me?" (St. Luke viii. 45). The multitude were thronging and pressing Jesus ; they were *all* crowding on Him, but *one* TOUCHED Him,—touched Him of intent, touched Him purposely, touched Him of design ; and He knew it and said, " Somebody hath touched me : for I perceive that virtue is gone out of me" (St. Luke viii. 46). And the woman came, and confessed, and was sent away with a blessing. We shall have to consider that another time.

But, just think what this ruler was feeling, all that time. Jairus wanted *Jesus*, he had not wanted the crowd ; he had wanted Jesus to come quietly, but he found he could not have Him without the crowd. And then, some troublesome woman stops Him to get a blessing, and *He* tarries to listen to her. Just you think—his little daughter was lying at the point of death ; he had left her *dying*, and had said, "Come, lay thine hand upon her, and she shall live." " She may be gone"—and then there is a blockade in the street, they cannot get on, and Jesus takes it quietly. He speaks to the woman, He is no hurry to proceed, and

F

this poor father, his heart bleeding all the time, is long-ing to be gone, but he does not utter a word! I think this is very beautiful. We contrast it, and say he should have said, as the centurion did, "Speak the word only, and " she " shall be healed," instead of " Come and lay Thine hand upon her." But, after Jesus had got up and was going to heal her, and there comes the interruption, he does not say, " This woman's malady will keep, to-morrow will do for her, or a month hence; she has had that complaint as many years as my little daughter has lived, and she can wait. Mine is an urgent case; hers is not." No. Jairus came and besought Jesus greatly, but when the Lord has risen up and is going, he leaves it all in His hands. That is wondrous faith! The moment he sees Jesus Christ take the matter in hand, he is contented about it. The moment Jesus turns His face to go with him, all is well. " Jesus takes up the case; it is in His hands, then He will go through with it. Now let the Lord take His time, so that He has once got up to go. There I leave her. I can be happy about her. I can afford to let Him cure this woman ; and as I see Him cure her, I have a pledge there in what He *has* done, of what He will do for me. He heals her; will He not heal my child?" This is a beau-tiful instance of real faith; the man says, " I am con-tent," when once Jesus Christ takes the case into His hands.

Now, this had detained them some time ; and very likely, this man's domestics, or the servants of the synagogue, or some other ministers of the synagogue,

had been thoroughly averse to such a man as Jairus
going to Christ. It seems, that he had got up of his own
mere notion and will, and had left them, probably complaining that he had gone away when he ought to have
been with his dying child—that, when she was breathing her last, instead of going with this harum-scarum
message to this Prophet, he should have been at home.
So they would be only too ready, when the child was
dead, to go and say—

"**Thy daughter is dead; why troublest thou the
Master any further?**"

The word may not have conveyed a very respectful
meaning—" Why troublest thou *this teacher* any further?
Let him go on teaching. It is not his business to raise
the dead. ' Why troublest thou the Master any further'?
Let him alone; he cannot do anything now. Your
place is at home with your sorrowing family and your
dead child; come back and leave him with this crowd
of publicans."

"**As soon as Jesus heard the word that was
spoken,**"—The ear of Jesus is very quick; He was not
intended to hear that, but He *did* hear it, and "**He said
to the ruler of the synagogue**" (it was the first thing
He *had said* to him), "**Be not afraid, only believe.**"

Jesus had never spoken a word to him before. The
man had besought Him greatly to go, but Jesus did not
speak. He had got up and had gone home with him,
but He did not say, " I will heal her." But, when He
finds these people coming and tormenting him, saying
it was no use—" thy daughter is *dead;* why troublest

thou the Master any further?"—and Jesus sees the poor man's faith will be sorely tried, He says a gentle word to him,—" Be not afraid, only believe." And remember, how sore was the trial of his faith. He had heard of Jesus healing the sick, and therefore seeks *healing* for his child. But Jesus had not hitherto raised the *dead*. Jairus has nothing, now, *nothing* to encourage him,— nothing to warrant a further request, when lo, the voice of Jesus says, " Be not afraid—trust Me even in extremities—only believe." And that is the word that Jesus Christ says to the tried, tempted soul, that has been long waiting and saying, " Will the blessing ever come? It is beyond hope; I can never be saved." He says, " Be not afraid, only believe."

" And He suffered no man to follow Him, save Peter, and James, and John, the brother of James. And He cometh to the house of the ruler of the synagogue, and seeth the tumult, and them that wept and wailed greatly."

You know that it was a custom amongst the Jews, to hire people to wail and make a noise at funerals,—to wail as a sign of mourning, and set up a noise with their musical instruments, and so forth. It was put on for the occasion. They used to do it just to express the sorrow of the bereaved family.

" And when He was come in, He saith unto them (unto these hirelings), **Why make ye this ado, and weep? the damsel is not dead, but sleepeth."**

Now, *how should we look on* DEATH ? Here you see one very young, in the flower—in the prime of her young life—one very fair to look upon, only twelve years old ; and she lay there breathless, stiff and cold. How must we look at her? "The damsel is not dead, but sleepeth." Was it not a thing to weep over? Was it not a thing to be very grieved about? Here we see death in youth, death under the fairest possible aspect —the death of a child ; and yet Jesus says, "She is *not* dead, but sleepeth." What is death? "In the day that thou eatest thereof, thou shalt surely *die*" (Gen. ii. 17). What is that? Does it merely mean that the *body* would lie in the grave? No ; it meant that while the *body* would lie in the grave, the *soul* would be dead—*the soul would die.* There would be a "*second* death"—the body and soul dead—dead for ever and ever. That maid is *not* dead. The death of the body *and the soul*—THAT is real death. But *she* SLEEPS ; her soul is a living thing, it has been quickened by the Holy Ghost, she is a child of God. How the light broke in upon her, we cannot tell ; but she is alive to God, and therefore she is "not dead." She has not passed away, she is not in the power of death—he who has "the power of death" is not her keeper (Heb. ii. 14), she only "*sleepeth.*" Her body is dead, but her *soul* LIVETH. She—the real, living, thinking person is alive, alive to God. She only sleeps—"she is not dead."

"**And they laughed Him to scorn.**"

They had lamented before in *un*-reality ; they laugh in *earnest* now.

"**But when He had put them all out**"—

These were not the people to have about Him at such a time; these were not to be the witnesses of what He was about to do.

"**He taketh the father, and the mother of the damsel, and them** (the three chosen apostles) **that were with Him, and entereth in where the damsel was lying. And He took the damsel by the hand, and said unto her**"—in tones and words of supreme tenderness, like a gentle mother awaking her child— "**Talitha cumi; which is, being interpreted, Damsel, I say unto thee, Arise. And straightway the damsel arose, and walked.**

This is the first time we have any record of Jesus' raising the dead. Three times He raised the dead, according as we have the record. First, He raised a little girl, twelve years old,—then, a young man, the only son of his mother,—and then, Lazarus, who had attained to mature years. He raised one,—a child; another,— a young man; another,—a man in full maturity and vigour. In the first case, the breath had just gone out of the body; in the second, the young man had been dead a day, and was being carried to be buried; in the last, Lazarus had been dead four days, therefore "he stinketh," said his sister. So we see three instances of the power of death, and Jesus, in each case, quickening the dead.

And we see also *three several representations of three spiritual conditions.*

(1.) We find people like Lazarus, and it is said, "Do not open the grave, for 'he stinketh.'" We find some so dead in sin, so saturated in corruption, so vile, that others say, "Do not open up the sepulchre, lest you should be poisoned, as it were, with what comes out of that dreadful corruption." But Jesus Christ has power to raise even that vile, dead sinner, and to bring him out of the deepest pit of corruption—"Lazarus, come forth." If men are as spiritually corrupt, as Lazarus was supposed to be physically corrupt, Jesus Christ shows His power over that corruption ; therefore we are not hopeless over wretched sinners, over vile and outcast sinners.

(2.) Then look at the young man cut off in his strength, beginning to be corrupt so that he had to be buried,—not sunk yet, but just beginning to sink, into corruption. What multitudes are there, who are just tolerable above ground, but who will not be tolerable above ground long, because corruption is eating away at their heart and life, and, ere long, they will be so corrupt, will be such as he of whom it is said, "he stinketh." The very moral life is all dying out, and corruption is doing its work ; the man is not yet a pest, but is *becoming* a pest. And Jesus says, "Young man, I say unto *thee*, Arise."

(3.) And then, there are others who seem as if they are free from corruption ; they look so fair, so beautiful. Those who are just dead, often look more beautiful than they did in life. It seems, as if life were abiding in them somewhere or other, or as if a new loveliness had impressed and beautified the features. And yet, there is *death*. But now, Jesus takes this young girl by the hand, and says, " I say unto *thee*, Arise."

In all forms and in all states, till Jesus Christ has brought the new life of the Spirit into the soul, there is death; but He speaks to sinners who appear as fair as this fair young girl—to those who are sinking into corruption spiritually, as the young man whom He raised at Nain was bodily—to those who are as vile spiritually, as Lazarus had become physically; He can say to them —He, the only one glorious Saviour—the *Lord*, "*I* say unto *thee*, Arise."

"And He charged them straitly that no man should know it."

They could not help people's knowing it. There was a great crowd outside, and every one *must* know it. These minstrels, and all who were so sternly driven out, would be sure to noise it abroad, for they had lost their fees because there was no longer any matter to wail about; and now they would feel themselves aggrieved. What did the Lord mean—"*See thou tell no man?*" Once He had said, "Go home to thy friends, and *tell* them how great things the Lord hath done for thee" (verse 19). *Here* He says, "Let no man know it." There is something exquisite about it. "Don't you go and boast of it; look at this tender child—she *is* a tender child—don't you go and make a show of her. Don't you let people go asking her what she felt when she was dying, and what she felt when she was coming back. Don't you be making her something, and somebody, and turning her head. Let her be kept quiet, modest, humble." True religion is a very delicate thing; it does not go and show itself, it keeps itself very quiet, *and lives.* There she was ; there could be no mistake. Her living was a sign that she was alive ; that is enough,—she lives, this little girl. They might see her if they liked. It was her being alive that would tell what Jesus Christ was, not her tongue. "She lives —that is everything ; her doings, her acts tell it. Let her live in her father's house, quietly, modestly. Don't you go and make a show of her. Don't you go and boast, that Jesus Christ has gone and done this to exalt you." When she was delivered from death, she became her parents' child really for the first time. To have a child really, the parent must receive it from Christ.

" And [He] commanded that something should be given her to eat."

It is a wonderful thing to think of—that the moment she is alive again—as soon as Jesus has given her life, she is to be given something to eat ! He does not say, give her something to *do*, but something to EAT. The Lord meant that this young life, which was to be lived for God, and to be a testimony for Christ, should be lived in the shade, in quietude. "She will live, there can be no mistake about that ; I want not her tongue yet, it is enough that she *lives.* She knows Who has given her life ; she needs that life sustained. Nourish her, strengthen her, fit her to live."

How wonderful for this little maid, in two years more, before she was fourteen, to hear up in Capernaum that He who said, " Talitha cumi," had been Himself stretched on the Cross, and that in the last agony of that bitter death, He did not release Himself, did not bring Himself down from the Cross, but died— *died*. He did not fail at last—*He died* that she, the little one, might only *sleep;* that she might *never* die, He tasted the bitterness of actual death. She would hear of His dying, and she would hear, too, of His coming to life again. Perhaps, she was one of the many to whom He appeared in Galilee; perhaps, she was amongst the "five hundred brethren" (1 Cor. xv. 6) who saw Him who had been brought to life again. It might be that, in that great assembly, she was there with Jairus and her mother, to look on Him who had given her life, and whom she knew to be the life of the soul. She was really alive; and when He stood once more amongst His disciples, He did the very thing, in token of His risen life, which He here commanded she should do. " Have ye here any meat? And they gave Him a piece of a broiled fish, and of an honey-comb. And He took it, and did *eat* before them " (St. Luke xxiv. 42, 43). So He " commanded that something should be given *her* to eat."

There are many lessons that may be learnt here. And last, let me ask all here present, " Have you ever really come beseeching Christ, and beseeching Him *greatly*, saying, ' I have a poor, sinful, lost, dying, dead soul—I *beseech* Thee to come and heal me, O Lord?'" Then if *this* lesson be learnt, the others will be sure to be learnt, too. And when Jesus Christ gives new life to any soul, He says, "Give ye her to eat"—yea, break for her the " bread that came down from heaven," that

she may eat and never die. If we are to " live to God,"
we must ever be feeding upon " the Bread of God,"
which giveth life to the world, and of which if a man
eat, he shall " not die."

VI.

THE HEALING OF A WOMAN WITH AN ISSUE OF BLOOD.

" A certain woman, which had an issue of blood twelve years, and had suffered many things of many physicians, and had spent all that she had, and was nothing bettered, but rather grew worse, when she had heard of Jesus, came in the press behind, and touched his garment. For she said, If I may touch but his clothes, I shall be whole. And straightway the fountain of her blood was dried up; and she felt in her body that she was healed of that plague. And Jesus, immediately knowing in himself that virtue had gone out of him, turned him about in the press, and said, Who touched my clothes? And his disciples said unto him, Thou seest the multitude thronging thee, and sayest thou, Who touched me? And he looked round about to see her that had done this thing. But the woman fearing and trembling, knowing what was done in her, came and fell down before him, and told him all the truth. And he said unto her, Daughter, thy faith hath made thee whole; go in peace, and be whole of thy plague."—ST. MARK v. 25–34.

ON the last occasion when I addressed you, we considered the case of Jairus, the ruler of the synagogue. Jesus is still in Capernaum—" His own city "—so-called because of the many wonders that He did in it. Jairus came, you remember, came and besought Jesus to come and lay His hand upon his little daughter, who was at the point of death—as good as dead; and He rose and went after Jairus. And then, as I told you, the record of another wonder came in the midst of that, like a wedge—a woman met Jesus and the crowd, as they were going along and expecting some mighty deed to be done, because of the petition of Jairus. We see the multitudes following, and, while they were going along the street, the circumstance occurred which we have to consider this evening.

"A certain woman, which had an issue of blood twelve years,"
—a defiling, deadly malady, that had wasted her frame, blighted her life, undermined her health,—that had brought her, probably, to the last gasp of existence, and destroyed her every hope for this life,—and had not only destroyed her hopes, and wasted her health, but had taken away all her substance. She had laboured under a malady as bad, almost, as leprosy, for *twelve years.*

What had been her state during that long period— those twelve long years? She had *suffered* under the malady; she had been pained by it; she had been willing to undergo a great deal, if only she could be delivered from the malady, which is here called by the strong name of "*a plague.*" She had not been careless about it, she had not been indifferent about it; she had groaned under it, she had hated it, she was longing to be delivered from it. And she had done—what would naturally follow in a case of suffering, under circumstances that were displeasing and distasteful to the mind—she had *sought relief.* All those twelve years she had been seeking relief; very likely, there had not been a day, in which she had not been alive to her sore and destructive malady. She had been asking continually, Where is there " *balm* ?" Where is there " *a physician* ?" Where is there relief? Where is there help? Where is there a cure? She had never been careless about it; but, all the time, she had been longing for deliverance, sighing for relief—

"**And had suffered many things of many physicians.**"

Now let us realise these two fundamental things, before we go further. (1.) She *felt* this disease,—she felt it to be *a burden;* she hated it and groaned under it, as Naaman groaned under his leprosy. And (2.) she wanted *help;* she not only felt she had a disease, but she, earnestly and truly, *desired to be delivered from it.*

As I have told some of you before, some people have got a deadly disease, that causes them no pain and gives them no anxiety—and then, all at once, they are *gone.* But it was not so with this woman; her disease caused her great pain and suffering, so that she was willing to suffer *other* things, if only she could get rid of that suffering. In those long years, she had, very likely, tried every doctor who was worth trying, in all Capernaum. She would go to hear what this doctor had to say, and what that doctor had to suggest. Somebody had said they were worth a trial; she had heard, perhaps, that they had done somebody good, so she would think, " Perhaps they can do *me* good." So she had gone to them till, the Evangelist tells us, she—

"had spent all that she had (on 'many physicians'), **and was nothing bettered, but rather grew worse."**

She had not confined herself to one and said, " If he cannot cure me, it is of no use to go to anybody else." No. The disease would not let her rest, so long as she had it. No doubt, the doctors had used the best of their skill, they had done what they could—they had caused her a great deal of suffering in the process, but she was *"nothing bettered"* after all the doctors had done for her. You remember a story I once told you, about the piece of steel flying into a gentleman's eye ; he went to the doctors, and they cut here, and hacked there, but made it none the better. It only pained the eye more than ever—*he* " suffered many things of many physicians," and was only *the worse* for all they could do. You know how that story ends, but that is not to our present purpose.

This woman had " suffered *many* things of *many* physicians, and had spent all that she had." She had not another guinea left, if there had been any more physicians to try. Now this disease was so sore, that she had been willing to do this—to spend her " all " for the sake of health, to spend her " all " in the mere hope of health. That was going a great way. When people are willing to sell their plate, to sell their house, to sell their bit of land—when they are willing to part with *even their furniture*, to make up another fee to go to the doctor with, then we may be sure they have a racking malady, that will not let them rest and be at ease.

This woman was driven to try everything she could,

she "had spent *all* that she had." The doctors in Capernaum had got all that woman's property; she had parted with it all, in seeking for relief and health.

And what had it all come to? That she was more hopeless, more suffering, more miserable, lower down— all her property gone, and she not a bit the better for all that the doctors could do for her.

Now this was just the simple case of the woman, "when she heard of Jesus "—that is in the crowd, "she came in the press behind, and touched His garment." Now these words are to be noticed,—

"When she had heard of Jesus."

What a good thing it is to *hear* of Jesus Christ ! Of course, when she heard of Him, she thought of her disease, of her load. It is a *good* thing to hear of Christ. Some day or other, you may find out that you want Him, that you need Him, that nobody else can help you, that you are in as miserable a condition spiritually, as this woman was bodily. It is a good thing to *make* men hear of Christ. We often lament deeply over this, that so few people round us seem to want it, or to care for this. They say, it is a nice story about Jesus Christ, but they do not want Him *in particular ;* they do not feel that there is something He can do for them, that nobody else in the universe can do. They do not feel that there is something that all physicians fail in, and that He alone can succeed in. They have no particular desire for Jesus Christ. Perhaps I am speaking to many now, who think they can get on without Him, who feel it is very interesting to hear of what He did and of what He can do, but who never realise that they stand in the same need of His power and grace. They go on just as before; they do not feel, " I want Him, and if I do not find Him, I am miserable, and shall be lost."

It is a relief to know, that we have even made people hear of Him, so that, if it please God,—perhaps in some great affliction, in some sore trouble, or in some deep sorrow—it may be brought back to the mind that perhaps He could save, that perhaps He could help. I say, it is a good thing even to *hear* of Jesus Christ.

This woman heard of Him, and, no doubt, she thanks God now, in Heaven, that she ever heard of Him, that she had her great trouble for twelve years, and that she had spent all that she had, till she could not go to the physicians any more, and that she endured all that suffering and all that misery, which was needed to make her "feel her need of Him."

But another thought presses on us here. It will not do to be content, if you hear of Jesus Christ and go on as before. This woman did not. Supposing she had done so, supposing she had sat down and had made no effort, and had not gone to Him—supposing she had let Him go on uninterrupted to the house of Jairus, who can tell that she would ever have seen Him again? Who can tell that she would ever again have heard His voice, that she would ever have had an opportunity of coming near Him again? When she had heard of Jesus, she did what? She came. *When she had heard, she came.* That is right; that is what we want to see,

G

that is what we long for. When *she* had heard, she *came.* Yes, there were many hindrances in the way, many obstacles in the way of her coming to Christ. If she had not been in real earnest, she would never have got there. If she had wanted an excuse, there were plenty of them. How was this poor, sick, weak woman, to break through the crowd that was pressing on Jesus? But she did not want to make any excuse. Now, people generally want an excuse for not coming—when they can get rid of *this*, when *that* does not prevent them, they will come, they say. But where there is real earnestness, where there is real sense of need, no excuse is wanted. And if you do want an excuse, the Devil, who wants to destroy you, will give you an excuse at once.

This woman, in her weak, delicate state, with her poor, miserable, shrivelled form very likely, from all she had gone through, was scarcely able to bring her body into the presence of Christ—much less to thread her way through *a crowd*, for, as Peter first, and then the others, said, "The multitude *thronged* Him." We know what it is for a crowd to press, and this was a pressing crowd. There was plenty of excuse for her, but she came through all; she got through the crowd, and came, and—

"touched His garment. For she said, If I may touch but His clothes, I shall be whole."

Now what did she mean? You know, that under the Old Testament law, God commanded Israel by Moses to wear a certain *fringe,* or hem on the garment. In

Numbers xv. you find it all written out : " Speak unto the children of Israel, and bid them that they make them fringes in the borders of their garments, throughout their generations, and that they put upon the fringe of the borders a ribband of blue.   And it shall be unto you for a fringe, that ye may look upon it, and remember all the commandments of the Lord, and do them ; and that ye seek not after your own heart and your own eyes, ... that ye may remember and do all my commandments, and be holy unto your God" (Num. xv. 38-40).   Very well.   The Lord gave them that, they were to make it, and to look on it, in order to "remember all the commandments of the Lord and do them."   And what did the wicked heart of man do with that ?   Of course, it made it a mere form, so that we find them enlarging the borders of their garments and saying, We are holy.   They were to look on them, to make them *remember* the commandments of the Lord to *do* them—but they go and put them *in the place* of keeping the commandments.   But there was the command for every Jew to wear this border on his garment.

And this woman said, "If I may touch but His clothes, I shall be whole ;" and " she came behind Him, and touched the *border* of His garment" (St. Luke viii. 44).   Whether she looked on it as peculiarly sacred, we cannot tell.   Very likely, she thought of its being the portion of the garment that was worn by the command of God, and, as such, it was a consecrated, a sacred thing ; and, He being a consecrated and holy person, it was the most *fitting* thing, as it was the most *easy* thing, for her to stoop and touch.

Now then, she had heard of Jesus Christ to some purpose. You know what Jehovah said to Israel that He would be called—" Jehovah-Rophi "—that is, " The Lord that healeth thee "—" The Lord thy healer." And she says, " I have got God—I have got the Lord that healeth here, and health goes right down to the very skirts of His garment "—just like the sacred ointment of the High Priest—" that went down to the skirts of His garments," says the Psalmist (Ps. cxxxiii. 2). " And so this spiritual power to heal (says the poor woman,) belongs to every part—" Bless the Lord, O my soul . . . Who *healeth* all thy diseases " (Ps. ciii. 3). " If I may but come near Him, if I may but touch Him, if I may but touch the things that He has touched, I shall be whole."

See how she had learnt the truth. She had gone to the doctors, *speculating*—" I will go and *try* what they can do for me." But she does not say, " I will go and *try* Jesus Christ." No, but " I SHALL be whole—I shall be WHOLE,"—there was no trying, no speculating, all was real *certainty*. We know this was so, because we know what the Lord said to her when she came. She came by *faith*—" Daughter, thy *faith*—not doubt, not speculation—but thy *faith* hath made thee whole." She had heard of Jesus, she had heard of what He could do, and she believed it. Faith came into her heart, and she said, " He can heal me—He will heal me. These doctors couldn't. I have only lost everything, I am without health, without strength, without a penny! Yet, if I may but touch His clothes—(*not*, I shall be relieved, I shall get a little ease, but) I shall be whole, I shall be cured, perfectly cured."

And Jesus says, That is *faith*. Now you see these fundamental truths stand out in bold relief,—she *felt* her malady, she groaned under it. Some think their prayers will save them, some think that penances will save them, some think attendance on ordinances will save them. *No! Nothing will save but contact with Jesus Christ.* This woman had gone here and there, to this doctor and to that doctor, as the poor Jews try to work out a righteousness of their own; but none could cure her. She had a malady beyond their reach. *So have we*, but the difference is, we do not *feel* it. None of us do, till we have been led and taught by the Holy Spirit. It is one thing to have a disease, it is another thing to *feel* we have it. Therefore, when God was picturing *conviction of sin*, He represented it by *leprosy*, —because what man that had that, could ever be unconscious of it? A man may have heart-disease, and be unconscious of it, and may drop off in his sleep. But a leper has only to look at his hand, or to look at himself in the glass, and he would know at once what he was. Therefore God pictures a sinner, convicted of sin, as a *leper*—he loathes it, he hates it, he groans under it; he asks, Who can save me? It makes a great man like Naaman, willing to travel all the way down the country, and bend at the prophet's lowly cottage-door. It must have been hard work for him to stoop to that—for a great captain, for the greatest man in all Syria, to come to the prophet of *Israel*. He must have been in a very sorry state, to have been made willing to do that. And this poor woman feels she will suffer anything, she will go anywhere, for relief ; and, at last, she hears of One who can do everything. And she says, " If I may touch but His clothes, I shall be whole ;" and she goes right through the crowd, and lays hold of the hem of His garment. But we must go on.

"And straightway the fountain of her blood was dried up ; and she felt in her body that she was healed of that plague."

Now we see, that as soon as ever she comes in contact with Jesus, as soon as ever she comes to Him by " faith," as soon as ever she comes to fetch a blessing, *she gets the blessing.* But nobody comes to Jesus Christ without the leading of the Holy Spirit. She came, stealthily, through the crowd, to get a touch of Him. He did not see her, but He knew it. He knew it, because He is God, because He knows all things. He knew what was in her heart,—He knew, when He got up to follow Jairus, that this woman would meet Him, and seek for healing.

"And Jesus, immediately knowing in Himself that virtue had gone out of Him (knowing that He had cured her), **turned Him about in the press, and said, Who touched My clothes ?—** *Who touched My clothes ?"*

Now this shows many things. Amongst others, it shows the wonderful love of Christ. "*He* is not ashamed to call" us "brethren"; and now He says to the woman, "Do not be ashamed of *Me:* you have come and stolen healing virtue for yourself"——" *Who* touched My clothes?" He will have her own Him, He will have her acknowledge Him. He says to this woman, "Tell out what has been done for you." While, on the one hand, He is not ashamed of His people, however diseased, however wretched, however ruined, however great the malady they are saved from,—yet, on the other hand, He will not have them ashamed of Him, He will have them come out and acknowledge Him. Jesus knew she was ready to do it—He knew that if she had faith to be *healed*, she had faith to *confess* Him. But He would have her state with her own lips, how she had come, what she had got, and how she had been healed.

And then there is another thing. Why is this written in this Book? Why are we discussing it continually? Has it any lesson for you and for me? It is intended to teach us this—God often chooses "the poor of this world rich in faith" (James ii. 5). And here was a great man carrying Jesus off, and this poor woman, a beggar—for her "all" was gone—intervenes. But Jesus stops. He is not in such a hurry to go to Jairus's house, though Jairus was the chief ecclesiastic in all Capernaum. Jesus is in no hurry. This poor woman stops Him in the way, and out of this poor woman's mouth, He will instruct the heart of this greatest ecclesiastic in Capernaum. Jesus wants to teach him something. You remember that when Jairus said, " Come and lay

Thy hands on her," Jesus had risen up, and said *not a word;* but, to this woman, He says, " Come and preach this sermon to Jairus, the ruler of the synagogue ;" and He brings her forward, with her simple story only, to tell Jairus the great truth. *She* came, saying, " If I may touch but His clothes, I shall be whole ;" and here was Jairus going, with a bleeding heart, home to his little daughter,—thinking that she will be gone, yet he must stop. It was a trial to his faith—yet Jesus stops him to hear what this poor woman has to say, of Jesus and His healing power. He says to her, " *You* tell Jairus."

And many an opportunity have those in high posi-tions, of learning their best lessons of Christ in this way. It is often by the bed of the sick, and suffering, and sorrowful—by the bedside of the very poor, too, that we learn our best lessons of God's power and grace.

Those, who imagined that they wanted nothing, might have said, " What ! this poor woman teach Jairus ! And Jairus might have said " *She* teach *me !* *I* know all the Old Testament, and I can expound all the law. I have counted every letter of it. What then can this creature teach me?"

But Jesus says, " Come and teach him." And she comes, and stands forth, and teaches, not only Jairus, but the apostles. **The disciples**—His chosen disciples —first Peter, and then the others—**said unto Him, " Thou seest the multitude thronging Thee, and say-est Thou, Who touched Me ?"**

A very natural observation indeed. A great many things are very natural, which are not exactly the right things. It was as much as to say that Jesus did not know everything. The disciples had not got hold of the truth that He, whom they were following, was God as well as man—that He could see behind as well as before Him. He, who clothes the lilies and cares for the sparrows, must surely know who "touched" Him, though He did not see her. Yet these disciples of His did not believe. So Jesus says to the poor woman, "Stand up and teach My disciples, enlighten their ignorance." And then, out of that thick crowd— who would ever have supposed it? who would ever have imagined it?—Jesus makes a dead stop,—Jairus wanted to get on as fast as he could to his little child; but he has to stop while Jesus looks round, and bids her tell what He had done for her; and

"The woman fearing and trembling."

No wonder she trembled, when every eye was upon her, and the Lord and Master had called her to tell whose power she had felt in her body. She felt she was well, that she had been made "whole," and that "straightway." And now, He who had done it, calls and says, "Who touched Me?" And she comes trembling, and confesses. She—

"Knowing what was done in her, came and fell down before Him, and told Him all the truth."

I think that is a wonderful word—"she *told Him all the truth*." That is what Jesus Christ expects. If we have already been saved, we have been at His feet, and there we have told Him "all the truth." We must keep nothing back, we must pour out before Him all our life, all our wicked life, all our sins—"she told Him all the truth." There is not a more blessed sight in all the world, than to see this woman at the feet of Jesus, and just telling Him all the truth. She might have said, as the hymn, that we have just been singing, says—

> " I need not to confess my life
> To Thee, who best can tell
> What I have been, and what I am ;
> I know Thou knowest it well."

She knew that *He* knew it ; but He wanted her to tell it out. He wanted Jairus and His disciples and the people to know all the truth—and she confesses all. And then Jesus said unto her,

"Daughter, thy faith hath made thee whole: Go in peace, and be whole of thy plague."

Now, what is this? *How* had her faith made her whole ? Faith itself does not save. If I believe that I have £10,000, that does not make it a fact. No such thing. Faith does not save, but it does this—it brought this woman to Jesus. She believed on Him ; she believed He was able to do this for her ; she believed He was able to cure her, able to cleanse her, able to save her. She believed that He could save her, because He was God, by His very *touch*. So, faith brought her to Christ. When she had gone to the other doctors, very likely she had *hoped ;* but when she went to Christ, she *believed.* When she went to them, it was to *try ;* when she came to Christ, it was with *certainty. She* says, " If I may touch but His clothes, I *shall* be whole." So *He* says—" Thy faith hath saved thee"—*She* had said, "I know that Christ has power to heal and to effect all that I want ;" and now *He* says, " Daughter, go in peace, and be whole of thy plague." She was not cured so that the malady might come back, but cured to go on her way rejoicing.

There are a good many lessons to be learnt from this, which I hope have been picked up by all, and that they will go with us—and may many whom I address to-night " Go and do likewise."

VII.

THE HEALING OF THE PARALYTIC.

*" And he entered into a ship, and passed over, and came into his own
city. And, behold, they brought to him a man sick of the palsy,
lying on a bed : and Jesus seeing their faith said unto the sick of
the palsy, Son, be of good cheer ; thy sins be forgiven thee. And,
behold, certain of the scribes said within themselves, This man
blasphemeth. And Jesus knowing their thoughts said, Wherefore think ye evil in your hearts ? For whether is easier, to say,
Thy sins be forgiven thee ; or to say, Arise, and walk ? But
that ye may know that the Son of man hath power on earth to
forgive sins, (then saith he to the sick of the palsy,) Arise, take
up thy bed, and go unto thine house. And he arose, and departed to his house. But when the multitudes saw it, they marvelled, and glorified God, which had given such power unto
men."*—ST. MATT. ix. 1–8.

THIS miracle was wrought when our blessed Master
had come forth from that, I may say, almost enforced
retirement, into which He had been driven by the un-
restrained zeal of one, on whom He had conferred an
inestimable benefit. From that retirement He came
forth, still in the early part of His ministry, to " *His own
city,*" Capernaum ; and there He entered into a house,
possibly the house of Simon Peter. Around Him in
that house were gathered what, for such a place, was a

great multitude, so that very soon afterwards, there was not room for any one to pass in and out in the house itself, or in the courtyard immediately around it. The miracles which the Lord Jesus had wrought, had attracted the attention, and compelled the serious consideration of many thinking persons. And, at the present moment, we find Him surrounded, not only by ordinary sight-seers, not only by those who were gathered from the immediate vicinity, but by scribes and " Pharisees and doctors of the law," from all parts "of Galilee," from " Judæa," and even from " Jerusalem" itself (St. Luke v. 17). It was, therefore, an important occasion—an assembly of considerable moment, an audience of great interest from almost every point of view ; and it was to such an audience, crowded together in an incommodious dwelling-place, that Jesus was now speaking words of eternal life. The words of grace, which were for ever falling from His lips, were now being poured forth, in the riches of His goodness, on this strange assembly.

It would be interesting to us, if we might stop and speculate on the feelings that animated this assembly. They must have been feelings of great variety,—feelings of wonder, feelings of astonishment, feelings of envy, of hatred, and of deep, determined malice—but we cannot stop to ponder this. We must proceed to consider somewhat concerning the miracle itself.

On this occasion, when every avenue to the presence of Jesus was firmly fixed and blocked up, so that there was not so much as room for *one* to pass in, we find *four* men—as St. Mark tells us—bringing one **"sick of the palsy, lying on a bed,"** (St. Mark ii. 3), to be healed by Jesus of his infirmity. Our attention is first attracted by this strange scene, by these four remarkable men,—four men, who had given up their day's occupation, and devoted themselves, of their love and goodness, to the interest of a fellow-creature,—four friends of a poor man, a *paralytic* man, a helpless man, a man requiring four persons—such was his malady—to bring him into that sacred Presence.

And we see them, bringing their burden to the outskirts of the assembly, and then they find *a difficulty*, an impossibility, in the way of their coming to Christ. They wish to bring that burden of theirs, and to lay it down at the feet of Jesus. They wish to bring the poor, helpless, agonising sufferer, to look up in the face, and hear the words of Him, who could do for this man what He had done for multitudes—recover him of his infirmity, and heal him of his disease. Yet, with all their good intentions, with the very best intentions, these men,—thoroughly determined to bring him, whom none else could help, into the presence of Jesus,—find the way blocked up. They knew no one else could effectually save him, and we find them, when carrying out this grand, sacred purpose of theirs, met by an insuperable obstacle. The crowd was so thickly pressed together, and every man so determined to keep his own place, that there was not room for *one* to pass through, much less for *four*,—much less for four men bearing, on his bed, one who needed the gracious help of Jesus.

Now, we hear much about difficulties, much about impossibilities. We hear the souls of men groaning, and complaining that they *cannot* come to Christ, that they cannot get at Christ, that they can neither see His face, nor hear His voice. They want the forgiveness of sins, they want comfort in their hearts from the knowledge of that forgiveness, they want to come—but they stop short. There are some difficulties in the way, obstacles present themselves, and they are beaten at once—they give in. They cannot see Him face to face, and hear the assurance of forgiveness, so they give it up, and sit down in the outer court, in a sort of sullen contentment.

How unlike is this to the *real* earnestness, how unlike to the real determination of those, who feel that they *must* have help, or die—that they must come to Christ and hear His voice, or else they will be lost ! The reason of it is just this—men do not realise fully, that, unless they come to Christ, unless they hear His voice and get the blessing from Him, they *will* be *lost,* because of a deep, settled conviction that they are helpless in themselves, and undone, and lost, and that He alone can help, He alone can save, He alone can speak the word which shall give liberty to them, and speak healing to their souls, and bless them for all time, and for all eternity.

Now, let us look again at these four men, and their sad, helpless, decrepit burden. They find difficulties in coming to Christ, the way is hedged up—the crowd is pressed together thick, close, fast. The obstacle is insuperable, there is not an inch for them to edge into the presence of Christ anyhow.   They stand and see the way closed against them—as physically closed, as the moral way seemed closed against the woman of Syro-Phœnicia, when Jesus said to her, " It is not meet to take the children's bread, and to cast it to dogs." (St. Matt. xv. 26).   They see the way to Christ firmly blocked up, yet they say, " We *must* go to Christ, we are determined to lay down our burden at Christ's feet. Whether it is impossible or not, *we mean to come* to Christ.   If the crowd will not make way for us to come, yet we are determined to get to Him, and for this reason,—if *He* cannot help this helpless one, none else can.   If *He* cannot save him, no one else can.   If this opportunity is lost, another opportunity may never come.   " *Now* is the accepted time, *now* is the day of salvation " (2 Cor. vi. 2).   We must come to Christ, whatever the obstacles in the way may be.

These men are men of faith.   " Love (said one of old) may creep, but faith will climb."   And so, faith in these men climbs over every obstacle.   Though it be a great high mountain, faith will climb over it, if Christ be on the other side.   These men come, and they find the way closed against them, but they do not, therefore, sit down and fold their hands and say, We cannot do it. They would have held themselves disgraced, if they had said such words.   They desired a blessing, they were determined to have the blessing, and " the kingdom of heaven should suffer violence, and the violent take it by force " (St. Matt. xi. 12), rather than that they would go away without a blessing.

These men will rise up in the judgment against all who say the difficulties were so great, that they could not come to Christ. It is placed here on the pages of inspiration, to show this,—that, where there is real knowledge, where there is real faith, difficulties will vanish, and obstacles be removed out of the way. Faith is not only a grace that climbs over mountains and housetops, but it is a grace that will take no denial, and is rich in ingenious devices. If there is no way *through* the multitude to Christ, faith will try to get up towards heaven, in order to come down before His face. So they made their way to the housetop. They could not get to Christ in the ordinary way—but, when they could not get to Christ in the ordinary way, they ask themselves whether there is not an extraordinary way. If a man *wishes* to get to Christ, *he will* get to Christ. If a man sets his mind upon anything, and says it is a matter of life or death, he will find ways and means. And so did these men—they devised means. It was not for themselves, but it was for another; it was not that they might be healed, but that he might be healed.

"**Their faith**" in this case is all the more remarkable. No doubt, it was pressed on them, infused into them by the faith of him (as we shall see presently), whom they were carrying as a heavy burden. Their hearts must have been moved by some mighty influence, moved by this man, cast down, weary, suffering, earnest, loving, wanting Christ, desiring to come to Christ—getting them to bring him to be healed of his malady, yet, in his secret heart, desiring to come that he might be healed of an infinitely worse malady, and get an infinitely higher blessing, than any mere freedom from physical suffering could possibly be.   But look at faith climbing—climbing to the housetop, in order to get to Christ.

I need not, I suppose, waste a moment of precious time in reminding you, that you must not think of our western buildings here.   The shortest way to the housetop, was on the *outside* of the dwelling-place, and, therefore, there was not so much difficulty, though quite sufficient ingenuity was needed.   No doubt, it was an original idea, and " faith " gave them that original idea, which led them to go up those steps to the roof of the house ; and there we find them, diligently, carefully, cleverly removing one thing after another, clearing away every obstacle, taking away every impediment in order to get their sick one to Christ.

Wherever there is real coming to Christ, there will be obstacles, sometimes very mountains of difficulty. In the Gospel, we read of one in faith trying to bring his son to the feet of Christ, and he asked Christ's disciples to cure him, and they could not ; and Jesus said, " Bring thy son hither."   We must expect that there will be difficulties in the way of our coming to Christ— " as he was yet a coming, the devil threw him down, and tare him " (St. Luke ix. 42).   Yes—only let him see real determination in any soul to get to Jesus Christ, and, if there are not difficulties in the way, he will make them, and put them in the way.   So here.

" They could not come nigh unto Him for the press,"
(St. Mark ii. 4) ; so they get upon the housetop.

And now, difficulties of another kind meet these
men. They have to uncover the roof, and to break it
up, carefully, lest they should attract too much attention, or cast any portion of the roof on the congregation below. They brake it up. Faith is not only
clever and ingenious, but it is also a very careful grace.
Faith can not only get up the steps on to the housetop,
but is also clever enough, and careful enough, to remove
the roof so that those beneath should not be disturbed,
in order to get into the presence of Jesus.

Thus we see the faith of the sick man, and the faith
of those who carried him up. Their faith stands here
on the inspired page, to tell the half-hearted and the
mere formal, pretended seeker after Christ, that if there
is a real sense of need, if there is real, determined earnest desire after Him who can meet every need, no
obstacle can thwart, no difficulty can baffle. They
stand here to prove, that if men keep away from
Christ, they will have no excuse when the secrets of all
hearts shall be disclosed. It will be said to them, " Ye
were not willing to come to Me, that ye might have life "
(St. John v. 40). If they were really willing, they would
go up the steps even outside the house, and break up
the roof, as did these men.

And now the man was let down—what a strange
scene it must have been in that assembly ! There were
gathered together Pharisees and doctors of the law
from Jerusalem, and country schoolmasters from all

parts of Galilee ; and, before all these captious and envious men, this poor paralytic was let down.   He came, professedly, for a *temporal* good ; he came, professedly, to be healed as other men had been healed. But, as he lay there, Jesus said,

"Son, be of good cheer, thy sins be forgiven thee."

Now, one of the great lessons from this passage is this,—how Jesus reads every thought and intent of the heart.   We see by His words to this man, that He interpreted what was in his heart.   "Son, be of *good cheer.*"   This shows us what was in the man's heart ; he was very sad, he was not of "good cheer."   His heart was very heavy, and there was only one thing that could make him of good cheer, and that was to know that his sins were forgiven.   Jesus does not say, "Son, be of good cheer, thy *palsy* is cured," but—"Son, be of good cheer, thy *sins* be forgiven thee."   Therefore, Jesus knew what would make the man of good cheer, that what would make him bright, and happy, and blessed, even though he remained a paralytic to the end of his days, was the assurance that his sins were forgiven him—"Son, be of good cheer, thy sins be forgiven thee."

And, remember, when Jesus Christ says a word like that, it is a word that goes right into the heart.   He *effected* what He *said.*   He did the thing that His words expressed.   He conveyed the good cheer along with the forgiveness of sins.   He made the man happy, though he was a paralytic yet, though he lay still in his palsy.   Nothing had been done yet to his poor body, which was, in all probability, fatigued and exhausted from being carried about. He was still suffering from the paralytic affection which rendered him helpless, yet we find, all at once, the sadness had gone—his sad days had ended, his groans had passed away, and happiness, peace, and life, and love filled the soul, that had just been crushed down under the burden of sin. The man came to be healed, but, in his heart, he was wanting a higher blessing. He was coming there to Jesus, in order that He who could heal diseases, might forgive his sins. He might have been thinking of what is said in one of the Psalms—" Who forgiveth all thine iniquities, who healeth all thy diseases" (Psalm ciii. 3). " Son (said Jesus) be of good cheer, thy sins be forgiven thee."

And now came *the contrast.* In those words, Jesus Christ had claimed the Divine prerogative ; in those words, Jesus Christ had assumed to Himself Divine authority. There was nothing wrong in their arguing thus—" Who can forgive sins but God only?" (St. Mark ii. 7). That, my friends, is *true.* They were perfectly right, their theology was sound enough *there—* " who can forgive sins but God only?" Where they were deficient was in this,—that He stood before them claiming to *be* God, and saying that He *was* God, and they could not see Him *to be God.*

It is not that they were wrong in saying, " Who can forgive sins but God ?"—but they were wrong in not seeing that *He* who healed the diseases, He who cleansed the lepers, and who was standing now in their midst, exercising Divine power over material things, could be none other than One *equal to* GOD.

That was the great mistake, that was the great controversy all along, that was the ground on which, at length, they nailed Him to the Cross—" Thou being a man, makest thyself God " (St. John x. 33). And *that* is the great controversy *still*, that is what the inquiring, anxious heart of man feels it *must* know.

> " So guilty and helpless am I,
>   I dare not confide in His Blood,
> Nor on His protection rely,
>   Unless I were sure He is God. "

The half-awakened, the *un*awakened man longs after a religion of beauty. Many are satisfied with all that is fair and beautiful in the life of Jesus, but the man who has gone into the depths of his own nature, and found there the foul uncleanness of sin, who has gone through the length and breadth of the Divine law, and found that it reaches to the thoughts and intents of the heart, who has seen the holiness of the Divine character, and viewed sin in the light of heaven,—that man knows, that none but *Almighty* power can lift him up, that no grace that is not *Infinite* likewise can atone for him.

There is the contrast. These men do wish for a teacher, for a restorer, for a Messiah,—but without Divine attributes. But the lost, helpless sinner, the poor paralytic lying before Jesus, knew that he wanted the *Divine* presence, the Divine prerogative, Divine power, Divine grace all exercised on him, or he never could be of " good cheer,"—*never*. He knew there was a sadness pressing upon his heart, that none but "the Living God" could ever take off. The man, who is *dead* in sins, never feels it. The man, *half*-awakened, may feel something, but not this great need. And this controversy was thus ever being carried on. Jesus stands and exercises the power of God on that man—"Son (He says) thy sins be forgiven thee."

What a word to be spoken in a world like this! What a word to be spoken with authority by Him, to one who knew himself to be a sinner! And what happiness would it be, if that word had gone the round of the wide world, and infused into all hearts the knowledge, that there was One on earth who could say, Son, thy *sins* be forgiven thee—that there was one whose sins *had* been forgiven by that One, and that men were everywhere led to argue thus—If that man has been forgiven, why should not *I* be forgiven? Why, if He can forgive truly the sins of one, should not all, who flock to His feet desiring forgiveness, hear the word, "Son, *thy* sins are forgiven *thee*?"

"And, behold, certain of the scribes said within themselves, This man blasphemeth."

These men, who were looking on, talked in their hearts. They did not dare, in that Divine presence, to do it openly, but, in their secret heart, they reasoned and complained, and said, "This man *blasphemeth*." Now, the word "blasphemy" in this and other passages does not, necessarily, mean to speak evil against any, but to detract from, or to lay hold of something in the Divine character, and to rob it of that. So they say here, "This man blasphemeth." "You are robbing God (they say)—you are robbing God of one of His prerogatives; you are taking what belongs to God, and arrogating it to yourself. 'Who can forgive sins but God only?'"

And they were perfectly right from *their* point of view. If Jesus had been no more than Peter, if He had been no *more* than a man, He would have been justly chargeable with this allegation. It all depends simply upon this—*who* it was that was saying this.

"And Jesus, knowing their thoughts"—

He saw into their hearts, He sees into all hearts, He knows every thought of every heart, and judges it. And He saw into theirs. He saw this—that *right* in *one* point, they were *wrong* in *another*. He who was God's Eternal Son, He who was God's anointed Messiah, He who was the Redeemer on whom help was laid for the helpless, was standing in their midst, and Him they were rejecting in their *hearts;* and so He said to them,

"Wherefore think ye evil in your hearts?"

They were not thinking rightly of Christ. "As a man thinketh in his *heart*, so is he" when he thinks of Christ. They were thinking in their hearts of Christ, and thinking *evil* of Him. And therefore He asks—

"Whether is easier, to say, Thy sins be forgiven thee; or to say, Arise and walk?"

Now, let us understand our Lord's meaning here. He does not say, Whether is easier, to *forgive* sins, or to *cure* a paralytic, by a word; He does not say that, He does not mean that. But—whether is easier to *say*,

Thy sins be forgiven thee, or to *say*, Arise and walk?
That is, whether it is easier to claim the Divine prero-
gative of forgiving sins, or easier and safer to claim the
Divine prerogative of healing diseases?

Of course, it is far easier to claim the power of forgiving sins,—because, a man may claim that power,
and, the heavens being closed to mortal vision—it cannot be proved or disproved by his hearers.   But, if he
claim the power of healing diseases miraculously, his
claim can be brought, at once, to the test.   If he says,
" I claim the power of forgiving sins," we say, " That
may, or may not, be so ; we must have *proof* of it,"
which may not be so easy.   But if he claims to cure a
paralytic, we can tell at once—we say, " Let us see him
arise and walk."

These men were thinking " evil " in their hearts concerning Christ. They were setting Him down as an im-
postor.   They say, " He claims the power of forgiving
sins, and He knows we cannot bring Him to the proof,
because we cannot go into heaven to see if the sin,
which is, professedly, forgiven on earth, is, actually, forgiven in heaven. He is safe there. He is not only
claiming the Divine prerogative, but He is going upon
ground where He cannot be confuted."

And then, Jesus meets them on their own ground—
" Whether is easier to say, Thy sins be forgiven thee,
or to say, Arise and walk."   You all admit it is *not* so
easy to *say*, " Arise and walk," because that can be
brought to the test ; and therefore you think that is
why *I* said, " Thy *sins* be forgiven thee."

"But that ye may know"—

We see here what the Lord puts before these men. What He wanted them to know was this—"that **the Son of man hath power on earth to forgive sins."**

He wanted them to know it, He was determined that it should be known.   It was His gracious will that we, upon whom the ends of the world are come, should know *the greatest of all facts.*   No knowledge under the sun can be compared in value to that—"that ye may know that the Son of man *hath* power on earth to forgive sins."   "That ye may KNOW."

Now, I ask, do we estimate knowledge as Jesus Christ estimated knowledge?   Are our minds made up about this—that the most important of all knowledge possible to us, is the knowledge of this one fact—"that the Son of man hath power on earth to forgive sins?" The Lord stands there in the midst of these captious people—people who were thinking evil in their hearts, people who were rejecting Him, people who would continue to reject Him to the end,—yet He says, "O that *ye* may know that the Son of man hath power on earth to forgive sins."   Jesus Christ will have that knowledge conveyed to all there—to the despisers and rejecters, as well as to the earnest and longing ; to all He would have that knowledge conveyed—"the Son of man hath power on earth to forgive sins."

We may have all knowledge and all wisdom about every manner of thing, but if we are without *that* knowledge, then what shall we do in those great swellings, when our sins rise up before us as a lofty mountain in their height, threatening to crush us beneath their weight? What shall we do when death looks us in the face, and the judgment is a reality to us, and we find ourselves in a grasp from which we cannot escape, if we have not found that knowledge of Him who can remove those mountains of guilt, and take away those iniquities, and put away those sins,—"The Son of man Who hath power on earth to forgive sins?"

Yes, that is a word that speaks to every soul in this assembly. It spake to the man lying still in his paralysis; it spake right to his heart in warm, living, loving accents, and he said in the depths of his heart, "He *has* the 'power,' He has removed the burden. I care little now for the palsy because my sins are forgiven— those sins, which would have shut heaven against me, and made eternity all blackness and darkness for ever, are all gone."

Christ spoke to those men who were rejecting Him, and accusing Him, in their hearts, of blasphemy, and said—"Oh men, whose mortal life is but a vapour, and who must yet live for ever and ever, are you sinless? And if you are not sinless, what will you do with your sins? If you are pining away in your iniquities, what will be the end thereof?" It was a word to them all. And it is that Divine, blessed knowledge, which He has commanded to be preached throughout all the earth, that will justify Him who sits on the throne, when He says to the impenitent, "Depart, ye cursed."—"That they may know that the Son of man hath power on earth to forgive sins."

If you have not yet your sins forgiven, if you have not the peace that comes from forgiveness, it is not because *the Son of man* has not *power*, it is not because the Son of man is not willing, but because "*ye will not come* unto Him that ye might have life." You do not feel your need of it, you have not that faith which will find steps up to the·housetop, or that will break up the roof when it gets there.

These words are words of *life*—they are words of everlasting life—" The Son of man hath power on earth to forgive sins." There are many dark spots on the earth. The earth is, but too often, a very dreary desert, there are mysteries and darknesses settling upon it. Death and Sin cast their dark shadow over this world, a gloom which no power can dispel,—facts against which the infidel may close his eyes, and not choose to see now; but the closing the eyes to them will never dispel them. Sin and Death cast their dark gloom from one end of the world to the other; and these words are the *only* words which, spoken to the soul, can ever dispel that gloom. And yet, men will not come to Christ for life, they will not seek Christ; they will rather give way to the doubt that leads to *mis*belief,—and from misbelief to confirmed *un*belief,—and from confirmed unbelief in revealed truth to belief (if such it can be called) in a dread Infidelity.

I have read of one, of whom it was said, that he had wandered in spirit to the outskirts of creation,—had seen the socket where the eye *should* have been, and had heard the shriek of a Fatherless Universe. What desolation! A socket, but no eye—a casket, but no gem—a skull, but no brain—a body, but no soul—a world, but no God—a Universe, but no Father! Well might the Universe shriek if it found it was Fatherless! Well might his heart fail when all reality was banished, and a mere dead desolation occupied its place.

But, the Son of man stood on the earth, bone of our bones, flesh of our flesh, with the Divine prerogative and Infinite grace of the Eternal God, and said, "That ye may know that the Son of man hath power on earth to forgive sins,

"(Then saith He to the sick of the palsy), Arise, take up thy bed, and go unto thine house."

Therefore, He hath power to heal sickness, *because* He hath power to bind up the brokenhearted—power to bring the sinner back again to his God and his Father, that he may never feel desolation more, but learn to cry, Abba, Father. Well may such an one say, " In Thee I have all, for Thou hast forgiven my sins." When the sinner comes to ask the question, What must I do to be saved? and would that all might be asking that question, for it is the one solemn question of importance for men to be asking, and the one question of importance for them to have answered,—I say, when you come to ask that question, let these words ring in your ears—" The Son of man hath power to forgive sins." And He who can say, " Thy sins are forgiven," can say, " Arise and walk."

There is nothing that *He* cannot do, who can forgive sins. Though it is easier to *say*, Thy sins be forgiven thee, it is infinitely more difficult to *forgive* sins.   An act of *power* could heal the sick, but it required *everything* in God to save sinners.   It required the whole might, and goodness, and love, and everything—GOD'S UTMOST.   The world could be created by His word, but the utmost of His grace and power was needed to blot out one single sin.

And when He has done *this* for you, you may be sure that He who has forgiven your sins, will heal your diseases.   If He has forgiven thee, He can *subdue* thy sins.   If He has forgiven thee, He can enable thee to walk in the ways of righteousness.   If by His own precious Blood He has blotted out all thy transgressions, there is not a want of thine that He cannot supply.   He who has done the greatest, can do all beside.   "Arise, take up thy bed, and go to thine house.

"And he arose, and departed to his house. But when the multitudes saw it, they marvelled, and glorified God."

I bring these things together—the prerogative of Christ's power and the healing of human disease.   The *Son of man* has the power of speaking the word of health.   *We* cannot do that.   We are driven to ordinary means and appliances, but if the Spirit of our Master who said, "Take up thy bed and walk," is in us, it will lead us to do what we can, to soothe and alleviate the sufferings of our fellow-men.   It is the very spirit of our Master to alleviate all such ; and let *us* seek to drink thoroughly into that spirit.   Our blessed Master never once caused one needless suffering, He never once gave, or inflicted on any, *needless* pain. His whole life was spent in " doing good," in " healing," and blessing, and comforting, and He says to us, " Go and do thou likewise."

Oh, to be like unto Him! But if we are to be like unto Him, we must have this knowledge—that our great, deep, dark sinfulness has no other healer but only Him, and that He is the actual Lord that healeth—Jehovah-Rophi. Let us not rest, or be satisfied, till we have broken up every obstacle, and trodden under every difficulty in the way, that we may come to His feet, and hear His word in the deepest depths of our anxious heart, " Son, Daughter,—thy sins, which are many,—thy sins, which are great,—thy sins, which are sinking thee into destruction, are all forgiven. Arise, go forth, and walk, and glorify God."

VIII.

THE CLEANSING OF THE LEPER.

" When he was come down from the mountain, great multitudes followed him. And, behold, there came a leper and worshipped him, saying, Lord, if thou wilt, thou canst make me clean. And Jesus put forth his hand and touched him, saying, I will; be thou clean. And immediately his leprosy was cleansed. And Jesus saith unto him, See thou tell no man; but go thy way, shew thyself to the priest, and offer the gift that Moses commanded, for a testimony unto them."—ST. MATT. viii. 1-4.

THIS miracle does not, perhaps, quite follow next in order, but those, which I have omitted, I have spoken upon, in the hearing of some here present. So I have preferred passing on to that one, which is recorded in the passage that I have just read. It is not certain how long it was after the Lord had come down from the mountain, nor is it certain in what locality He was, when this man met Him and presented his petition. But it is remarkable, that St. Matthew should begin the narrative with these words,

"When He was come down from the mountain"—because it may have been some time after He had come down, before this poor leper came in contact with Him. It seems, therefore, as if St. Matthew would draw a contrast between Jesus *on* the mountain, and Jesus *come down* from the mountain—between Jesus dealing with persons when He was on the mountain, and Jesus dealing with persons when He was come down from the mountain. The mountain on which He had been teaching, overlooked the Sea of Galilee. When He was up in the mountain, you remember His disciples were with Him ; He had called them to follow Him, to be partakers of His grace and of His salvation, and to learn the blessed truths He came to teach. He had spoken many things to them, which are familiar to us all—many things to guide the Christian's life, many things to comfort the Christian's heart. He had said, " Blessed are the pure in heart, for they shall see God. Blessed are the poor in spirit ; for theirs is the kingdom of heaven. Blessed are the peacemakers ; for they shall be called the children of God. Blessed are they which are persecuted for righteousness' sake ; for theirs is the kingdom of heaven." He had said, " Ye are the light of the world. A city that is set on a hill cannot be hid. Ye are the salt of the earth "—and many other such like things He had said to them, when He was there up on the mountain. But now He had come down from the mountain. This poor, leprous man had no right to be on the mountain —he had no right to be in a great assembly of people, or amongst the dwellings of men. He was an outcast, for he was *a leper*, and so he had his dwelling outside the city. A leper was shut out from the ordinary duties of life, shut out from home and friends, shut out from

I

the ordinary possessions and occupations of men; therefore this man could not go up to Jesus in the mountain. Jesus must come down to where *he* was; He must come away from the multitudes that surrounded Him, and from the lofty eminence where He was teaching —down to some place below, where He might come in contact with the leper.

So it is in fact. Jesus has *come down*—He has come down from the mountain. What for? He has come down to the place, where poor, sinful sufferers may touch the hem of His garment—to the spot, where even the poor, outcast leper, who was obliged to cry, " Unclean, unclean," and to cover his lip, and to dwell outside the city, may come near. Jesus has come down to the place where lepers dwell.

Remember, at this time specially, when we are about to commemorate the Incarnation of our Blessed Saviour, that He had come forth, He had " come down " from Heaven. " I *came down* from heaven, not to do Mine own will, but the will of Him that sent Me " (St. John vi. 38). We are told that He " emptied Himself," and " made Himself of no reputation, and took upon Him the form of a servant, and was made in the likeness of men " (Phil. ii. 7). *That* was coming down from the mountain, indeed, and if He had not come down from that mountain, He never could have met with sinners—just as, if He had not come down from this mountain, this leper never could have met with Him. Let us never forget this, when we think of the work of Christ—*He has come near to sinners.* None will ever be able to complain, that Jesus did not come near to sinners in their distress. He *did* come down from the mountain, for He actually laid aside His glory, and took our nature, that He might be here on earth, that He might be in a place where He could meet with sinners.

"**Great multitudes followed Him.**"

But they were not pressing on Him, evidently, as they had been when He was going to the house of Jairus. They followed Him down the mountain side, but He was on in front. And, as He came down from the mountain—the disciples and the multitudes following behind—

"**There came a leper**"—

Yes, a man "full of leprosy" (St. Luke v. 12). We saw, the other day, that, as Jesus was going, followed by a multitude, to the house of Jairus, there came a poor woman who said, "If I may touch but His clothes, I shall be whole." And just as it was then, so is it now. "There came a leper." *He* did not say in his heart, "If I go and touch the clothes of Christ, I shall be cured"—he dared not do that. That was altogether out of the question—he was a defiled and unclean person. But "there came a leper,"

"**And worshipped Him, saying, Lord, if Thou wilt, Thou canst make me clean.**"

Now, do we really understand what the disease of *leprosy* is? I am not going to say much about it. It was a kind of living death. Just what Isaiah says of the people of Israel, morally and spiritually, *that* the leper was *physically*—"from the sole of the foot even unto the head there is no soundness in it ; but wounds, and bruises, and putrifying sores " (Isa. i. 6). The man was altogether "an unclean thing " (Isa. lxiv. 6), yet the disease in him was living, acting, moving. It. poisoned all his blood, it destroyed all his peace, it left him not a single moment of comfort, it filled him with shame and confusion of face, it banished him from friends and home. As it was unclean, and hateful, and defiling, so was it fatal, and destructive to the whole life. Now, you see, this man had this terrible disease ; and as the woman, whom we spoke of last week, could not help knowing her disease, so this man *knew* that *he was a leper;* and he loathed himself in his own sight, because of his leprosy.

This is a picture, and it is intended to be a picture. You all know the history of Job, and that when his friends came to see him, he was so covered with this terrible disease from head to foot, that he took a potsherd and scraped himself withal. That was Job's *physical* condition, as he sat in the ashes, and his friends "sat down with him upon the ground seven days and seven nights, and none spake a word unto him : for they saw that his grief was very great " (Job ii. 13). That was his condition of body, and that is the picture God drew. And what do we find Job saying, at the end ? He comes and tells God that he has found that his soul is, spiritually and morally, just what his body had physically been. " Behold, I am *vile* " (Job xl. 4). He had found it out, he had found out that his *soul* was leprous—"I am vile." Multitudes do not know that. Few people really know it. Few come to find themselves altogether "an unclean thing," and that they need health in their *souls*, as this poor leper needed omnipotent, gracious, Divine power to give health to his *body*. Job's body was leprous ; and when God, in His mercy, gives physical life and health back, Job says, "That disease was a picture of my soul's state—'Behold I am vile. . . . I abhor myself, and repent in dust and ashes'" (Job xlii. 6). He had hated his own flesh, he had "abhorred" his own flesh, as he sat among the ashes. *Now*, it is not his body, but his soul, that finds it has the disease of leprosy—the disease of *sin*, which is spiritual leprosy ; and now he abhors himself, because he sees that he is "vile." The leper is *a picture*, a picture of all sinners who have not had their souls cleansed. That is a picture of your soul, if you have not had the saving work of Christ wrought in it.

Now, let us look at *the leper's thoughts*, for a moment; let us see what were his thoughts, when he came to Christ. Of course, he had got Job's thoughts about being "vile" in body, and Job's feeling about his physical state—"I abhor *myself*." He felt it, and he came to Jesus Christ to be cleansed, to be made whole, to be made fit for the ordinary avocations of life. But, what were his thoughts about Him to whom he came ? He "worshipped *Him*." He seems to have had very *lofty* thoughts of Him ; we cannot tell what he knew of Jesus. Perhaps some good, kind messenger of mercy had reported the mighty works of Jesus, and the Spirit of God had so enlightened him, that he knew that He, who did the " mighty works," was " the mighty God " (Isa. ix. 6). And he *" worshipped* Him." He had some true, right, lofty thoughts of the dignity and glory of Him, to whom he came. This does not mean merely, I think, that he prostrated himself in Eastern fashion—he did not call Jesus by some ordinary name of respect, Rabbi, Master ; but by the high name that belongs to the Living God. He calls Him *Jehovah*— " LORD."

Well, but what other thoughts had he about this Lord, whom he came to worship ?

"If Thou wilt, Thou canst make me clean."

Thou CANST. Now, remember, this leprosy could not be cured by human means. This man never thought of spending his. money on the physicians, like the woman we spake of—he knew that it would have been throwing money away. He knew, as a Jew, that he could only be healed by a miracle—he knew that his disease was not only separating and defiling, but that it was absolutely *incurable* by human means. He did not spend his money on physicians, he knew they could not cure him, unless they were endued by God with miraculous power. He knew that, of old, the Syrian captain had come, and stood at the door of Israel's prophet, and had been healed,—but *that*, he knew, was God's work. He knew what was said, in the Old Testament, concerning this disease,—of the peculiar ceremonies, of the work of the priest, of the sacrifice

to be offered, when God vouchsafed to cleanse the
leper; and the man had never thought of wearying
himself, by subjecting himself to any processes of human
instrumentality. But he comes to *Jesus*, and says,
"THOU canst." He puts Jesus, at once, out of the
range of all human healers, he puts Him on a platform
lifted up over all human means. "THOU canst—Thou
canst do what only GOD does. Thou canst perform
what only Divine power can effect." "Thou *canst.*"

He had advanced far. When we can get a man, a
woman, or a child, to find out that they have a deadly
disease of soul—when they find their souls as "full of
leprosy" as this man's body was, as full of all sinful
passions, of all corrupting desires, of all that is defiled
and earthly—only let them find this out and say, "My
soul is full of sin," and let them find out that Jesus
Christ came down from the lofty, high mountain, and
stood on the same platform as sinners, that He might
heal their diseases, might be within their reach—that
He *can* heal them, that there is no spot or stain on a
human soul, that is beyond the power of Christ to
heal—"Thou canst"—I say, when the soul has got so
far, and says, "Lord, I have got this disease, and
THOU—*canst*—heal this disease of mine," it has got a
great way; and we can be hopeful, when we see that.

But this man says, "*If* Thou WILT." He puts an
"if" in it. He seems to say, "Perhaps He will not
be willing—He has done a great many things, He has
healed the woman with an issue of blood, He has
raised the daughter of the ruler of the synagogue at

Capernaum, He has turned water into wine, He healed that paralytic man, He stilled the raging sea—multitudes brought their sick to Him, and He healed *them.* He has healed multitudes already, but who can say that He will heal *me?* He *can* heal me, He can do everything—but I do not know that He *will* do it for *me.*" This is the feeling of the man—" I know He is a Saviour, I know that He can save, I know that He can cleanse—but then the question is, Will He cleanse *me?*" Here the man seems to doubt *the willingness of Christ to deal with leprosy;* or, perhaps, he thought, " If I were some other leper, some other leper with great claims, some other leper with interest and influence and position, He would ; but, being such as I am—(very likely, a very poor leper) *will* He?" " *If* Thou wilt."

We may thank this leper for his doubtfulness. We may thank him, for putting forth this "If thou wilt,"—if it saves *us* from this dishonouring thought of Jesus. But what multitudes of spiritual lepers, in all ages, just feel the same thing ! They get so far—they believe that Jesus *can* cure leprosy, even the leprosy of the soul ; they believe that He can put away and wash out sin, that He can subdue their iniquities, that He can overcome, and trample down, everything that is evil in them. They get so far ; but *then* they say—" *If* Thou wilt "—" if Thou *wilt.*" "Will He care for *me?* Am I not too advanced in leprosy? Is not the disease too powerful and too universal in me, for Him to deal with it? Am I not so completely a leper, that I am beyond

His willing tenderness? Am I not so worthless and despicable, that He will not care to pick me out of the mire of my great ruin? If I were *so-and-so*, He might do it, but not for *me*." Is not this the feeling of multitudes of men? They get so far—Christ *can*, but *will* He do it? It is just this that we have to deal with, to-night—*the real willingness of Christ—to heal real spiritual leprosy.*

Now, first, we may ask, If He had *not* been willing, *why* did He come down from the mountain at all? Why did He make Himself of no reputation? Why do we keep this Christmas season? Why was He born in Bethlehem? Why was He crucified on Calvary? Why did He live and die on earth, if He is to be met thus, and if it is to be said—"*If Thou wilt?*" Can we dare to look Him in the face, and—when He has laid aside His glory, and suffered on Calvary—address Him with an *If*, and, with an "If Thou *wilt?*" When He has done all this, suffered all this, manifested Infinite love, "love strong*er*" than "the death" of the Cross— dare we address Him thus? Why all that, if He be not willing to save "even to the uttermost?"

But, if it is so—if we are too deep down, if our leprosy is too terrible, our sin too multiplied, then we ask, *Where* is the limit to the willingness of Christ? Is there *any* limit to the willingness of Christ to save? Is there any limit to the tender compassion in the heart of the Father? Can ever a limit be placed, by anybody, to the *willingness* of Christ? No. He is willing to save to the very utmost.

Here was a man, who was not only a leper, but (St. Luke tells us, chap. v. 12) "full of leprosy"—*full* of it —"from head to foot." And *he* comes to Jesus with an "If thou wilt." Now, let us not dwell longer on the man, on *his* feelings, but on Jesus Christ. When He was appealed to on this point, He did not stay to argue the point; He might have said—"Why am I here, if I am not willing? Why am I not still in the glory, which I had with My Father before the world was?" But, in tenderest compassion, the moment He was appealed to, He "put forth His hand and touched him." " *Touched* him." Who can touch a leper, and not be defiled? Who dared come forth and *handle* that leprous man? Here was One, who was above all defilement.

"Jesus put forth His hand, and touched him."

The man had said, "If Thou wilt, Thou canst *make me clean.*" He had never expected the hand of grace to be put on him; he never thought that, in his uncleanness, that hand of purity would *touch* him. But Jesus did lay His hand on him. What a touch was that! Does it not reveal something of the heart of Christ— that touch—that pitying touch of *His* hand? No dainty touch is the touch of Jesus, but the gentle, loving touch of infinite tenderness. Does it not show us some of the deep, Divine compassion of Jehovah the Healer, that would make the man thoroughly aware of His more than willingness—when, ere He said " *I will,*"—" He *touched* him?" What must the leper have felt, when Jesus said " I will," and when he felt that *touch?* No friendly hand had ever been, compassionately, laid on him, he had never been "touched," since the filthiness of leprosy was on him. Now he feels the touch, this Divine, hearty, healing touch—and Jesus says, **"I will: be thou clean."**

Now, you will admit—all faithful expositors admit— that *that* Word is *God's* Word. No one can say " I WILL," but God. It shows us what and who He is, when He says *"I will!"* It is God saying, that what He purposes, He *will* effect,—" I will." Let God say, "I will," and it is done. "I will: be thou clean."

Now, remember, this man had not asked for mere *relief*, he had not asked for *ease* from pain, but for the whole misery to be wiped out, to be done away—for his flesh to "come again as the flesh of a little child;" he had asked to be *made over again*, as it were—to be made whole—and Jesus says, " I will : be thou clean." This stands on the page of Scripture to tell us this— that, while there is the power in Christ that is attributed to Him, He repudiates the very idea of unwillingness. He would not have us entertain the thought, for a moment, that He is unwilling to touch, to heal, to save, the most unclean.

Where is the flaw then? Where is the hindrance? Why are not lepers cleansed? What leaves men still in their sins, still under the slavery of sin, still in the uncleanness of sin? Where is it? It is not in Jesus Christ. The man admitted that He had the *power*, and Jesus, presently, proved that He had the *will*. Where then is the hindrance? It is because, while God says that man is a spiritual leper, man will not *believe* it, and does not seek, therefore, to get his leprosy cleansed—he is not anxious or willing to be cured. And, because it is a *hidden* leprosy, a leprosy concealed from observation, a leprosy that cannot be detected by the natural senses, therefore the man does not come to have it cleansed, therefore he does not feel his need of One who has the power, and who has the *will*, to cleanse him from its foul and deadly uncleanness.

What is the one great necessity of all? It is this—" Lord, teach me what I am in myself. Lord, teach me my need—teach me that I am a poor, unclean sinner," ought to be the prayer of every uncleansed soul.

"And Jesus saith unto him, See thou tell no man; but go thy way, shew thyself to the priest."

How delicate, and how impressive, is that command! "See thou tell no man." Jesus would not have this man flourishing about, and glorifying himself, and dancing, as it were, for joy, because he had got rid of his dreadful disease. He would not have him go with boasting tongue, and say, "See how highly favoured I am." No. "See thou tell no man." Jesus would have it found out in other ways, by quieter means. "Go, shew thyself to the priest;" let us have this fact made sure, and indisputable.

"And offer the gift that Moses commanded, for a testimony unto them."

There was an ordinance of the ceremonial law (I cannot enter into it to-night), by which the priest was appointed, to examine cases of supposed leprosy, to determine what was the condition of the individual, and, in case of cleansing, judicially to pronounce that the sufferer was healed, and fit to return to the ordinary business of life, and the dwellings of men.   We cannot enter into this subject now, but you see that the *priest* was the person appointed, under the law, to decide whether the disease were gone.   Jesus says, "Go, obey that law—shew thyself to the *priest.*"   The priest was a type—a type of Jesus Christ, the great High Priest. This man was not to go out in the world, all at once, and blaze this abroad, and make much of it ; but, to go quietly to the *priest*, to have dealings with him, to have communion with him.   "Let *him* tell you that your leprosy is cleansed."

There might be other points ; but it was necessary, that the Jewish mind should have evidence which none could gainsay, that this man *was* actually cured.   Everybody knew that he was a leper ; now he is to go, and let the priest declare whether the leprosy is really cleansed —and, if the leprosy *be* cleansed, let them say whether or not there is a prophet in Israel.

Let us look for the application to ourselves.   "Offer the gift that Moses commanded, for a testimony unto them."

Yes—when a man or woman is cleansed from leprosy, let them go to Christ, and ask Him to deal with them, and, then, let them yield themselves to Him as their God, let them give themselves up "a living," willing "sacrifice" unto Him—to be silent or to speak—to do or to suffer—as He appoints.

And now, in conclusion, what lessons have we to

learn from this? First, we have to make these inquiries, Have *I* indeed this spiritual disease in *my* soul? Have I this spiritual leprosy, this fretting leprosy within me, resulting in spiritual sores, spiritual wounds, spiritual bruises, all putrifying within—all leading to an eternally fatal end?

Now, let me testify from God's Word, that you have it, whether you know it or not. And alas! if you do not know it, you are not likely to go to the true Physician, for cleansing and relief. If you *have* found it out, then come—not as this man with an " *If* Thou wilt, Thou canst,"—but saying, " Lord, Thou canst, and I *know* that Thou wilt," and leave Him not, till He has said, "I will, be thou clean." "Go, wash in the Fountain opened for 'uncleanness,' and thou shalt be clean." Leave Him not till you have heard His word of power, and found that Fountain,—which cleanses the disease of the soul, and purifies its leprous stains,—effectual to your complete salvation.

IX.

THE CENTURION'S SERVANT HEALED.

" *Now when he had ended all his sayings in the audience of the people, he entered into Capernaum. And a certain centurion's servant, who was dear unto him, was sick, and ready to die. And when he heard of Jesus, he sent unto him the elders of the Jews, beseeching him that he would come and heal his servant. And when they came to Jesus, they besought him instantly, saying, That he was worthy for whom he should do this : for he loveth our nation, and he hath built us a synagogue. Then Jesus went with them. And when he was now not far from the house, the centurion sent friends to him, saying unto him, Lord, trouble not thyself : for I am not worthy that thou shouldest enter under my roof : wherefore neither thought I myself worthy to come unto thee : but say in a word, and my servant shall be healed. For I also am a man set under authority, having under me soldiers, and I say unto one, Go, and he goeth ; and to another, Come, and he cometh ; and to my servant, Do this, and he doeth it. When Jesus heard these things, he marvelled at him, and turned him about, and said unto the people that followed him, I say unto you, I have not found so great faith, no, not in Israel. And they that were sent, returning to the house, found the servant whole that had been sick.*"—ST. LUKE vii. 1–10.

OUR Blessed Lord had been speaking the gracious words, which are recorded in the previous chapter. And

"When He had ended all" those precious **"** sayings

in the audience of the people, He entered into Capernaum."

Now we have, already, spoken a great deal about this CAPERNAUM—it was called the Lord's "own city," because He lived there so much, and did there so many of His mighty works. We have had this town of Capernaum brought before us, on one or two occasions, and, you remember, that it was in this very Capernaum, that certain things had already happened. A certain nobleman had gone from thence to fetch Jesus, beseeching Him to come and heal his son. We have, already, considered *that.* It was also in this town, that the chief ruler of the synagogue had gone to Jesus, on behalf of his sick and dying daughter. And then, a woman with an issue of blood—and her history we have also considered—came to touch the hem of His garment. *Here* then 'had the chief ruler and a nobleman gone to Jesus —one on behalf of his son, the other on behalf of his daughter—and here we are told, that a certain centurion sent to Jesus, on behalf of his servant. The first, then, had come about his *son;* the second had come about his *daughter;* and the third had sent about his *servant:* the nobleman for his son,—the chief ecclesiastic for his daughter,—the centurion for his servant.

Now, let us inquire, for a moment, about this centurion—who and what he was. He was a captain in the Roman army. You know that Rome, at that time, had overrun the civilised world ; there was hardly a nation that pagan Rome had not subdued. Cæsar lived in his palace at Rome, and governed these outlying provinces; and here he had put his foot on the neck of Galilee. And, at this time, Capernaum was garrisoned by Romans—and the Jews there felt exactly as we should feel, if there were a French garrison in this town. We know that the Romans had garrisoned Capernaum, amongst other places, with Roman soldiers; this centurion had soldiers under him, holding that town for the Emperor.

What, for instance, do the French feel now that the Prussians have taken possession of their cities, occupied their strongholds, possessed their public buildings and the chief places of concourse, and proclaimed themselves masters? Just as the Jews regarded these Romans in Capernaum, and this centurion, who was the captain of the soldiers who held it. He was a captain with a regiment of soldiers under his command; and under him, they commanded and regulated that town. Well, this man, then, was a captain in the Roman army, whose chief commander, and whose soldiers too, probably, were all worshippers of idols. Here is the servant of a heathen Emperor, holding this Jewish town, and a servant of his,

" **who was dear unto him, was sick, and ready to die.**"

St. Matthew tells us a little more on this point—that he was a paralytic, and very "grievously tormented." (viii. 6). This servant had, evidently, had a paralytic stroke, and was held under very severe sufferings, at this time ; but he was " dear " to his master.

Can we find out how this had come to pass ? It was not merely that he was " dear unto him," but that

K

he was *precious* in his sight. It was not only that he esteemed, but that he *valued* him—that is the word,—the master *valued* his servant very greatly, and loved him very much. What sort of a notion had he about a servant, about *his* servant? He lets it out, presently, when he says, "I say to *my servant*, Do this, and HE DOETH IT." This was the man ;—we see he was a real, true, intelligent servant. "He not only does what I tell him, but he does not need the way chalked out exactly where he is to go, nor to be told what to do in such and such particular circumstances—but I simply say, Do this, go and transact that business, and I believe the man has intelligence to do it, and I believe he has integrity to do it. I trust him, because he has intelligence and integrity. I say to him, Do this—transact this business, and what happens? It is *done.*"

That was the man who now lay sick—a man who had so endeared himself to his master, acting in all intelligence, and in all integrity, in his position,—had so wound himself round and round his master's heart, that when he was sick, the heart that he had wound himself round was well-nigh breaking. The centurion had a servant—who was "dear unto him,—precious unto him,—and he was sick"—stricken down—no longer able to do his business, though he still had the intelligence and the will; but there he lay—"grievously tormented."

We see here the picture of a good master, and clearly, too, the picture of a good servant. There are immense complaints made of servants by some people ; they tell you there is not a good *servant* to be found ; and, if you go amongst another class, they will tell you there is not a good *master* to be found, almost anywhere. And why is this? Not because it is impossible for any one to be *a good master.* If anybody was likely not to be a good master, it was a centurion in the Roman army—the commander of a garrison-town of conquered, subject people. Yet there he was—a good master—I do not mean, merely good in paying wages, and executing righteousness, but a master who cared for his servant, and had a feeling of affection for those who served him, and were round about him. And, surely, it is not impossible to be *a good servant.* If ever it was difficult to be a good servant, it was there, in a Romish garrison in a town, where it was difficult to be even decently moral, or commonly upright. This man was a private in the Romish idolatrous army, that was putting its feet on the neck of the conquered people. We know what soldiers are, when they are let loose, in a conquered town, to pillage —and what, too, is the arrogance of the people, who feel they belong to the conqueror; and surely there would be every temptation to be immoral, to be godless, to partake of the open notorious sinfulness of the heathen, in the place where this man was found.

Yet here, in the most unlikely place in the world, we find a good master, and a good servant ; and the two so bound together, that, when the servant is afflicted, the heart of the master is filled with grief.

"**And when he heard of Jesus, he sent unto Him**

the elders of the Jews, beseeching Him that He would come and heal his servant."

Now I have, already, spoken about the great blessing of *hearing* of Jesus, about the great blessing it is, if—when conviction of sin comes into the heart, when trouble comes into the mind, when the soul begins to ask, "What must I do to be saved from the terrible eternity before me?"—if that man has heard of a Saviour, and such a Saviour. It is a *great* blessing to have "heard of JESUS."

People could scarcely help hearing of Him in Capernaum, where He had been doing such wonderful works. Surely, it would have been a strange thing, if there had been any, in this town of Capernaum, who had *not* heard of Jesus Christ! I daresay, many were as ignorant, as if they had never heard Jesus Christ's name, but, in this case, it was a blessing even to have heard of Christ, and of what He could do.

And another thing is remarkable. If there was anything the Jews hated above all others, (except a publican—they hated the publicans, because they regarded them as traitors, and guilty tools of the people who were trampling on them,) it was the soldiers who kept them in subjection. They did not look with a friendly eye on these Roman soldiers, who were there to keep them subject. To go back to my illustration—if the French were here, garrisoning our town, claiming our money and our provisions, and keeping us in subjection, we should not be likely to regard them with very kindly feelings; they would not be likely to get any of us to do any great kindness for them. Yet we find, that this Roman centurion goes to the very "elders of the Jews"—to those who stood at the head of religion in Capernaum, to Jairus and all the rest,—and gets *them* to go to Jesus, for him, on behalf of his sick servant. The captain of a regiment would be a proud man, and hold his head up ; he would not stoop to ask favours of those, whom he was so accustomed to regard with contempt—yet, for the sake of a *slave*—not a hired servant—not one who was hired by the year and received wages,—but for one whom, according to the Roman law, the centurion held as a slave, he could go and ask the Jews—he asks *them* to go. He puts everything in motion. His dear servant, so grievously tormented, is *so* "dear" to him, that he stops at nothing. Very likely, he went to the nobleman whose son had been healed—very likely, he asked the ruler of the synagogue, whose little daughter Jesus Christ had raised, and, perhaps, even the woman who had had an issue of blood—to join in the deputation. He asks them all to go to Jesus, and plead with Him on behalf of his servant, of his slave, who was *"grievously tormented."*

What a picture is this man ! When he looks on the servant, whom he loves, in grievous torment, he cannot bear the sight. How earnest should we be, when we read what was said of one—" In hell he lift up his eyes, being *in torments ;*" and you remember his words, —" Send Lazarus, that he may dip the tip of his finger in water, and cool my tongue, for I am *tormented* in this flame." (St. Luke xvi. 23, 24.) How earnestly ought we to be desiring, that Jesus would put forth His exceeding great power, to stay the possibility of any one's falling into those torments! Look at this man —so eager is he, when he sees his servant in torment, that he asks those elders of the Jews, if they will go to yonder house up the street, where Jesus had entered in the afternoon of that weary day, when He had healed the leper after preaching that long sermon,—he asks them to go with all reverence and all respect, and beseech Him to come and heal his servant.

It is a touching, but a very instructive, sight. Look at these men—they hear, they are willing, they go. You might say, there never was a man in a position where he was less likely to win the respect, the confidence, the esteem of those amongst whom he lived, than this centurion—yet he had so got it, that they were, evidently, willing to do anything for him. He has only to ask, and away they go and do it. How strange it is ! Why is it that this man is so respected? People say, " What can *I* do? *I* can never influence anybody." If a Roman centurion could influence Jews in Capernaum, there is no child of God who need despair of exercising influence for good on anybody. No one ever had greater difficulties to contend with, or greater prejudices to surmount, than that man when he went there ; and now he asks the Jews to go, not for himself, but for his poor slave! Who cared for his slave? When did any Roman centurion care a fig for his slave? No,—no more than he cared for his dog. *But this man did.*

Why? Because there was something in him, that caused him to feel and act as he did.

"When they came to Jesus, they besought Him instantly, saying, That he was worthy for whom He should do this."

What strange language is this! Look at the estimate these men have of the character of this Romish centurion. They do not say, " He is a Gentile dog." That is the way the Jews then spoke of Gentiles. They do not say *that*—they do not say he is not worthy to be helped—this Gentile soldier, with soldiers under him. They do not go to Jesus, coldly indifferent, because they are frightened at his power as a soldier, who could visit it on them, if they did not do it ; but they go with all their hearts, and say, " He is not a common man, he is not an ordinary man—he is a "worthy" man— worthy of a miracle. " He was *worthy* for whom he should do this."

That man had evidently won their *hearts !* What must there have been in him, to bring the Jews so to estimate his character? There he was in their midst, and they would, naturally, have hated the very sight of him—yet they will go to Jesus, and beseech Him, and that "instantly," to heal this man's slave. There is no excuse for people's not having influence. Let us only act from the same principles, from the same motives, in the same way, that this man did, and we shall get influence. We need not make a noise about it. Don't think that he made a noise,—very likely, he made no particular profession of kindness, when he and his regiment came in.   Very likely, he came in quietly, and let people find out the truth about him—preaching by his life, rather than by his lips.   *Where* is the worthiness in their estimate ?

"**He loveth our nation, and he hath built us a synagogue,**" though he was the servant of the conqueror, one of the hated Roman nation.

It *was* a blessing for this man, that he had been sent to Palestine from Italy, that he had come in contact with Divine truth !   Here was a man who had, evidently, been seeking the salvation of his soul, a man who had been led to ask, What will become of me ? who had been led to believe that his soul was immortal, and to ask what would become of that soul, and whether he could be delivered from the heathenism in which he dwelt.   In coming into " Immanuel's land," he had learnt the truth that was only to be found *there*—of the Eternal, and of the way to the Eternal, and of the meeting-place with the eternal Judge and Lord of all. And he had found there, though darkly and dimly yet, that hope was rising within him.   He had heard there of a Mercy-seat, he had heard there of the great truths of the Old Testament dispensation, which told him that God was in the world, that God was to be approached by sprinkled Blood.   " He loveth our nation, and he hath built us a synagogue."   Well might he love it !   He could never have learnt the way to God, in Italy,—he could never have learnt, in Italy, how he might approach the Lord of all.   But in that nation, despised though it was, were " the oracles of God "—" the testimony of

Jesus " in types and symbols. Dim and dark it had been really. Now the great Light itself was beaming around them—though it was shining " in darkness." If a man has eyes to see, he can grope his way even by starlight ; but the man, who has no eyes, stumbles even when the sun is shining at its brightest. So was it with *this* man— the Spirit of God had opened his eyes to see the need of his soul, and to see what could supply that need— and though it was but starlight with *him*, he groped his way on. And thus they speak of him—**"he loveth our nation."**

And what does love do ? Love always acts. When love gets into the heart, it *acts*. "He hath built us a synagogue." He said, " I want all you Jews to learn, more particularly than you have yet been able, about the truths of your own Scriptures. I want you to have the prophets read every sabbath-day—and to have a place where you can hear the testimony, which has given me some little hope. I will build you a synagogue," —perhaps the very synagogue of which Jairus was the chief ruler. He had built a synagogue for the Jews. This was *how* the man had come to be a blessing in Capernaum—he built them a meeting-place, where men might hear Moses, and hear the prophets, and hear the testimony of Him who was to be born for them—of Him who should bear their sins.

"Then Jesus went with them."

In the other Gospel, we are told that Jesus said, " I will come and heal him." He had not said *that* to the nobleman ; to him He had said—" Go thy way, thy son liveth ;" He did not even speak to Jairus—but just got up and went.   But, in this case of the centurion's poor slave, He acts differently, and says, " I will *come* and heal him."   And He goes—making his way on to the centurion's servant.   After He had started, the centurion hears that Jesus is coming ; and now he sends his own natural "friends, saying unto him, Lord, trouble not Thyself ; for I am not worthy—(he uses another word—it is not befitting—it is not beseeming) that Thou shouldest enter under my roof."   Therefore *he* thought himself "*not* worthy."   You know what the Jews thought about it ; *they* said, "He *is* worthy."   Then we see what he thinks of himself—" I am not worthy."

That is just as it should be.   A true Christian never thinks himself worthy, but he makes everybody else think that he is worthy—not by his profession, far from it, but—by his life of practical godliness.——" Wherefore neither thought I myself worthy to come unto Thee, but much less do I expect that *Thou* shouldest come to *me*, and do these great things."   " He stood afar off and would not lift up so much as his eyes unto heaven, but smote upon his breast." (St. Luke xviii. 13).   " I am not worthy."   It is the spirit of the poor publican. What had this man learnt?   He had learnt evidently, first, that he was not worthy that Christ should come to him—and then, next, that he could not do *without* Christ's coming to him.   A great trouble had taught him that.   He feels first, that he is not worthy ; and then, second, that he cannot do without Christ.   He is not worthy to come to Christ, yet he must have Him and His very present help.

"But say in a word, and my servant shall be healed."

What a grand thought concerning Christ! You know how he illustrates it. It shows how he had been turning the thing over in his mind. *That is the way* to get at the truth, not to sit down and say it is very fine, —but to turn it over and over till you get at the truth. Now he brings it out—

"I also am a man set under authority, having under me soldiers, and I say unto one, Go, and he goeth; and to another, Come, and he cometh; and to my servant, Do this, and he doeth it."

" I also am a man set under authority—I am *not the highest.* I am only a captain—there is the Major, and the Colonel, and the Commander-in-chief, and then the Emperor. I am *under* authority, and very low down too; there are many over me—yet I have non-commissioned officers and privates under me, and though I am not their chief master, what do I do? I say to one, Come, and he never thinks of *not* coming. I say to another, Go, and he never thinks of disobeying. He comes, he goes, *because* I *tell him,*—and yet I am not the Emperor, nor the General, not even the Colonel, but only " a centurion." *He* goes, and *the other* comes, and I say to my servant, Do this. When I give him anything to do, he does not expect me to mark it all out for him. I say, *Do* it—transact that business, transact it satisfactorily,—let it be done, let it be complete, not in a foolish or slovenly way—but let it be *done.   And he does it."*

"When Jesus heard these things, He marvelled at him."

Because He had all the faculties of man's nature, and was capable of exercising all those faculties, therefore He was capable of marvelling.   He was capable of feeling every feeling of humanity, without a spot or stain, and so He " marvelled."   What a thing truly to marvel at, Jesus seems to say to us ! He says in His heart, " I have found none like this ; this man knows Me, he appreciates Me, he thoroughly comprehends and understands Me."

The man says, " I am under authority : Thou, Lord, art *not* under authority, for Thou art God over all.   I am *under*—Thou art ' *over* all, God, blessed for ever.' (Rom. ix. 5).   And therefore if *I* say, Go, and he goes ; Come, and he comes ; Do this, and it is done, *Thou*— who didst once say, Let there be light and there *was* light,— *Thou* who didst once command all things into being—surely THOU needest not to come.   I am not worthy that Thou shouldst come—Thou canst say the word, and my servant shall be healed."

"And Jesus marvelled at him, and turned Him about and said unto the people that followed Him, I say unto you, I have not found so great faith, no, not in Israel."

" Not in Israel "—not amongst all the Jews—born Jews—who had had the Bible in their hands ever since they had been able to hold it,—" not in *Israel*" with all its prophecies, with all its prophets, and priests, and symbols—"I have not in *Israel* found any that know Me as this man knows Me."

"And they that were sent, returning to the house, found the servant whole that had been sick."

Now, let us just pick up the threads of this discourse. Look at the illustration of what the poor leper said— " *Thou canst.*" Here was a poor centurion, in the dimmest possible twilight, but he sees the power of Jesus to heal and to save, power to deliver one from grievous torment, and he believes that Jesus is *God*,—that, by *a word*, He is able to do it. He knows he is not worthy to come into His presence, yet he asks Him. He is bowed down in the lowest humility, yet he glorifies Jesus by the most wonderful faith. It is the bough of the tree, that is most heavily laden with precious fruit, that bends lowest to the earth. Here is a man with most wonderful faith, yet bowing down ; conscious of his unworthiness, he comes lowly, loving, anxious, in earnest, pleading even for another ; and he finds that Jesus accepts the challenge, and delivers the servant that is so dear to him, from his grievous torment, so that he goes on his way rejoicing.

There are, here, a great many wonderful lessons to be gathered up—about Jesus and His power,— about grace and its operation in the heart,— about what should influence, guide and govern us, in all our dealings with our fellows, and in seeking blessing for those whom we love. We have a sight of startling power, revealing Jesus as a Saviour who can deliver from *grievous torment,* yea, even from *eternal* torment.

And He will be "enquired of to do this" for us, (Ezek. xxxvi. 37), and to do this for those who are "dear" to us; and then He will do this for us *perfectly,* "by the word of His power." (Heb. i. 3).

X.

THE WIDOW'S SON RAISED.

"*And it came to pass the day after, that he went into a city called Nain; and many of his disciples went with him, and much people. Now when he came nigh to the gate of the city, behold, there was a dead man carried out, the only son of his mother, and she was a widow: and much people of the city was with her. And when the Lord saw her, he had compassion on her, and said unto her, Weep not. And he came and touched the bier: and they that bare him stood still. And he said, Young man, I say unto thee, Arise. And he that was dead sat up, and began to speak. And he delivered him to his mother. And there came a fear on all: and they glorified God, saying, That a great prophet is risen up among us; and, That God hath visited his people. And this rumour of him went forth throughout all Judæa, and throughout all the region round' about. And the disciples of John shewed him of all these things.*"—ST. LUKE vii. 11–18.*

I SOMETIMES try to fancy what a condition we should all have been left in, if the Lord Jesus Christ had gone back into Heaven without having raised Himself, or without having raised any other persons, from the dead—without showing, in fact, that He had power over *that* great work of the Devil. He was "manifested to destroy the works of the Devil" (1 John iii. 8), who "through fear of death" had kept multitudes, even of God's saints, " all their lifetime subject to bondage." (Heb. ii. 15).

Now, the great enemy of man, the great enemy that every one has to meet, some time or other, is *Death.* If we can conceive it possible that Jesus Christ should have healed sicknesses, should have recovered the paralytic, and yet never have come face to face with the great enemy, Death, itself—we might have felt that, while Jesus could modify some of the great evils of life, He had *no* power over the *greatest* calamity of all. Yet we know, that it was said of Him, hundreds of years before He came into the world, " O death, I will be thy plagues ; O grave, I will be thy destruction : (and in this matter at least) repentance shall be hid from mine eyes." (Hosea xiii. 14). And in this passage, this evening, we see *Jesus* brought *face to face* with *Death.*

I have already pointed out to you, that the miracles of Jesus Christ are not only intended to show what He could do, and to show His mighty power with regard to *physical* things—physical diseases, physical sufferings, physical death,—but to show, by the operation of His power over *bodily* diseases, the operation of His power over diseases of the *soul.* If He heals the diseases of the body by a word, it is to show that He can, also, by a word, heal the diseases of the soul. If He cleanses the physical leprosy, it is to show that He can cleanse the leprosy of the soul.

And now here, in this miracle, Jesus is brought face to face with the great calamity, the great enemy, the great sorrow, of all mankind. And I just sketched out, or hinted, a few weeks ago,—when I was speaking of the ruler of the synagogue, who besought Christ to come and heal his little daughter, who was at the point of death,—that we have, in the Gospel, *three instances* of Jesus Christ's coming face to face with this deadly enemy of all—with Death. There, in the *first* instance, we saw death in its *mildest* form. The life had but just gone out of the little girl,—she lay there, I do not say in the innocence—but in comparative freedom from the manifold corruptions and evils—of human life,—a dear, well-protected, pleasant child, beloved by those with whom she was connected by the ties of kindred,—with the breath just gone out of her. Death appears there in its weakest, in its mildest form. We look upon her, and can scarce believe that it *is* Death. There is something of touching beauty in it, something that appeals to our tender feelings, and makes us say, Is *that* Death? And we hardly believe it, as we look on the little child, with the breath only just gone out of her body.

We looked, then, at *the other extreme*—when Christ came in contact with it at the grave of Lazarus; there was nothing beautiful, nothing fascinating about *that*. Death had come in, and worked corruption there. "Lord (said his sister), he stinketh." (St. John xi. 39). It was death stinking; it was death in a state of advanced corruption. You cannot remove the door from the sepulchre, without death making its horrid corruption known and felt.

Here, we have a *middle* instance—this was a "young man"—growing up into cheerful, bright, useful man-

L

hood.   There is neither the weakness of childhood,
nor the decrepitude of age here, but the full strength of
humanity.   Death had done its work on him,—death
had so long had hold of him, that he was *ready* to be
carried out of the city, and *to be buried out of sight.*
Here we have the strong young man, in the stronger
grasp of death, but death is not breathing out its
horrible stenches yet.   There is nothing yet to repel
any from the sight of the young man, as he lay on his
bier.   There is nothing yet of death in its horrid im-
purity, but yet death has begun to tell.   You look on
the countenance, and you see that death has imprinted
its mark on him.   There is no fair beauty, as in the
little girl of Jairus, to lead us to think it only a soft and
gentle sleep.   It is *death*, but not yet death in its filthiness and corruption.

We have, then, in these three instances, wonderful
pictures of the *spiritual death* that rules in the world in
these three forms.   Sometimes we see it hidden under
a fair and fascinating beauty; sometimes we see it
veiled under the fallacious garb of—what man in his
unwisdom even comes to call—innocence.   You look,
and you say, " Can there be spiritual death in that
child, in that up-grown person, so free from all corruption, so careful in all their moral life and actions?   Can
there be spiritual death there?"   Yes.

Then we go to the other extreme, and see it breathing forth a very moral pestilence, walking along our
streets, living in our lanes, and, as at the grave of
Lazarus, you say, " Open it not, it *stinketh.*"   It is a

very fountain of corruption—it pours forth its horrible vapours everywhere. That is Death stinking in the very nostrils of the world.

And then, again, we have spiritual death in its *strength.* We look, and we cannot feel but that the soul is *dead to God.* It is alive, it may be, to many other things, to many good and useful things, but it is dead to *God.* It is death in its strength; it is death,—not yet pouring out the excess of corruption, but it is death,—not presenting the comparative innocence and beauty we have spoken of,—but there *is* spiritual death in the soul, and it is working its dread results. Its power is exhibited in the case of this young man, a man in his prime, subject to death.

" It came to pass the day after,"

You remember the day *before*—we were speaking of the day before, last Tuesday, and of how the centurion, who loved the Jewish nation, and had built them a synagogue, sent Jews to Jesus to tell Him of the sickness of his servant who was dear to him. You remember all that; and the next day *after*, Jesus left Capernaum, and passed down on the western side of the Lake of Galilee—(I cannot point it out to-night, for there is no map,) a very long day's journey it must have been; and, at the close of the day, He came along the foot of Mount Tabor, and of what is called the Lesser Mount Hermon, in order to come to this place, which is mentioned nowhere else in the Bible, but the remains of which exist to this day; and the burying-place there, *outside* the city, exists to this day. Jesus was accompanied by His disciples; and many, who had experienced His wonderful works, were with Him.

"Now, when He came nigh to the gate of the city, behold, there was a dead man carried out, the only son of his mother, and she was a widow."

In the compass of these two or three lines, we have a most wonderful history. The Holy Ghost did not take many words to describe this calamity—"a dead man carried out."

That is sufficient—it *ought* to be sufficient—to make men think, when they see dead men and dead women carried out. We have seen them carried out every day, till the sight is so familiar, that we cease to think about it,—but the heart must be hard indeed, that ceases to have a solemn thought, when it sees "a dead man carried out."

Oh, what the sin we love has done in the world! There is not a sin, there is not a sorrow, there is not a suffering, there is not a dead man carried out, that is not because of *sin*. If there had been no sin, there would have been no death; and if there had been no sin, there would have been no sorrow. Then, how is it that sin is the best-beloved thing in the world, till grace comes into the heart,—that sin which has created all the suffering, caused all the sorrow, brought all the death? There would never have been a grave dug in the world, if it had not been dug by sin. If there had been no sin, there would never have been a dead man, nor a dead woman carried out.

It is a *complete* misery that our Lord looks on here—

" There was a dead man carried out, the *only* son of his mother—and she was *a widow !*"   It was not the first time that she had followed a corpse out of the city ; she had followed at least *one* before.   She had followed her husband, the father of this son—and this now was her "*only* son "—therefore her last prop was cut away from under her ; her last sustaining hope was taken away from her.—" The *only* son of his mother, and she was a *widow.*"

Now, you know, there is passage on passage in the Old Testament, that point it out as the highest of all sorrow, to be in bitterness for an " only son." (See Jer. vi. 26 ; Amos viii. 10 ; Zech. xii. 10).   So then, this poor widow might well weep and sorrow over *her* increasing and unmitigated calamity.   There must have been something very *peculiar* in her case.   What was it that guided the steps of Jesus that long, weary day, all the way from Capernaum, where He had been working and toiling all the day before ?   What brought Him all those long miles in the burning sun, toiling on His weary way ?   *What ?*   The disciples did not know, the multitude did not know, but *Jesus knew.*   He knew, when He was healing the centurion's servant the day before, that there was, lying, perhaps, in some little cottage in the village of Nain, a dead son—perhaps a subject of grace.   Jesus knew that—and He knew that the young man was the " only son of his mother," and that " she was a widow ;" and the compassionate heart of Jesus brings Him over the hills of Galilee.   How little did she think, as she followed the bier, to consign the body of her son to the grave, that she had any interest in the heart of the great Healer! How little did she think, when she was closing his eyes the night before in her cottage, that there was a heart feeling for her, beating for her, far away in Capernaum! *She* was not thinking of the Deliverer; and she little thought that a heart,—the greatest and tenderest human heart that ever beat—knew *her* sorrow, and was making arrangements to come down for *her* deliverance. · She little thought that Jesus Christ was thinking of *her*, who was so little, so unworthy, to be thought of. She had a great sorrow; perhaps she had been nursing it—perhaps she had been saying in her heart, " My sorrow is greater than I can bear." And when her son was carried forth to the tomb, her thought was—" This is the last drop in my cup—now my last prop is cut away." Her case must have been one of much sorrow, for " much people of the city was with her." Their hearts were stirred.

Let us look at the contrast. What could *they* do? They could feel for her, they could weep for her, they could go with her, but they could only go with her *to* the grave. They could help her to *bury* her son. They could comfort *her* in their own very poor fashion; they could walk by her side, they could shed tears on her behalf, they could sustain her trembling steps, they could promise her temporal assistance and present help; but so far as regarded *her son*, they could only help her to take him to the grave.

But there was One who could do *more*. No doubt she trembled (as every Jew trembles still), and was tormented (as every Jew is tormented still), with the terrible fear of Death; and she had yet to learn that there was One, who had power over "him that had the power of death" (Heb. ii. 14). And *He* was coming, hastening to her, full of tenderest sympathy, compassionating her sorrow. He could do something that these could not. They could weep with her, but they could not dry up the fountain of her tears. They could help her to bury her son, but they could not bring him to life again. They could do many things to soothe her, but *one* thing they could *not* do. They were destitute of that, without which all comfort and sympathy is very poor; they lacked *the real power to help* and sustain.

Now there is that in Jesus Christ, which makes Him just what we poor, sinful, helpless creatures want. We do not only want pity, but we want real help,—we want One who has the *power* to save. We do not only want the compassion that mourns and suffers with us; but we want One who has the *power* to remedy the suffering and the ruin that sin has wrought.

"When the Lord saw her, He had compassion on her, and said, Weep not."

How vain, how very empty, it often sounds when one is in deep sorrow, to hear somebody say words such as these—"Don't be sorrowful; don't give way to your sorrow!" How vain and empty it sounds, because we feel the sorrow is crushing us, and we cannot help feeling the bitterness in our very heart; and we say, Why do *you* tell us not to weep?" But, when these words

come from the lips of *Jesus*, it is a very different matter.
When the Lord said to her, "Weep not," He had, remember, the *power* and the *purpose* to dry up the very
fountain of her tears, and to turn her very sorrow into
deeper joy.   What lesson do we learn here but this,—
if we are Christ's, (and if we are not, let us see the
blessedness of being such), let us bring our sorrows
under Christ's notice, for we are told that "when the
Lord *saw* her, He had *compassion*."   He cannot see
without having compassion, and His compassion is
infinite.   He is "touched with the *feeling* of our infirmities" (Heb. iv. 15).   There is not a sorrow that we
bring before the eye of Jesus Christ, that He does not
compassionate.   He may not see fit to remove that
sorrow at once ; He may see that we need it for a little
while to press upon us.   But when He says "Weep not,"
it is with the power to dry up the fountain of tears, and
there will be a day, when He will say this to each of His
ransomed ones.   He will "wipe away all tears from
their eyes." (Rev. xxi. 4).

**"And He came and touched the bier: and they
that bare him stood still.   And He said, Young man,
I say unto thee, Arise.   And he that was dead sat
up, and began to speak."**

Now, we have placed before us here, one of the most
wonderful instances of the exercise of the power of
Jesus.   Not more wonderful was even the resurrection
of Lazarus, than that of this young man.   Death has
been the conqueror of millions on millions, in every age
of the world.   Death has mowed down successive

generations for six thousand years ; and death had never before met his match—had never been made to feel that he was a miserable slave, and that he would be cast out and overcome. Death was here, holding this young man in his strength and his prime ; but he finds that there is a voice which even *he* must obey, that he *must* give up his captive. This young man, who was being carried to the tomb to be buried out of sight, must be given up to Jesus Christ. Death cannot hold him any longer, when JESUS says " Young man, *I* say unto thee, *Arise*."

What should we feel if we had not this consolation, that the great enemy of our race, the great enemy who has cut down those nearest and dearest to us, and who is beyond our power, is *subject to Christ*,—subject to Him who is all goodness, all compassion, all grace? " Young man, I say unto *thee*, Arise." He can do it with spiritual death, as He can do it with physical death. No other power but that of Jesus Christ can break the fetters, loose the bonds, and let the captive go free. But He *can* do it.

" Young man, I say unto thee, Arise. And he that was dead sat up, and began to speak."

Jesus Christ has power over the death of the body, and He has power over the *greater death of the soul*. He can say, " I say unto thee, Arise "—and he, who was spiritually dead, shall sit up and begin to speak. Yes—there is not a living Christian, there is not one who is really Christ's, who does not answer to this description—who does not know that he was dead and now he lives; he was blind, now he sees; he was deaf, now he hears.   He sits up, and begins to testify and to *prove* that he lives, by speaking words of grace, of wonder, and of praise.   He had been bound in the clammy grasp of death; and now he is raised up again, to be a monument of the Saviour's grace, obedient to the Saviour's word.

"And He delivered him to his mother."

No doubt, when Jesus delivered him to his mother, she felt as if she had never possessed him before, and very truly she might; for what do we possess, what possession have we, of any real, lasting, abiding good, if it has not been delivered to us by Jesus?   Parents have not their children, till they are delivered to them by the hand of Christ.   The friend has not his friend, till that friend has been received from the hand of Christ.   "He delivered him to his mother."   Then she *had* him; then he was a son indeed—hers for ever, hers without end, without possibility of separation.   She might have had sons that were hers by nature, and yet have been eternally separated from them : but now that her son has been delivered unto her hands by the gracious Lifegiver, none shall pluck thence what *He* has consigned to her.

It is a grand, glorious thought, which is suggested by these words—that in the great Day of Ingathering, in that great day when all who have believed, have been washed, and sanctified, shall awake out of death, when "all shall be changed," and "the dead shall be raised incorruptible" (1 Cor. xv. 51, 52), *then* there will the final delivering of one to another, of parent to child, of friend to friend, of relative to relative, if only they are one in Christ. "He delivered *him* (the risen one) to his *mother.*" He was hers now—brought out of the grave to be hers for ever. So will it be then—ours, and ours for ever, when Christ,—the gracious Captain of our salvation, our King, and the Conqueror of death and the grave,—shall give one to another for ever and ever.

Well might there come **"a fear on all: and they glorified God, saying, That a great prophet is risen up among us, and, That God hath visited His people. And this rumour of Him went forth throughout all Judæa** (it goes before Him, for He was on His way to Jerusalem) **and throughout all the region round about."**

"And the disciples of John shewed him of all these things."

Jesus Christ had raised the *dead.* He had raised a man in the presence of two companies of people, in the presence of the people of Nain. It was a case that there could be no mistake about—no illusion—a young man, in his prime, had been raised from the dead. Surely God *had* visited His people. Ought *we* to take so coldly these works of infinite grace—when Jesus Christ has come and said to the dead "in sins," "Arise"? Ought we not to feel that this is the Word of *God,* and "that *God* has indeed visited His people"—that God is here in the midst of us? It meant something very wonderful, as it went from mouth to mouth of the Jews, who had ever lived in fear of death—that *Death had met his Conqueror.* Ought we not to rejoice when life comes into the soul, and the man speaks the praises of Him, who has called him from the power of Satan unto God?

This, then, is indeed one of the wonderful works of Jesus Christ. It teaches us, with regard to the death that is still in the world, that He lives who *can* and *will destroy* death. His long-suffering is salvation, but the " dead in Christ " shall " awake," and arise, and enter into their glorious Home of eternal rest, and life, and joy.

But it teaches us this, too,—how many in this assembly are, as it were, stretched on the bier, and if they only knew and properly realised that, there would indeed be weeping over their state. They are *dead,* " dead in sins," in love with sin, under the power of sin, in the very hands of Satan—dead and ready to be buried out of sight.

We may well believe that many of those, who had been weeping over the death of her son, went away weeping for themselves. They had been weeping over a small calamity, compared with that of multitudes walking in sin, who might well be wept over—whom angels might well weep over, because they see that Death holds them,—*spiritual* Death. They do not hear God, they do not know God, they do not love Him, they do not fear Him ; they are not seeking God's pardon, and His favour, and the joys that *He* can give. Death is carrying them out of the city, it is doing its utmost on them, and corruption is making them its prey.

Let us, then, while we compassionate every sorrow, and weep with them that weep, (and if there are any

Christians here to-night, they may well go out of the city weeping over the dead, over the dead in *sins*),—let us cry to the great Captain of salvation, to come over the mountain and raise the dead, that there may be a great spiritual resurrection. And then, there will be one given to another—given, never to be taken away—given spiritually and eternally—" He delivered him to his mother."

XI.

THE HEALING OF THE IMPOTENT MAN AT BETHESDA.

" *After this there was a feast of the Jews ; and Jesus went up to Jerusalem. Now there is at Jerusalem by the sheep market a pool, which is called in the Hebrew tongue Bethesda, having five porches. In these lay a great multitude of impotent folk, of blind, halt, withered, waiting for the moving of the water. For an angel went down at a certain season into the pool, and troubled the water : whosoever then first after the troubling of the water stepped in was made whole of whatsoever disease he had. And a certain man was there, which had an infirmity thirty and eight years. When Jesus saw him lie, and knew that he had been now a long time in that case, he saith unto him, Wilt thou be made whole ? The impotent man answered him, Sir, I have no man, when the water is troubled, to put me into the pool, but while I am coming, another steppeth down before me. Jesus saith unto him, Rise, take up thy bed, and walk. And immediately the man was made whole, and took up his bed, and walked : and on the same day was the sabbath. The Jews therefore said unto him that was cured, It is the sabbath day : it is not lawful for thee to carry thy bed. He answered them, He that made me whole, the same said unto me, Take up thy bed, and walk. Then asked they him, What man is that which said unto thee, Take up thy bed, and walk ? And he that was healed wist not who it was ; for Jesus had conveyed himself away, a multitude being in that place. Afterward Jesus findeth him in the temple, and said unto him, Behold, thou art made whole : sin no more, lest a worse thing come unto thee. The man departed, and told the Jews that it was Jesus, which had made him whole."*—ST. JOHN v. 1–15.

WE are not quite sure, what "feast of the Jews" this was. St. John evidently meant his Gospel to be read by the *Gentiles*, because he is very particular to describe this as a feast of the *Jews*. It was most likely, I think (in spite of all that has been said against it)—the Passover ; but it is not a matter of much importance for us to know, or we should have been told, as we are in other cases—whether it was the Feast of the Dedication, or of Tabernacles, or of Purim, or what not. But *this* is important—that we should know that Jesus was ever found, at the stated time, in His Father's house, though mourning over all the declension and apostasy that He found there. In the house of sacrifice, in the house of prayer, in the house in which His Father had put His Name—there Jesus ever was found at the stated time.

"**After this there was a feast of the Jews : and Jesus went up to Jerusalem. Now there is in Jerusalem** (says St. John, at the very time when he was writing his gospel) **by the sheep market,**" or the sheep gate, "**a pool, which is called in the Hebrew tongue Bethesda, having five porches.**"

You know quite well that it was necessary, that there should be a place called a sheep gate, a place called a sheep market, in Jerusalem ; because people, coming to the Passover and the other feasts, could not bring their sacrifices with them. There was a sheep gate—a sheep market, and, within that, (says the Evangelist) "*a pool*"

—a considerable quantity of water, called in Hebrew *Bethesda*—that is, House of Mercy—with five porches, five colonnades, under which, sheltered from the weather, these poor, " impotent folk," **"blind, halt, withered,"** could lie on their mattresses, on little couches, on what is here called their " bed "—" **waiting for the moving of the water."**

I am not going to dwell, to-night, on the miracle of the moving of the water, nor on what the healing was, which this great multitude of impotent—of helpless folk, blind, halt, and withered, had come at that particular time to wait for.   You will notice one thing—" *A great multitude*" had gathered in the five porches, though it was absolutely certain, that only those who could get down *first*, would be benefited by the miracle of healing at that particular time, whatever that miracle was.— Whether God had, after taking away His prophets for four hundred years, established that one little testimony of His presence, to encourage them in hoping that the great mercy would come, is not our subject to-night. We have to look at the miracle, not of the moving of the water, but at that which was wrought by Jesus Christ.

" And a certain man was there, which had an infirmity thirty and eight years."

In all the miracles wrought by Jesus Christ, one great feature stands out—everybody that He healed *knew that he wanted healing;* everybody that came for mercy knew that he *wanted* mercy, that he could not do without mercy.   This poor man does not come to

Jesus, but Jesus comes to *him*—he was groaning under the weight of a long and severe malady, a malady he had had for eight and thirty years. We are not told *what* that malady was. It was, evidently, by his own sin, that he had brought it on himself. Thirty-eight years ago, he had sinned himself into this sickness. For thirty-eight years, he had endured the miserable consequences of that particular sin. We say once again, with all solemnity—there is no sickness, no suffering, no death, that is not *the consequence of sin.* There are some sicknesses and some sufferings in the world, because of some particular sins. Some, by their own sin, bring special sufferings on themselves ; and this was so more largely, when God's actings were more outward and more manifest than they are now. God had said to the Jews, " I will appoint over you terror, consumption, and the burning ague " (Lev. xxvi. 16)—" He will bring upon thee all the diseases of Egypt." (Deut. xxviii. 60). That was in the day, when everything was more manifestly *outward* than it is at present. The Jews had *many* ordinances ; we have only *two* now,—Baptism and the Lord's Supper. Things are more entirely *inward* now, in the dispensation of the Spirit.

This man had sinned, and he was made to bear " the sins of his youth." (Job xiii. 26). For thirty and eight years he had to bear this great infirmity—this, very likely, exceeding suffering. And he had been seeking mercy, seeking help, by the pool of Bethesda. He knew quite well that, here and there, dotted about Jerusalem, there was this man, and that woman, and that

M

child, who had been carried at a particular time, and dipped in the troubled water, and had come away from the House of Mercy with *health*, having gone there with sickness. He knew it, because report told him so—a report that was true; there were monuments in Jerusalem of the healing power of the waters of Bethesda. He hears of them, and it encourages this wretched man, —for he was very unhappy and friendless, as we shall see,—to go and wait in one of the covered porches of that pool,—on the bare chance, *on the bare chance* of there not being a crush to get into the water,—on the bare chance of being able to crawl near the pool, or that a more friendly hand than he had ever found yet, would take him and put him in, to get the benefit it conferred. He had suffered thus for thirty-eight years. How many times he had come to the Pool of Bethesda, when this "moving" was to take place, we are not told. Very likely, he had come many times to that House of Mercy, with a bare hope of finding health, and had been "sent empty away." He had come to Bethesda, and gone away unhealed. He had come seeking help, and found none; yet he could not let the bare chance of getting some measure of health pass by, without trying if it were within the reach of his poor, crawling powers to get there. So here we find him again, seeking health where he could not get it, seeking life where there was not any likelihood of his finding it. He finds, however, that that blind seeking for mercy, that blind desire for mercy, though it leads him to the place where he could *not* get it, yet brings him into contact with

One, who never sent one empty away, who never sent one unhealed away.

Look at the connection in which Christ stands to the Pool—what it *could* do, and what it could *not* do. The Pool could give health to those who had *some* remaining strength, to those who could get on their feet and push through the crowd, to those who were able, to some extent, to help themselves ; but, for those who could *not* help themselves, for those who were helpless and friendless, that Pool could not be of value. *It could not come to them*, it could not flow over them, it could not bring mercy to their feet—to the spot where they lay. The Pool had no power to heal those, who were absolutely without strength.

This man stands in a distinct position from the rest. A man with a paralysed *arm*, might manage to get to the water-side ; a man with only one particular wound, might push his way through the crowd ; but one, who was stricken down with *total* infirmity, had no chance. The Pool was not for *him*. He knew, that a man who was sound on his feet, that any with strength to push his way, could get in before him ; he knew that,—yet there he lies in one of those arcades, hoping against hope, hoping against sense and reason, that, perhaps, there might be mercy for *him*. So, when a man comes to know that he wants mercy, he will seek for it everywhere, that there is the barest chance of finding it. This man was helpless, he was friendless ; yet he managed to crawl to the place, where he could see that others had been healed. It inspired a faint, glimmering hope in his mind, when he thought of one man in one street, and of another in another street, of Jerusalem, who had been healed ; he had, perhaps, heard of some miserable wretch, who had found a friend to put him into the water, and had gone away with health ; and, ever since, that had given him strength to *hope*.   So, rather than pass the day by, he will crawl, on the bare chance, to the Pool.

But,—it brings him *this time* into the presence of CHRIST.   Only let a man find out that he is in an utterly ruined, miserable, wretched state, and, sure enough, Jesus Christ will find out that man.   Whenever sickness is realised, the Physician will manage to get in contact with the sick one.   It is only when man is in a calmly confident, in an indifferent, hardened state, that he will not realise it, and that he will not come under the Physician's care.   This man did not go *seeking* Jesus ; he did not know about Him.   He would have crawled right up to *Galilee*, if he had known anything of the healing power of Jesus! all he had heard of was, that in the moving of the water of that Pool, there was some power of healing.

"When Jesus saw him lie, and knew that he had been now a long time in that case, He saith unto him, Wilt thou be made whole?"

Why, the man might have turned round and said, "What have I crawled here *for?*   Why am I *here?*   Why do you ask me such a question? Do you mean to mock me?   Do you mean to add insult to my present pitiable condition?   Why am I here, if I am not willing? Why am I at all these pains to come? And why am I lying here?"—The words of Jesus are *strong* words; they mean, " Are you willing to be made whole?—*Are you willing to be made whole?*" They are very serious words; they are words that come from the fountain of Divine wisdom. Jesus must have the whole subject out with that man. There are multitudes of people whose sins are unpardoned, whose souls are unsaved, who are outside, as it were, the House of Mercy—are *they* willing to be made whole? Are *they* willing to be made sound? Are *they* willing to be made thoroughly whole from head to foot?

It might be, that there was something in the words as they were spoken, that opened up in that man's heart many wonderful thoughts; for when Jesus speaks, the Holy Spirit of God is acting, too. And the Holy Spirit, I have no doubt, was acting in that man's mind, and opening up in that man's mind many a startling thought, as Jesus asked the question—" Wilt thou be made whole?" We come and ask sinners, " Are you willing to be made whole?" And if they answered us *honestly*, they would say, " we are *not* willing for any such thing. We are willing to be made contented on *earth*, and to be made happy in the world to *come*." But they are not willing to be made " whole," to have their *souls* renewed. They are not willing to be renewed in the image of Him that created them,—they are not willing to be made thoroughly sound all through, and to have their spirits thoroughly imbued with the love of holiness and with the hatred of sin—with the love of God, and with alienation from everything, that is not in accordance with His pure nature, and His holy will. "We are willing not to go to hell," but we are *not* "willing to be made whole," would be the language of multitudes, if they spake truly.

This was not a *foolish* question; it was not an unnecessary question, but one that ought to go into the mind and heart of everybody—"Am I willing?" You want Jesus Christ to save you *against* your will. You are willing to be saved from the fear of punishment, but you do not want the responsibilities of health. Multitudes of people do not want to be made well; they like to have some croaking complaint or other left to them. But are you willing, in spirit and mind, to be made *really well?* willing to have all your desires pointing upward to the things of God, and all on earth looked on in its true light, as fading and passing away? Are you willing to come out of the world, to have *your whole life changed,* your whole current of thought changed, your hatreds changed, your loves changed, your actions changed? Are you willing to be made anew, to be "born again," to be made in the likeness of Jesus Christ, and to have the mind of Jesus Christ? That is quite another thing.

Then the man says—he does not answer the question—

"Sir, I have no man, when the water is troubled, to put me into the pool; but while I am coming, another steppeth down before me."

That is his account of himself. Now, poor man, look

at his condition. He says, "Look at me—I am not only what you *see*, but I haven't a *friend* in the world ! This is my miserable condition; if I could get some one to put me into the water, I should be *well*, but I have *no man* to put me into the pool." What a deplorable condition ! No man cares to do it, no man will do it. He was so friendless, perhaps so loathsome, that no one would do it for him. One would imagine, that *anyone* would have done this for him. But no ! nobody would. Nobody cared for this man's *body*, and his feeling must have been akin to his, who said, " No man cared for my *soul*." (Psalm cxlii. 4). No man cared enough for this poor, wretched sufferer, even to put him into the Pool. Truly did he need a Friend ; and there *is* a Friend in need " that sticketh closer than" any " brother." (Prov. xviii. 24).

"Jesus saith unto him, Rise, take up thy bed, and walk."

Now, look at this man. He looks up in the face of this blessed stranger, and he sees that there is power, as well as love, in it. He sees that look, and *the look of Jesus Christ* must have been very wonderful. He turned once and " looked upon Peter "—(St. Luke xxii. 61). And when He looked on this poor man, what did He see ? He knew how that suffering was the fruit of sin —that this man was not only the heir of the miseries of sin *generally*, but that he had brought this, in *particular*, on himself. And when Jesus Christ looks on sin, it is with an inconceivable hatred, and with an inconceivable pity. And, with that look of pity and compassion, there must have been a look of *power*, when He said, "Rise, take up thy bed, and walk."

Well now, the man does not answer. Why did not the man say to Jesus,—when He said, "Rise, take up thy bed, and walk,"—"Don't you see that I *can't* 'rise?' Don't you see I am absolutely helpless? that I am altogether without a single particle of power in me? And you tell me to 'rise,' when I can hardly *crawl!* Why, if I could take up my bed and walk, I could have got into the Pool long ago, and have been *well!* Are you mocking me again? You said, just now, like mocking words, and now you tell *me*, who am powerless, and have no more ability to walk than the very stones my bed is resting on, to 'rise and take up my bed and walk!' Don't you see that I *can't* get up? Where is the *power* to do your bidding? Surely, your words look like cruel mockery."

But the history goes on. He did not say a word, but, "immediately," he took up the little mattress he was stretched on.

"Immediately the man was made whole, and took up his bed and walked."

Now, what is the point here? "Art thou willing to be made whole?" *He was;* and as he looked in the face of Jesus, there was trust and hope springing up within him; and he kept looking stedfastly in the face of Jesus, as the word came, "RISE."—There was power. He felt it, he knew it, he did not stop to argue, he did not stop to say, "*How* can it be done? Such things don't happen. If you were to take me up, and put me into the pool, that *would* be something like." But he does not say anything ; he rises up, takes his mattress, and is healed—made whole every whit.

Why are not sinners healed? That same Jesus Christ still lives, still says, "Come unto Me, and I will give you rest"—and "Him that cometh to Me I will in no wise cast out." (St. Matt. xi. 28 ; St. John vi. 37). He is, still, as powerful to save to the uttermost, as when He said, "Rise, take up thy bed, and walk."

Then we ask once more, *where* is the flaw? It is just this—Art thou *willing* to be made whole? Settle *that* question, and every other question will settle itself. The real flaw is "Ye *will not* come" (St. John v. 40), ye are not willing to be made sound, to be really saved, to have Jesus Christ cleanse you from sin, and to have the law of Christ regulating and ruling your whole life and conduct. You love earth better than heaven, sin better than holiness, death better than life. Only settle the question of *willingness.* No charge can be brought against Jesus Christ, either as to His power, or His willingness, to save. No ! but *ye* are not willing, ye do not *want* to be made whole. Jesus Christ is wanted—He is wanted when a man sees the great abyss opening before him,—He is wanted when the man has lived all his life, and wasted it, and ruined himself, and *death* looks him in the face. When Death goes from one room to another in his house, when he goes into his very bed-chamber and says, "Here I am, and I must be attended to"—*then* Jesus Christ is wanted ; but He is not wanted for His own real worth. Jesus Christ never said, "I am come to save men from *hell.*"   No, never !   What He *did* come for was this, "He shall save his people from their *sins.*" (St. Matt. i. 21).   And a people who are saved from their sins, need never fear hell.   Jesus Christ is come to save sinners from themselves, from their own hearts, from their own lusts ; and when they are saved from their sins, they are saved from all that is really hurtful.

"**The Jews therefore said unto him that was cured, It is the sabbath day : it is not lawful for thee to carry thy bed.**"

The Jews, you see, did not like Jesus Christ.   Why, these rulers of the Jews—for it *was* the rulers—were as much opposed to Him as the Sadducees and infidels, as the very heathen of Tyre and Sidon.   They were always trying to get hold of something to find fault with in His works, and now they say this.   And what does the *man* reply ?

"**He that made me whole, the same said unto me, Take up thy bed and walk.**"

Why, what had Jesus Christ done ?   He had just got hold of that man's *heart.*   He had come and brought health into his poor body, and given him the great blessing that he had been waiting for, these thirty-eight years—and, in giving that great blessing to the *body,* Jesus had taken possession of his *heart.*   And when He had got the man's heart, He had got the man's *mind.* He says, "He who could do that for me, His word is law to me.   He healed me, He set me upright, He has made me a man again, and His word is law.   He that made me *whole*, THE SAME said unto me, *Take* up thy bed." Let a man *really* get the pardon of his sins, let him really get spiritual health, and he will not be quarrelling with Christ's restrictions, with Christ's admonitions, with Christ's word, with the law of Christ that says, Do this, or do that, Abstain from this, or abstain from that.

"Then asked they him, What man is that which said unto thee, Take up thy bed and walk?"

Just look at what the human heart is, if you can ! Look into the heart of these men—see how they answer this poor man. *He* had said, "*He* that *made me whole*, the same said to me, Take up thy bed." *They* say, "What man is that which said unto thee ?" What ?— What do you think they would have said ? Why, "What man is that which *healed* you, which hath done such great things for you "? One would have thought they would have been asking, "Where is there One who can do what the Pool cannot do—One who can give health to such a poor wretch as you—One who could rescue such a one as this, from his abject, loathsome condition ? What man is that which *healed* thee ?"

They did not want to know *that*. They did not want to know of One who could say, "*Rise*, take up thy bed and walk." They knew, that, if they heard of One who could do this mighty work, they would hear of One whose *word* was *law*—law to *them*, and that they must bow their proud hearts down, and submit to His law. Therefore, they leave out all about the miracle. "No, not that—what man is that which said unto thee, *Take up thy bed*, and walk?" So ·we find, if we begin to talk to a man about his sins, about his need of a Saviour, about being made whole, he will be sure to find some convenient quibble or loophole. These men allege the *sabbath*—a question of the law—of the sabbath day. The *healing* was the thing that proved, that there was a mighty Prophet amongst them. That proved it to the man. *They* knew that if they came in contact with Jesus, He would be their master, and they did not want a master, they did not want a Lord. They knew that if they were to admit Him, they would have to admit something else. They knew not that they were diseased, that they had leprosy, that they were more *spiritually* wretched, than this poor man had been *physically*. If they had known their disease, they would have said, "Where is the Healer, because our law tells of one—Jehovah-Rophi? Is *He* in the midst of us, for we need health?" No—they said, "Who is He that said to thee, Take up thy bed and walk, that we may catch Him in that matter?"

The man did not know, but Jesus met him—

"Jesus findeth him in the temple"—

Then, he knew that the way to God was *there*. Jesus finds him *there*. You may be sure of this—if Jesus Christ heals a man's soul, that man will be found in the temple, in the place of the sacrifice, in the place of the Mercy-seat sprinkled with blood. You will always know where to find a man's mind, when he has had spiritual health bestowed upon him—it will be *there*, he will attend there.　He may tread devious paths, he may tread rough paths, but he will look—from the city of Babylon far away, from the whale's belly, from the very depths below—towards that *Mercy-seat.*

" Jesus findeth him in the temple and saith unto him, Behold, thou art made whole ; sin no more, lest a worse thing come unto thee."

Jesus here is showing Himself to this man, as the Searcher of his heart, as the Lord of his spirit ; He shows that He can see right down there.　Why?　Eight and thirty years, this poor man had been suffering for the sins of his youth ; he had brought this misery upon his own head.　He had begun this dreadful suffering *before* Jesus was *born* in Bethlehem, yet Jesus says, " I know it all ; you cannot conceal anything from Me.　*You* know what I mean,—you know *when* it was, *how* it was, *what* it was, that course of guilt which ended in this. ' Sin no more.'　*That* sin brought these thirty-eight years of intense suffering upon you.　But if you go on, if you go back, then see what remains for you.—Sin no more, lest a *worse* thing come unto thee."

Jesus does not mean, that the man will not get to heaven, if he does not maintain absolute freedom from all sin ; because we know, that "if we say that we have no sin, we deceive ourselves." (1 John i. 8).　Every day we do what we ought *not* to do ; every day we leave *un*done what we ought to *do* ; and " there is no" spiritual " health" in the nature that remains to be crucified and mortified.　But Christ says, " I have healed you, I have saved you ;. and what is your life to be?　It is not to be a life of sin. You are not to go back, like " the sow that was washed to her wallowing in the mire." (2 Peter ii. 22). " Sin no more, lest a worse thing come unto thee."

"The man departed, and told the Jews that it was Jesus, which had made him whole."

Perhaps in the very simplicity of his heart, he went and told the rulers, because great issues were depending on it ; but we cannot enter into that, now.

But we see that there is One, who is the Helper of the helpless—the Friend of the friendless—the Healer of the diseased—the Saviour of the lost. And we see *how* it is that people are not saved, how it is that they go on in all their love of sin, and the world, and in alienation from Christ and His Word. It is because they love it—*they love it;* they are not willing to be made whole; they are not willing to be made new creatures—they are not willing to be washed in the Blood, and clothed in the Righteousness, of Jesus Christ, and to have their feet guided thus into the way of truth and peace.

XII.

THE FEEDING OF THE FIVE THOUSAND.

" When Jesus heard of it, he departed thence by ship into a desert place apart ; and when the people had heard thereof, they followed him on foot out of the cities. And Jesus went forth, and saw a great multitude, and was moved with compassion toward them, and he healed their sick. And when it was evening, his disciples came to him, saying, This is a desert place, and the time is now past ; send the multitude away, that they may go into the villages, and buy themselves victuals. But Jesus said unto them, They need not depart ; give ye them to eat. And they say unto him, We have here but five loaves, and two fishes. He said, Bring them hither to me. And he commanded the multitude to sit down on the grass, and took the five loaves, and the two fishes, and looking up to heaven, he blessed, and brake, and gave the loaves to his disciples, and the disciples to the multitude. And they did all eat, and were filled ; and they took up of the fragments that remained twelve baskets full. And they that had eaten were about five thousand men, beside women and children."—
ST. MATT. xiv. 13–21.

IF you refer to the opening verses of this chapter, you will see the alarm felt by Herod at the wonderful works which were being wrought by Jesus, and the terror awakened in his conscience at the thought, that John the Baptist, whom he had beheaded, had risen from the dead. The Evangelist takes occasion from that circum-

stance, to relate the details of John's cruel murder, and
tells us that the disciples of John buried his body, and
then came and told Jesus.   They came and cast their
burden of sorrow on Him, who is ever ready to bear
our sorrows ; they came and told Him, who alone could
heal the deep wound, which had been made in their
hearts.   And we read, this evening, that—

**"When Jesus heard of it, He departed thence by
ship into a desert place apart."**

It appears, that the effect of this intelligence on our
blessed Lord was to make Him go "apart," seeking
solitude, seeking a place where He might be alone, yet
not alone, but with His Father.   John's cruel death
was but a foreshadow, a *faint* foreshadow, of that far
more terrible death, which He Himself would be called
on to endure.   John had come to Israel, and Israel, in
the person of the king, had rejected him ; and Jesus
sees this as a foreshadow.   Therefore, He would retire
alone,—alone, at least, with His disciples, into some
inaccessible solitude, that He might ponder these things.
Remember, our Lord Jesus Christ was *man* as well as
God, and He needed everything, that a poor, weary,
sinless man could need, to cheer and strengthen Him.
We must remember that He needed rest, that He
needed food, that He needed solitude, that He needed
prayer, even as His people do ; therefore we have Him
before us here, as an example that we should follow
His steps.   "He departed . . . into a desert place
apart."

We find, that He embarked in a ship from Capernaum, and the little vessel made toward the northern part of the lake; but the people saw it, and went along by the side of the lake, following Him on foot. As the little vessel went up the lake, they went along the side,—two hours' good walking would carry them to the head of the lake, so that they could trace His steps, and see Him, wherever He might disembark.

"They followed Him on foot out of the cities."

He had been doing great wonders, and great acts of love, and His name was in everybody's mouth. Everybody that had a sorrow, that had a sickness, that had an infirmity, had thoughts about Jesus; and these multitudes follow Him by the lake-side as He goes, Himself seeking a solitude. From the latter part of this narrative, we see that it was a great multitude that followed Him: we see how deep an impression had been made, and how alive the inhabitants of Galilee were to the works of Christ. We know what miracles Jesus had done in their midst; all were thinking of Him, all were discussing Him, all were wondering, either what they could get from Him, or else what He was. He could not get the solitude He wanted—"there were many coming and going," and the very disciples "had no leisure so much as to eat." (St. Mark vi. 31.)

Such was the excitement, such was the anxiety, such was the pressing on Christ, of the multitudes of Galilee, that they think nothing of running for hours by the side of the lake, if they can but get to the spot where Christ will disembark. They go on foot, men, women, and children, in that great, rushing crowd, and think nothing,

N

consider nothing, if only they can meet with Christ.
And Jesus, who had gone before them, had landed at
the north-east part of the lake; and it is remarkable,
that there was—and travellers tell us there is, still,—a
grassy spot there, just suited for such an extraordinary
gathering as this.   When they arrived there, Jesus
" went forth " from the brief period of solitude,

**"And saw a great multitude, and was moved with
compassion toward them, and healed their sick."**

We find, in another Gospel, that He looked on them
" as sheep not having a shepherd," and " was moved
with compassion toward them." (St. Mark vi. 34).   He
might well be moved with compassion, when He looked
on that multitude; there they were, with all their sick,
all their paralytic, all who had a weary burden of care.
Many towns on that western side of the lake had
emptied themselves—there were " about five thousand
men, beside women and children."   And Jesus looked
on them; He knew every one of them, He knew the
heart of every one of them, He knew the sin of every
one of them, He knew the perverseness and selfishness
of the multitudes of them.   He knew every single thing
in the heart of every one of them, He knew they were not
five thousand *good* men, with *good* women and children.
He knew that many were following Him from mixed,
and many from carnal, motives ; He knew, as the sequel
proves, that, whatever He did before them, however
great His compassion, however great His work of love,
they would forsake Him and go back to destruction.

He looked on the multitudes,—a disciple might have

looked on them and said, "See the zeal for Christ ! See how earnest these people are, every one of them will be converted to His faith, and become His disciples,"—*a disciple* might have thought that, but Jesus could not. He knew them all, He knew what was in every heart, and what was in every mind, in that great gathering ; and, as He looked on them, He had but one feeling—a feeling of deep, tender, yearning compassion over them. He "was moved with *compassion* toward them, and healed their sick." He did not make them all first bow down to Him, He did not make them submit to some hard condition, but He healed their sick, and showed that His compassion was not a mere empty name, or empty feeling, but that He was ready to put forth the arm of His power,—that whoever felt a desire for help, whoever felt a want, had a Friend ready at hand,—that whoever had a longing desire in his heart for a great boon, there was Jesus ready to meet that longing, and to supply that need. Whatever evils they groaned under, they brought to His feet ; and He was not found wanting—" He healed their *sick.*"

Yes, it is so. Men bring their physical sufferings and their temporal wants, but alas ! their great *spiritual* necessities are unknown. His compassion was more for what they did *not* feel, than for what they did feel ; He was as much concerned for the health of the soul, as He was for the health of the body.

We must remember, while considering this miracle, that it stands out prominently in the Gospel history ; it is recorded by every one of the four Evangelists, and

occupies, therefore, a very important place.   Another
gospel tells us, that Jesus taught the people "many
things." (St. Mark vi. 34).   He sat down there, on that
quiet afternoon, and they sat down beside Him on the
hill-side, and the light atmosphere carried His words—
words such as "never man spake," to the outward ear
of that great multitude.   "He began to teach them
many things."   These "many things" are not recorded,
but we can easily imagine what they would be.   He
would tell out their necessities, deeper than those of
lepers and paralytics, He would tell that there was a
supply for all their need in the riches of Divine grace,
He would expand these truths to them according to
their understanding.   And, it seems, as if the great
Teacher and the great multitude had forgotten that man
was man, and had human necessities, and that night
was coming on—so that the disciples have to come and
remind Him,—

**"This is a desert place, and the time is now past ;
send the multitude away, that they may go into the
villages, and buy themselves victuals."**

Now, can we blame the disciples here?   Are they
blameworthy?   Surely, it was well to remember that
people have infirmities, that men *are* men, that a day is
but a day, and that "the night cometh, when no man
can work."   Though they might have trusted their
Lord's provident care, though they might well have
thought no place a desert where their Lord was, still it
was a desert.   Jesus had Himself gone to that desert
place that He might be alone, and it was a large

gathering of people who had watched Him go, and followed Him there. The disciples come and say, " This is a desert place, and now the time is far passed; send them away, that they may go into the country round about, and into the villages, and buy themselves bread ; for they have nothing to eat." (St. Mark vi. 35, 36). There is nothing unreasonable in this, neither does it indicate want of faith, or want of thought; but, possibly, there was in the hearts of the disciples, an anxious care for their Master,—for that Master who, they knew, had been seeking solitude, that Master who had said to them, " Let us go over the lake in order to get rid of the multitude, and let us have solitude."

" But Jesus said unto them, They need not depart ; give ye them to eat."

This was an extraordinary gathering. The Lord had detained the people a great length of time ; it had been a day much to be remembered, it had been a day that none of them could ever forget so long as eternity lasts, it had been a day of marvellous opportunity, a day of unspeakable privilege—to have sat at the very feet of Christ, and to have heard the very words of Christ. And Jesus says—" As I have called them to long listening, and to a long mental effort, there is provision for them ; they need not depart, give ye them to eat." Christ can provide for every one whom He attracts to Himself. None, who have been attracted to Christ, need depart from Christ for the sustenance of their spiritual life. " They need not depart, give *ye* them to eat." You remember the conversation which took place between Jesus and Philip, as it is recorded in the Gospel of St. John, and that "two hundred pennyworth of bread" was not enough—six or seven pounds worth —"that every one might take a little."

"They say unto Him, We have here but five loaves, and two fishes."

They could not have imagined what our Lord was about to do, and, therefore, there is nothing extraordinary in their looking on the provisions they had, and in their estimating what they had to feed the multitudes with.   I think, if they had *not* done it, it would have indicated,—not so much want of faith, but rather, *fanaticism.*   There can be no faith, unless there is a word of God on which faith is to rest.   That which believes *without* a word of promise, is not faith, but fanaticism.   These men had no reason to believe, at this moment, what Jesus would do ; therefore they estimate their resources.   When the Lord calls us to a work to be done for Him, and in His Name, He expects us to take a careful inventory of the stock in hand, of what we have to go to war with, what we have to go to work with, and what materials we are called to use.   We must always estimate, very carefully, the ordinary means, the natural means, at our disposal, to carry out every work of God that He calls us to undertake.   If a man rushes off to some work for which he is totally unqualified, with only a wild fancy that he is undertaking a work for Christ, and therefore is sure to have Christ's help, *that* is not faith, that is not obedience, that is running before he is sent.

It was well for these disciples to see how many loaves and how many fishes they had, and for them to be driven to see how very ill-prepared they were, to do the work which Jesus, nevertheless, commanded them to do. It was very well for them to take stock, and to realise distinctly, that *they* could not feed the multitudes, that they had not the power, that they had not the resources. It was well for them to look at the little loaves, and the little fishes, which a little boy could carry in his basket, —and then, to look at the spreading thousands, and then, to compare the greatness with the littleness. "Five loaves" and "two small fishes" were all the resources they had, for so great an emergency.

"He said, Bring them hither to Me."

He asks these men to bring that little basket of provisions to Him ; He asks them to do, what He bids every one of His servants do, when He commands them to serve Him—"bring them hither to ME." Bring your poor, weak intellect, bring your poor, weak body, bring those poor, feeble endowments, which God has given you, and with which He expects you to glorify Him. "Bring *them* hither to Me"—these five loaves and two fishes. He did not say, "Take them, and distribute them." No ; but first He says—"bring them hither to Me." They felt how poor they were, they felt that a little child could carry all their stock ; and Jesus says—"bring them hither to *Me*."

You may depend upon this,—if God is not glorified by any of us, it is not simply because of our poverty of endowments, whatever those endowments may be, but

it is because these poor endowments—if poor they are
—"barley-loaves" and "small fishes," are not brought
to HIM.   He asks us to do that,—first, to find out how
poverty-stricken we are, and then, to bring our poverty-
strickenness to Him.   If we think that *we* have enough
to feed multitudes with, we shall find diminution, not
multiplication.   If we think we have *enough*, without
requiring Divine grace, we shall be miserably mistaken.
Jesus Christ would make them feel their weakness, and
their poverty, and how unable they are,—and then, He
would have them bring all to Him, that they may see
His grace and power.   And then He said—"Make
the men sit down." (St. John vi. 10).

This might be for two reasons.   Jesus Christ is God
as well as man, and, as God, He is a lover of order,
and will carry it out.   "He commanded them to make
all sit down *by companies* upon the green grass," (St.
Mark vi. 39),—they sat down in regular ranks.   "God
is not the author of confusion"—He is the author of
order as well as "of peace." (1 Cor. xiv. 33).   It may
have been, also, to answer another end.   We may say
that this was, if not *the* greatest, yet *one of the greatest*,
of the miracles of our Lord; and it was to be wrought
in the presence, of some six, it may be seven or eight,
thousand people.   It was to be wrought in the presence
of the multitudes, who had come after Jesus from anything but unmixed motives.   It was to be wrought
before the face of the representatives of all Galilee.
"Make the men sit down,"—it was to be done with
ceremony, with careful order, with various preparatory

steps. "And they sat down in ranks, by hundreds, and by fifties" (St. Mark vi. 40), tier above tier, company above company. And He "**took the five loaves, and the two fishes, and looking up to heaven,**" the seat and source of His Divine authority and power, "**He blessed, and brake**" what He had blessed,—He put the Divine blessing on those very loaves and fishes, "**and gave the loaves to the disciples, and the disciples to the multitude.**"

There was not a loaf for each disciple, but the bread multiplied from His hands to the hands of the disciples, and multiplied from row to row, and from company to company, till the great miracle had been completed; and the "**five thousand men beside women and children**" "**did all eat, and were filled,**" in the afternoon of that weary day, on which they had run by the side of the lake, and had sat by the side of the mount, listening to Jesus. It had been a day of excitement, it had been a day of toil; but now their weariness was refreshed, their hunger was satisfied. "They did all eat and were *filled*,"—that great city-full of people, from the loaves and fishes which a little boy had carried in his little basket.

Now, this miracle was wrought in the light of day, it was wrought in the presence of multitudes of people, and it has been brought down to our day, undisputed. The infidel can find no better way to disprove it, than by saying that this means that they sat down to bring out their own satchels, which they had, providentially, provided themselves with in the morning,—as if, when they had left home in the morning, they knew where Jesus would land, and where they would be in the afternoon ! No. When Infidelity has no better argument than that, we can only come to the conclusion, that it is beaten out of the field. Therefore, this was the fiat of Christ,—the Divine power of Christ was put forth, filling multitudes " by the word of His power." The *little* of *man* had been felt and seen, the *much* of *God* had been felt and seen, and all that multitude did " eat, and were filled."

In another Gospel, we are told that the Lord said— " Gather up the fragments that remain, that nothing be lost" (St. John vi. 12), and here, that—

" That they took up of the fragments that remained, twelve baskets full."

Every one of the twelve Apostles had a basket, and those " *twelve* baskets" were " full," though a little boy's *one* basket, originally, had easily carried all. Thus we see the Divine power teaching us a great spiritual lesson. I do not think, that this miracle is recorded in these four Gospels simply to proclaim to us the Divine power of Christ, because belief in that rests, most of all, on the fact of Christ's own resurrection from the dead. But here we find an act of power and love, to show us, I think, His grace, and His power, and His willingness, to supply all the need of our souls. What was the great purpose for which Jesus Christ came into the world ? His purpose was not only to heal sick *bodies*, but to redeem sick SOULS—to save lost sinners. Therefore, everything He conferred on the body, and every incident in His life, had a bearing on the great end of His mission. So that, when He takes bread and gives it to these multitudes, Christ shows how the great purpose of love was to be accomplished, how the "Bread of Life," "which came down from heaven" (St. John vi.), was to be given by Himself to the ministers of His truth, and that it would be theirs to distribute, theirs to give, and that it would multiply again, and again, and again, in their hands, and yet that each should, after all, have a basket for himself. "Gather up the fragments, that nothing be lost."

How precious is Divine truth! I know, these words convey a general truth; I know, it is our responsibility to see that "nothing" is "lost," that *time*, that *influence*, is not lost. I know, our Lord says to each one, "Use every talent, every bit of a talent, use it to the utmost, that *nothing* be lost. Gather up every fragment, and turn them to account." But, I think, there is also a *specific* charge in the words. I think the Bread is Divine truth,—the Bread that men are to live on for ever,—the "Bread which cometh down from heaven, that a man may eat thereof and not die." (St. John vi. 50). And I think it is of that "Living Bread" (51) that Christ says, "Let every fragment be gathered up, let every little bit of truth be carefully cherished, carefully preserved, diligently used—let nothing be *lost*."

How many truths in the Divine Word are there, from which men turn aside and say, "My mind does not lean in this direction, or, in that direction; I keep to this part of the truth, or, to that part of the truth!" "No,"

—says the Lord—" Let *nothing* be lost, gather them all up."

I have one concluding lesson from this miracle—it is a very solemn one. The ministry of Christ was exercised in grace, and exercised in love, to those who were not really His. He looked on that great company, and He knew what would be the sad result, He knew from what motives, and with what feelings, they had all gathered round Him ; but He ministers to them all the words of everlasting life,—He lays on them, in deep compassion, in holy faithfulness, in hallowed tenderness, the responsibility of rejecting Him and His work. He looks on them, and, without reference to anything which was to happen hereafter, without reference to their going back and walking no more with Him, He ministers to all alike. This is a great lesson to the disciples of Christ in every age.

It is a great, cheering thought, that we only tread in the steps of our Master. If we have our sorrows, our disappointments, some going back, others falling off, we know that it was just the same with Him. He breaks the bread that they may eat, and not be weary, and not be " faint,"—He speaks the words of everlasting life,— and, if they refuse that word, if they say it is " a hard saying," if they go back and walk no more with Christ, —then, on them must be the dread responsibility. He called, but they would not hear ; He sought to win them, but they refused to come ; He sought, in tender compassion, to shepherd them in His fold, but they refused His invitations.

As we look on that great company, we cannot but be reminded of the words of the Psalmist, as we see them there being fed, and then going away,—going back from Christ—" They are ranged in Hades like sheep, and Death is their Shepherd." (Ps. xlix. 14). As they would not be shepherded by Christ, and ranged in Christ's fold, they must be ranged in Hades, with Death for their shepherd.

Let *us*, then, look up to that Shepherd, who is able to multiply bread to us,—the Bread of heaven, eating whereof we shall live and live for ever,—to that Shepherd who is able to multiply consolations now and evermore. And let us learn so to value that Living Bread, that not a fragment even may be lost, but let us gather up every one for our own edification, and for the strengthening and refreshing of our souls.

XIII.

THE WALKING ON THE SEA.

" *And straightway Jesus constrained his disciples to get into a ship, and to go before him unto the other side, while he sent the multitudes away. And when he had sent the multitudes away, he went up into a mountain apart to pray; and when the evening was come, he was there alone. But the ship was now in the midst of the sea, tossed with waves; for the wind was contrary. And in the fourth watch of the night Jesus went unto them, walking on the sea. And when the disciples saw him walking on the sea, they were troubled, saying, It is a spirit; and they cried out for fear. But straightway Jesus spake unto them, saying, Be of good cheer; it is I; be not afraid. And Peter answered him and said, Lord, if it be thou, bid me come unto thee on the water. And he said, Come. And when Peter was come down out of the ship, he walked on the water, to go to Jesus. But when he saw the wind boisterous, he was afraid; and beginning to sink, he cried, saying, Lord, save me. And immediately Jesus stretched forth his hand, and caught him, and said unto him, O thou of little faith, wherefore didst thou doubt? And when they were come into the ship, the wind ceased. Then they that were in the ship came and worshipped him, saying, Of a truth thou art the Son of God.*"—ST. MATT. xiv. 22–33.

WE have, in thought, accompanied our blessed Lord across the Sea of Galilee into that "desert place," where, as the day was advancing, as the *first* evening of the day was setting in, the disciples reminded Him that they were in a desert place, and besought Him to send the multitudes away, that they might buy food for themselves; and we have considered the work of Jesus, that great and glorious work, whereby the loaves and fishes multiplied *as they passed* from His hands to the disciples, and from the disciples to the multitude, till all—"five thousand men, beside women and children," "were *filled*." All had sufficiency, and the ministers of that food found that there remained, for *each* of them, a basketful of the precious fragments. And, as the evening, the *second* evening of the day, came on—the afternoon had passed, and the second evening had set in,—

"**Straightway Jesus constrained His disciples to get into a ship.**"

It appears from these words, that the disciples felt some degree of unwillingness, at least of unreadiness, and, if we look at St. John's Gospel, we shall see the reason why there was a necessity for this constraint to be exercised. When the miracle was over, the people said—"This is of a truth that prophet that should come into the world;" and we find, from St. John, that they had, in their minds, the purpose of taking "Him by force to make Him a king." (St. John vi. 14, 15). The idea rose in the minds of the multitude, who had been fed with bread by the wondrous grace of Jesus, that He was the One to deliver them from the thraldom under which they were groaning, and to lead them to the freedom and independence that they were all sighing for. They felt that He, who multiplied the loaves, was surely another, and a greater, Moses,—and that they might gather themselves together under Him, to free themselves from the Roman yoke. Well might the Lord *constrain* His disciples to get out of this scene of mere earthly, worldly thoughts, in order to learn something deeper, higher, more necessary for them to learn. Therefore, He separates them from the people with their thoughts of earthly greatness, and of Israel's presently restored dominion,—therefore, He constrains them " to get into a ship,—

"And to go before Him unto the other side, while He sent the multitudes away."

There are some thoughts which must arise in our minds, as we look at these words. Those disciples could not have helped feeling, that, however dark that night might be, however fiercely the tempest might rage, however terrible the boisterousness of the winds and waves, however near they might be to shipwreck,— there was this comfort, they went into the darkness, they breasted the danger, *at the command of the Lord.* It was He who constrained them to get into the ship, it was He who brought them into the storm,—going " up to the heaven," and " down again to the depths," to see the great and terrible " wonders " of the God of Creation and of Providence, " in the deep." (Ps. cvii. 24, 26). It was *He* who " constrained " them. And might they not have derived infinite comfort, might they not have ridden through the terrible storm, with minds calm and peaceful, if they had truly known *who* and *what* He was who constrained them,—if they had known Who it was, that was leading them as "blind by a way that they knew not," and that was leading them across that Sea of Galilee by "paths," which they, its familiar fishermen, never knew? (Isa. xlii. 16). If they had but known Him, if they had but known what was to be shown to them, they might have been calm amid the tempest's fury, they might have had peace, even while the Lord was away on the Mount.

First, then, He sent His disciples away; and then—with words of power and authority—He dispersed those thousands to their homes; and then,

"He went up into a mountain apart to pray; and when the evening was come, He was there alone."

We look here, again, at our blessed Lord from two points of view,—we look at Him as the great Intercessor, and we look at Him as the great Example. We look at Jesus up in the mountain, while His little Church was floating there, next door to shipwreck, on that tempestuous sea,—we see the Lord there, bearing their burden, pleading their cause, bearing them on His heart. And however much He needed, as "the man Christ Jesus," the strength that comes by fellowship with the Father, yet is He ever presented to us as our great, glorious, interceding High Priest, lifting up His hands for us, pleading our cause. And, *because* "He ever liveth to make *intercession*, He is able to save to the *uttermost*" (Heb. vii. 25), and, therefore, that they might know this, He would bring them, as it were, into "the uttermost" of danger and distress. We see Jesus here, interceding for His disciples on the mount, and

O

bearing them on His heart, while, at the same time, in the mysterious communion of His Divine and human nature, He communes with the Father. " He was there *alone*" —yet "not alone, because the Father" was "with" Him. (St. John xvi. 32). He is away from His disciples, He is away from the multitude, He is away from unreasonable and wicked men,—He has got rid of the world, and is "alone" with the Father—alone, yet *not* alone.

Now look at Jesus, for a moment, as the *Example* of His people. What a day had that been to Him! Remember, He was "perfect man," and to be a perfect man is not to be an angel, it is not to be free from the conditions, and weaknesses, and sufferings of humanity. It is to be just what we are, "yet without sin." And what a day had that been to Him, what a day for His human frame! If we consider what had taken place in the morning before He came over the sea, and then, the great, glorious work of the afternoon, what must it have been for the mind, what must have been the wear —what the pressure—what the work of the human soul, that dwelt in that human body of Jesus! And then we see —as He said to His disciples on another occasion, "Come ye yourselves apart into a desert place, and rest awhile," (St. Mark vi. 31)—that what He needed to refit Him for His work, was communion with Heaven. And we can never walk on earth as we ought, we can never understand earth as we ought, we can never do our work on earth as we ought, unless we have close fellowship with Heaven. Only as being lifted up, as it were, in the mount with God, so that we are not alone, can we have strength and wisdom; it is only as we look down from the mount of communion to the earth below, that we can understand it.　It is only by dwelling there that we can get wisdom, and that we can get strength, to "walk worthy" of our high vocation.　Christ is our Example in prayer, as He is our Intercessor with the Father.　But while He was there in the mount in prayer,—

"The ship was now in the midst of the sea, tossed with waves; for the wind was contrary."

In another Gospel it is said—"He saw them toiling in rowing." (St. Mark vi. 48).　Now, just ponder this for a moment.　The Lord had "constrained" those disciples of His to get into the ship, that they might pass over before Him to the other side, and no sooner do they go away, than trouble comes—no sooner do they get away from Him, than a great tempest comes. People generally imagine that if they belong to Christ, that if they are real Christians, real servants of God, He is bound almost in honour to make things go smoothly for them.　Men say, "What is the use of serving God, if our life is to be a life of tempest, of difficulty and trial?"　Here we have the disciples sent into the ship, and into the boiling, raging, tempestuous sea—Christ sends them down into circumstances where every nerve must be strained to the utmost, where their whole strength would be tried to the last extent, where their faith would be put to the severest test, and they be led to say,—"Our Master could not have known what He was sending us into, or He would never have constrained us to get into the ship. Surely, His wisdom cannot be so great as we have been led to suppose, or He would not have placed us in circumstances of such difficulty and trial, and of almost utter destruction."

The ship was in the midst of it all, and the disciples were "toiling," and toiling hard, with "rowing." These were the disciples of Jesus,—this was the infant Church of Christ—and the Lord, and Master, and Head of all was in the mount in prayer. And, while He was in the mount in prayer, they were tossed, apparently at the mercy—or rather, apparently at the mercilessness, of these waves. But THE LORD had sent them into it,— the Lord knew *why*, and He knew *where* they were going, and what all their circumstances would be. *He* had bidden them go into those circumstances, and they would have been very happy in them, if only they could have realised Who He was Who sent them,—if they had known that He was the great Captain of salvation, who could not make a mistake, who would not place them in circumstances of difficulty, from which He could not, presently, lead them forth with joy.

We look here at the condition of Jesus, and we look at the condition of the disciples. A melancholy, trying, miserable condition it is, if we look at it apart from Him ; but if we look at it in connection with Him, remembering that He sent them, that He led them, that He was in the mount, praying—then it is not a desperate, and it is not a dismal condition. But they were long tried, and tried just as the Church has been tried, ever since Christ went up into the mount. When

He went into the " far country," He did not say whether He would come in the first watch, or in the second, or in the third, or at the cock crowing, or in the morning. All He did was this,—He said to the infant Church, " Go into the ship, and pass over to the other side, 'and, lo, I am with you alway, even unto the end of the world.'" (St. Matt. xxviii. 20). He constrained His Church thus, as it were, to go into the midst of the sea, and He went up to be in the mount with the Father—He went up there to pray, to make intercession, and the Church has been long tried, watching, waiting, hoping—but the weary toiling has gone on, the darkness has deepened, the tempest has increased.

It was not till the disciples had been very deeply tried, it was not till **"the fourth watch of the night "** that He came; but, " in the fourth watch," He did come.

" Jesus went unto them, walking on the sea."
He came, " *walking on the sea*." In this miracle, as in the last that we considered, we see the power of Jesus over material things, over the inanimate creation. He, who could multiply loaves and fishes for all that great multitude, has power over all things—" He is Lord of all." (Acts x. 36). The sea shall praise Him. So we find Him even walking *on* the sea. O happy, blessed sea! we might well say, to have existed for so great an honour, to have become a very pavement for the King of glory to walk upon! He came " walking on the sea," just as He makes " His angels spirits," and walks " upon the wings of the wind" (Ps. civ. 3, 4).

"**And when the disciples saw Him walking on the
sea, they were troubled, saying, It is a spirit; and
they cried out for fear.**"

I know not whether it is quite true in *all* things, but
I think, if it is not universally true, it is true to a very
considerable extent,—that, there are very few truths
that the soul of man thoroughly gets hold of, unless
that soul has been exercised troublously about those
truths.   I believe, many truths come to us very easily,
and we fancy we have got hold of them, whereas, if
they be put to the test and tried, by some great storm
arising, we find that we have not got such hold of them
as we imagined.   It appears to me, that the *firmest* hold
the soul gets of any truth, it gets *through trouble*, in some
shape or other.

The disciples had had a sermon, as it were, preached
to them in the afternoon; they had seen the Lord do a
thing, that *ought* to have taught them Who and what He
was—but it did not teach them.   They were there in
the ship, they had had a lesson acted before them, and
solemnly impressed on them, but they had not learnt it;
and, therefore, they must get hold of that truth through
great trouble.   They had seen Jesus claim to be the
Lord and Master of material things, but they had not
learnt that truth.   In the calmness of the afternoon,
they saw Him multiply the loaves and fishes, and
they ought to have known that He was Lord of
matter, as He was Lord of mind, and as He was
Lord of the soul.   They ought to have seen that
He had power over all creation; but all they could

say of Him was, that He was a Prophet, and *the* Prophet.

We find, for St. Mark tells us, that they were "sore amazed"—"sore amazed in themselves beyond measure, and wondered" at *this* miracle, because "they considered not the miracle of the *loaves;* for their heart was hardened" (St. Mark vi. 52, 53). Now, I believe, the interpretation of this is, not that their heart was hardened after the miracle of walking on the sea,—but, that their heart was hardened after the miracle of the *loaves*, so that they did not understand, they did not learn, the lesson which was taught them, in the quietude of the desert place, on a lovely afternoon. We do not learn our lessons well when the sun shines—we do not well learn the truths of God when all is calm and peaceful; the mind seems to take it in, perhaps, but, when the tempest comes —it is gone! The disciples had seen Christ multiply the loaves and fishes, and would have taken Him by force, and have made Him a king. *That* was not the lesson to be learnt,—that He should take Herod's place, and rule as a temporal prince; but "their heart was hardened," so that they did not learn it *then.*

They *did* learn it, and fell at His feet and worshipped Him, when He had come into the ship; but they learnt it out of *trouble.* The Lord sent them trouble—He made them " **troubled,**" and they said, **"It is a spirit."**

What the idea in their mind was, we cannot tell. Just as when the damsel, "named Rhoda"—" when she knew Peter's voice," "opened not the gate for gladness, but ran in, and told how Peter stood before the gate," they said—" It is his angel." (Acts xii. 13-15).   So, perhaps, these men thought their Master, whom they had left with the multitude, was dead, and that His Spirit was appearing to them ; or, it may have been an indefinite cry of terror at the thought, that they had come into contact with the unseen world.   They were sorely " troubled" there, and almost in the jaws of the deep. And they learnt in trouble, what they might have learnt in the sunshine ; they learnt on the troubled sea, what they failed to learn on the calm mountain side.   The same lesson is taught in both miracles, but the circumstances of the learners are very different indeed.

Another Gospel says, He " would have passed by them" (St. Mark vi. 48), just as, on the way to Emmaus, " He made as though He would have gone further" (St. Luke xxiv. 28).   He will always have the voice of prayer called forth, He will always teach us our need. If we have not had our sin brought to remembrance, if we have not been made to cry to God for the forgiveness of sins, we are " yet *in* our sins."   Depend upon this, you have not got the forgiveness of sins, if you have never been caused, by the Spirit, to plead for forgiveness.

" But straightway Jesus spake unto them, saying, Be of good cheer ; it is I : be not afraid."

" And Peter answered Him and said, Lord, if it be Thou, bid me come unto Thee on the water."

We must not lose sight of the great leading facts of this miracle, and circumscribe our thoughts to the case of Peter.   When Jesus said " Be of good cheer, it is I ;

be not afraid," what did He intend to convey to the minds of the disciples? It seems to me, that He intended to convey *this* to their minds—His universal lordship—His universal power over all creatures, and over all circumstances. They did not know that they might "be of good cheer" in a storm, they did not know that they need not be afraid when a shipwreck was near, they did not know that their Lord and Master was One who could control all elements, and that He was the Ruler of all material things.

When people begin to think, when they begin to exercise their minds, they find that material things occupy a very important place in the Divine economy; and when they think more closely, they begin to feel a certain kind of *terror* at material things. "The wind bloweth where it listeth, and thou hearest the sound thereof, but canst not tell whence it cometh, and whither it goeth" (St. John iii. 8), but it bloweth, and seems to be doing its own will, and a very terrible will. We look into the various powers and forces of, what we call, Nature, and stand, sometimes, almost aghast, as we hear their voice speaking, as if they were their own masters, and had none to rule them. People say, that these very laws are forces which have existed from eternity, and that they must go on and on, working their own way by their own power. It is easy in a calm, quiet, happy time, at the side of the mountain, to think that you know all about it—but let the mighty tempest get you in its grasp, let it make you feel yourself a poor little prisoner, and you ask, " Is there none to control this power? Is there no Lord to rule these material forces?" Jesus stood and said, " It is I—be of good cheer, be not afraid." Yes,—it is a comfort to every thinking mind, that all these material things, world upon world, system upon system, have all got a great " Lord sitting above the water-floods," and, in spite of all,—never shipwrecked, never overthrown,—remaining a King for ever. (Ps. xxix. 9, P. B. V.). The Lord, then, would teach His disciples, through great trouble, when they were tossed up and down like a ball on the waves, that He was THE LORD. They did not see it, when He multiplied the loaves and the fishes ; so He must teach it them in trouble.

"And when Peter was come down out of the ship, he walked on the water, to go to Jesus. But when he saw the wind boisterous, he was afraid."

We shall not dwell on Peter now ; he was always putting himself forward. However, he is ready in this deep affliction " to go to Jesus," he wanted to be the first to embrace his Lord, he wanted to be the first to get near to Him. It shows some wisdom that he did not go till he was bidden, and till Jesus had said— " Come." And Peter *did* walk on the water. He walked on the water in very deed, and he might have continued to walk upon it, till he had embraced the feet of his Lord as He stood on the water, if it had not been for one thing—that, instead of keeping his eye upon the Lord, who had bid him come, he looked and " saw that *the wind* was boisterous." He ought, simply, to have kept his eye on JESUS, the Lord of that raging sea—instead of that, " he saw the wind boisterous," and therefore, " he was afraid."

How can we keep our troubles under our feet? How can we keep our dark circumstances under, and turn them into a solid pavement on which to rest our feet? How can we keep all our perplexities and diffi- culties and trials under? Not by looking at them, not by dwelling on them, not by examining how great they are—but by looking *at the Lord.* Then we shall be enabled to " tread upon the lion and adder ; the young lion and the dragon shall we trample under feet," (Ps. xci. 13), yea, the very waves of the sea. That is the point—the eye must be fixed on Christ, and fixed on Him as *the Lord,* the Controller, the mighty Ruler of, and over, them all. When Peter looked down, he began to sink. Your trials and difficulties will not bear you up, if you look at them ; they will not bear you up if you think of *their* power, and not of *His* grace. So, when Peter was—

"beginning to sink, he cried, saying, Lord, save me, And immediately Jesus stretched forth His hand, and caught him."

How often does He do this to every one of His faithful servants ! What child of God has not felt that he was sinking in his troubles, yea found them over- whelming him ?

"And said unto him, O thou of little faith, where- fore didst thou doubt ?"

The Lord knew what was in Peter's heart. We are told, that it was when Peter *saw* that the wind was boisterous, that he was afraid ; but it was the heart, not the eye, that was radically wrong.   It is *the heart* that is wrong—there is doubting of heart, and, therefore, the eye looks at the wrong thing.   "Wherefore didst thou *doubt ?*"   There was not much "faith" in that " honest(?) doubt."   Why was Peter to be rebuked for doubt ? He was in circumstances of great temptation, surely he might be excused for doubting?   Doubt is a great enemy, any sort of doubt is a great enemy, and ought to be fought against.   It is a hard enemy, too, to con- quer, and, as we throw one over, another rises in its place ; we must keep the warfare going.

Surely, Peter deserved rebuke.   Look at what he had seen during the last four-and-twenty hours, and see if he did not deserve rebuke.   He had seen those great wonders that his Lord had done, and therefore, he *ought* to have trusted Him.   If the Lord could do what He did yesterday afternoon—if the Lord could do what He was doing, at that moment, before his eyes, He did not deserve to be doubted—He deserved to be trusted implicitly.   It is not for us to walk on the water, God has not bidden us walk on the material element, but He did bid Peter walk upon it, and, therefore, Peter would have been justified in believing, that the Lord would sustain him as he walked on the water.   Having seen, and seeing now before his eyes, the Lord's power over material things, Peter ought not to have doubted.

And we may turn and apply all this to ourselves.   If the Lord whom we love has said to us, "Go into that difficulty—Come into this place—Meet that danger,"—

we have had such experience of His power and of His affection, that we deserve to be rebuked, and to be asked, "*Wherefore* didst thou doubt?"—if we *do* doubt.

"**And when they were come into the ship,**" into which "they willingly received Him" (St. John vi. 21) —surely, they did *willingly* receive Him—"**the wind ceased.**"

And what now was the result? A very different result from that, which followed the miracle of the loaves and fishes. *Then* they said, "This is of a truth that *prophet* that should come into the world." (St. John vi. 14). But *now*, we find in the 33d verse,

"**Then they that were in the ship came and worshipped Him, saying, Of a truth Thou art the SON OF GOD.**"

That was the lesson they had to be taught—"Thou art the *Son of God.*" They would think of the loaves then; they did not see nor understand this when they saw that miracle, not because it did not prove the same truth, but because of the state of their *heart*,—"their heart was hardened," *therefore* they did not understand. Our hearts require to be taken care of, and watched. Jesus Christ was not to be a mere temporal prince,— succeeding Herod—conquering Rome; but He was the "Son of God"—the Lord of all creation, and the Lord of all hearts.

And well might the people of Gennesaret, that rich bit of country on the N.W. of the Lake, next day, when they "had knowledge of Him," (ponder this word in the 35th verse—when they *had knowledge of Him;* that is what we want)—do as they did—" they sent out into all that country round about, and brought unto Him all that were diseased ; and besought Him that they might only touch the hem of His garment, and as many as touched were made perfectly whole." Yes,—virtue from the head of the great High Priest goes down to the very hem of His garment ; and as many as touched *that*,·were made *perfectly* whole.

Let us, then, ponder this lesson ; and in the various trials and difficulties that befall us in life, let us seek the radical consolation—to realise that we have been led into them, by the wisdom and love of our great Guide, and that there are no circumstances, of which He is not the Supreme Disposer, the Mighty Ruler,—for He is the Almighty GOD.

XIV.

THE OPENING OF THE EYES OF ONE BORN BLIND.

" One thing I know, that, whereas I was blind, now I see."—
ST. JOHN ix. 25.

YOU perceive, in these words, that this man trusted the
evidence of his senses. He was satisfied that that
evidence was quite sufficient. "One thing I *know*,
that, whereas I was blind, now I see "—I know *that*—I
know it." The evidence was all-sufficient to him, in this
case.

The history of this miracle comes next, I think, in
our course. Our. Lord, in the preceding chapter, had
been declaring the truth concerning His own glorious
character. He had said to the Jews, " Before Abraham
was, I am. . . . Your father Abraham rejoiced to see
my day, and he saw it, and was glad." (St. John viii.
58, 56). Well, the result of it was that they disowned
Him ; they rejected His claim, and "took up stones to
cast at Him ; but Jesus hid Himself, and went out of
the temple, going through the midst of them, and so
passed by." (St. John viii. 59). They could not touch
Him.

But, **"as Jesus passed by,** (presently, a short time after) **He saw a man which was blind from his birth."**

Our Lord wrought more than one miracle on *blind* people ; and this was very significant, showing how men need to have their eyes opened, the eyes of the mind, the eyes of the soul. Jesus meets now with a man who was stone-blind. The blindness had not fallen upon him in his lifetime, but he was *born* blind. There was a radical defect in his physical nature. And it seems that the disciples called the attention of our Lord to him, in a very remarkable way. He was sitting there by the wayside, and had, very likely, asked an alms of them ; and then they ask Jesus a question which has puzzled many.

"His disciples asked Him, saying, Master, who did sin, this man, or his parents, that he was born blind ?"

It was a strange question for them to ask. It will be seen to be a strange question, if we examine it closely, if we scrutinise it very narrowly ; but there was one leading thought manifest in the minds of these disciples—they could not divest themselves of the idea, that if a man were a great *sufferer,* he must be a great *sinner*—I mean, an *outrageous* sinner, so as to have brought the suffering upon himself. We know, indeed, quite well, that if there were no sin in the world, there would be no suffering. By sin came death and all our woe.

There would have been no deaf people, no blind people, there would not be any under the crushing weight of poverty, or of sorrow, if it were not for sin.

Sin has brought all this misery into the world; yet we do not *hate* sin. I mean, the world at large does not hate sin. It requires the Holy Spirit within us, to make us hate sin *as* sin. Some people hate some sins, —the covetous man hates prodigality—many a man hates drunkenness, swearing, and licentiousness; but he does not hate sin *as sin* in the sight of *God*. I say, it requires the Holy Spirit to make a man hate sin *as* sin. Sin has brought all suffering into the world; but it does not follow, that, because some are *greater* sufferers, therefore they are *greater* sinners. They *are* sinners, and they need the Blood of Jesus Christ to wash away their sin, and the Holy Spirit to lead them to hate sin, and to free them from the dominion of sin. But it does not follow that they are *greater* sinners than others, because they are greater sufferers. Still there was, in the mind of these men—it is in the mind of man naturally—of man unenlightened, unregenerate,—this notion; and till the mind is thoroughly enlightened, it will think as these disciples plainly did. Some people came, you remember, and told Jesus " of the Galilæans, whose blood Pilate had mingled with their sacrifices. And Jesus answering, said unto them, Suppose ye that these Galilæans were sinners above all the Galilæans, because they suffered such things? Or those eighteen, upon whom the tower of Siloam fell, and slew them, think ye that they were sinners above *all* men that dwelt in Jerusalem? *I tell you, Nay;* but, except ye repent, ye shall *all* likewise perish." (St. Luke xiii. 1–5). He knew they had this same thought

P

in their minds. He knew that they had set it down, that, because this man was a great sufferer, therefore he had been an outrageous sinner above all people. "*Who did sin*, this man, or his parents, that he was born blind?"

They thought there would not have been blindness, except as a judgment on some action, or course of action, of which he, or they, had been guilty. "*Who* did sin?" We ought to be very careful about this. We ought to be very careful in judging. We may set it down as a great truth, that "*all* have sinned, and come short of the glory of God" (Rom. iii. 23); that *all* need an infinitely efficacious salvation to deliver from sin. But, it is very dangerous to take up stones and throw them at others, because they are great sufferers. Sometimes, indeed, there are things in the world that make us say, "Verily there is a God that judgeth in the earth" (Ps. lviii. 11). I am not going to enter, to-night, into the question of the sad state of things, that we see abroad in the world now; but no thinking person can forget, that, some years ago, in that country which is now in such suffering, a woman was elevated as the Goddess of Reason, and worshipped, as such, by the population of that now terribly afflicted city. There has been nothing like *that* in any city, that has had the Bible and the Gospel of Jesus Christ made known to it; there is nothing in the pages of history like that, where God has been so set at nought. And, remember, that nation has *never repudiated* that fearful act; and, while we pity the sufferers, and refrain from judging in any wise, we cannot help asking sadly, Why have they not *disowned* that rejection of the Blessed God—the worship of the creature as *God*—declaring the creature to *be* God? We must remember this, and yet it requires the greatest care, lest we should speak beyond what we have any right to speak.

The disciples ask Jesus this question, as if nobody could be born blind, or as if nobody could be grievously afflicted, unless they were outrageous, flagrant sinners.

"Jesus answered, Neither hath this man sinned nor his parents; but that the works of God should be made manifest in him."

That is to say, they had not sinned *so, as to cause him to be born blind*—not, that they had *never* sinned. Jesus says something that is very instructive here.

"I must work the works of Him that sent me while it is day; the night cometh when no man can work."

Now, *what* is the work of Him, who sent Jesus into the world? What would He represent Him as doing? Is it God's will that men should be "born blind?" Is it pleasing to God that men's hearts are so blind and so dark, that they cannot see the Saviour, that they cannot see the Truth? No. Jesus says—"I am come *a light* into the world" (St. John xii. 46).—There is no light in the world, but only that "Sun of Righteousness." "I AM the Light of the world." (St. John viii. 12).

Now, what did Jesus do to this blind man? He did a very curious, a very remarkable thing.

"He spat on the ground, and made clay of the spittle, and He anointed the eyes of the blind man with the clay."

He spat, and mixed the earth with it, and made a little lump of wet clay, and put it on his eyes. Why, you would say, That was more likely to *make* the man blind, than to *cure* him! Jesus covered over the sightless eyeballs with the earth He had just mixed at His feet, so that the man was no *more* blind than he was before; but Jesus put a symbol on him—a symbol indicating that his eyes were *really* closed up. This is itself very significant. It is a very curious thing. You remember, Jesus said something very different to Bartimæus; he was told simply that he had the petition he desired. "According to your faith, be it unto you." The man was brought to Jesus, and Jesus stood still, and spake to him; and *he saw*. But this man has a *covering* put over his eyes. He comes in a different way; Jesus has something to do—something to teach *him*. He would let everybody see the symbol of darkness upon him; and the man with the symbol of darkness upon him, feels the touch of Jesus, and hears Him say,

"Go, wash in the pool of Siloam."

Now, we must always remember this, that our Lord Jesus Christ has various ways of giving sight to the hearts of His people. He *speaks*, in some cases—"Let there be light," and there *is* light. In some cases, He seems to make the darkness more visible, to make the man *feel* the darkness more deeply, to make him feel how he is groping, and that the very clay of the earth is covering his sightless eyeballs. Jesus found, indeed, blindness and darkness in this man ; but He makes him feel that the earth is covering his eyes, and sends him groping to the Fountain.

How variously suffering brings men to the light,—and we must not judge harshly if a man is not brought to Christ, just as we were brought to Christ. One man is led in one way, and another, in another way. The light shines quickly in on some, and, on others, more gradually. They may not have seen clearly all the marvellous workings of Jesus Christ, but the test is this—

"One thing I know, that, whereas I was blind, NOW I SEE, whether it be by a word, or by the curious darkening process, adopted by Jesus in this case.

"He went his way therefore, and washed, and came seeing."

Why, there's a volume in those three little sentences—He *went*,

He *washed*,

He *saw*.

What a declaration in these few words—almost monosyllables—have we here! Jesus said, Go, and he *went;* Jesus said, Wash, and he *washed;* and came back with the blessing. Why? Because he just *did what Jesus told him.* It is the obedience of faith—"Go and wash," —" He went, and washed, and came seeing."

Now, there is all the Gospel in this. Why, you say, "You are always telling us that, about every little miracle that you expound. You tell us this—'it has all the Gospel in it.'" *And so it has.* St. John says, **"Siloam, which is by interpretation, Sent."** That is singular. We might expect this in a Dictionary, but St. John puts it in his Gospel. And why? *Jesus Christ* is the SENT, Jesus Christ is the true Siloam, Jesus Christ is the One "sent;" and He says to all sinners, weary and heavy laden with the burden of sin, "Come to the Sent One—Come to Siloam—Come unto Me."

What is real faith? It is to believe in Jesus Christ. *How* is true faith proved to exist? By obedience to the word of Jesus. When this blind man was told to *go* to Siloam, he *went.* If he had not wanted his sight, he would never have gone there,—if he had not believed that Jesus Christ had wisdom and love enough to direct him to the *right* place, he would never have gone. But he *did* believe, and he *did* go. That is, he trusted Jesus Christ when Jesus said, "Go, wash in the pool of Siloam"; and he went, feeling how deeply he needed the blessing, which Jesus Christ gave him to understand he would find there.

Now, if there are any who hear me, to-night, who feel they need what Jesus Christ, as the true Siloam, gives,—if God has taught you to feel the burden of sin, the guilt of sin, and that, if it remains on you, it must sink you into the depths of judgment at last,—if you know, therefore, that you need pardon, and cleansing, and washing, and that it can be found at the true Siloam, and you hear Jesus saying, Come unto *Me*—then the question rests with *you*—do not delay to go to Siloam, where all that is evil is cleansed and put away for ever. This man went and washed, and came *seeing.*

> " There is a Fountain filled with Blood
> Drawn from Immanuel's veins : "

and they who wash in that precious Blood are cleansed "from all sin"—from every stain.

We know how it was with Naaman—how he " went away in a rage," when the prophet sent to him, saying —" Go, and wash in Jordan seven times "—but, afterwards when better advised, he *went,* and *washed,* " and his flesh came again like unto the flesh of a little child, and he was clean." (2 Kings v.) So this man—" he went therefore, and washed, and came seeing."

Now, remember, this very miracle was wrought by Jesus Christ—not indeed directly, but it was a real miracle, and wrought by Him, nevertheless. The power in the water was *His,* as the word that bade the man " Go and wash," was His.

A remarkable thing happened, after his return. There were certain people who formed what was called the Sanhedrim, the great council of the nation ; and when the neighbours began to look at the man, they said—"**Is not this he that sat and begged ?**"—They now see him with his eyes *open ;* they knew that he had been blind from his birth, and so they asked him, and he told them the simple story, how Jesus Christ had done this great miracle of love and mercy.

And then they went off to the Pharisees—to this great Council sitting at Jerusalem, and brought the man

before this Council.   It was " on the sabbath-day," that
Jesus did this miracle.—A great controversy arose, and
the parents of the man were called; and, finally, the
man was cast out of the synagogue, excommunicated,
and ruined, as far as regards temporal things.

When he was put upon examination, he gave the
simple answer of my text,—

**"Whether He be a sinner or no, I know not; one
thing I know, that, whereas I was blind, now I see."**

He says, " I cannot tell whether He who opened my
eyes is a sinner, or not, I have never seen Him."   You
must remember, the man had never *seen* Jesus; Jesus
had touched him when he was blind, and sent him to
Siloam, but the man did not see Him,—he simply heard
His voice, and went, and did what he was told, in the
power of a Divinely inspired faith.   " This one thing I
know, that, whereas I *was* blind, *now* I see."

This is a picture.   Here we have the dividing line in
the man's life.   It may be a wide line, it may extend
over many days or months, or years; or a man may
be able to put his finger on a period of his life, when he
could say, " *Then* I was *blind* "—and then to say, " *Now*
I *see.*"   Who has done the work?   Who made the clay?
CHRIST.   It is the work of Christ; Christ gave sight to
the blind.   The man had been blind before; now he
could see the sun in the heavens, he could see the blue
sky and the green fields; now he could understand the
difference between colour and sound.   He couldn't
before.   The blind man knows nothing of colour,
beauty, or deformity.   Like the blind man, who was

once asked what *purple* was like, and replied, "A clap of thunder," he had no sense of the impossible comparison—he had never *seen* colours. All he could go by was the sense of *sound*, and so he said that. You say, it was a foolish thing to say, and it *was* foolish; but it was all he knew, or could know.

Just so, many do not see, in Jesus Christ, what is good and true; they have no means, until He gives them sight.

"Now I see." We must take care; this man said it with truth. His judges said it in another sense—"We see"—but *they* saw *wrong;* they saw only by their own unenlightened understanding.

And now, lastly, let us consider the interview, which took place between Jesus and the healed man, when all the toil and turmoil was over. When he was excommunicated from the synagogue, and sent to beg as he had begged before—for they would have nothing to do with him—Jesus met him, and said to him,

"Dost thou believe on the Son of God?"

That is a question that we may well ask every man and woman—" Dost thou *believe* on the Son of God?" If we *believe* in the Lord Jesus Christ, we have salvation. If we are true *believers*, we are truly pardoned, truly saved. "Dost thou believe (He says not, on *Jesus*—not, on the Son of *man*, but) on the *Son of God?*" *That* was the great point—to know what Jesus was. Was He a mere man? Was He a mere child of Adam? No. He was the "Son of *God.*"

Now, look at the man; he does not jump at a conclusion.   He thinks about it;   he is cautious, he is careful.   He is not like people who jump into things; he is careful, and will make sure.

"He answered and said, Who is He, Lord, that I might believe on Him?"

He wants *knowledge,* that he may believe,—he wants knowledge of JESUS.   We cannot believe, unless we know.   All is fancy, not faith, if we have not knowledge at the bottom of it.   "Who is He, Lord, that I might believe on Him?"   Now, are we really anxious about this?   Can we say this — "I have found out that I want something, that I want something which only the Son of God can give me—something that only Omnipotent and Infinite grace and love can bestow on me?" "Who is He, Lord, that I *might* believe on Him?"

Many say, "We know about Jesus Christ, and when we come to die, we'll think about Him."   But this man wants to know Him, wants to believe on Him *now;* and Jesus says, **"Thou hast both seen Him, and it is He that talketh with thee"** *now.*

What a wonderful thing for Jesus to say to this man! "Thou hast *seen* Him—*thou* hast seen Him."   But he couldn't see Him till Jesus had opened his eyes; he couldn't see Him without the work of Christ being wrought on him—he couldn't see Him, till Jesus sent him to the pool of Siloam.   He never could see Jesus with the eye of flesh, till He had given him *opened* eyes.

What have *we* seen and heard of Jesus?   A great deal; but how little we *know* of Him!   We still need teaching; and we may still ask, as we lift up our eyes to Him, "Who is He, Lord, that I might believe? Tell me all about Him. Explain to me all about His grace, all about His love, all about His greatness."

"And he said, Lord, I believe. And he worshipped Him."

There are a great many people in the world, who glory in their *un*belief. This settles the question. Only let the eye of the understanding and of the soul be opened, only let that eye see the gracious Saviour as He is revealed in the Word of God, and then there will be no more unbelief. " Lord, I believe." He believed because Jesus had opened the eyes of his mind, and revealed Himself to those eyes of the mind; and he saw in Jesus, the Physician—the Good Physician—the gracious Saviour—the Son of God, who is able to save even to the uttermost. He saw in Jesus all that he needed, for time, and for eternity.

Now, to sum up all this, On which side of the line do *we* stand? We all *see*, or else we are *blind*. We were *all* " born blind," — there's no doubt of that. That is certain ; and we have continued blind from our birth—how long? Has the change come? Have we been made to *see?* Is there a time, is there an hour, in our past life, when Jesus Christ drew near and spake to us, when He put clay, as it were, on the eyes of our understanding, and made us *feel the darkness?* Yes— He made this man *feel* his physical darkness, when He placed those heavy, sticky lumps there, making him feel his case to be more hopeless than ever. Has He done this to *us?* St. Paul says—let a man " become a fool, that he may be wise." (1 Cor. iii. 18).   No man is wise, who does not know his folly and his ignorance. No man sees really by this spiritual sight, unless he is made to feel that he is, by nature, blind.   Are we blind still?   Have we ever seen the love of Christ, with the eyes of our heart?   Have we ever seen the grace of Christ in coming down to bear our sins, in His own body, on the tree?   Have we been enabled, as we look with opened eyes, to say—"He loved *me*, and gave Himself for *me?*" (Gal. ii. 20).   Or are we blind still?

If any here, who have been born blind, are *still* blind, all I can say to them is, Go and wash in the Pool that is called "sent."   Go to Jesus, who is the true "sent" One, and Who, alone, is able to anoint your eyes with eyesalve, that you may see His glory and His preciousness, and that you may be blessed, and rejoice for ever in His love—seeing His face, and having His Name in your foreheads.

XV.

THE HEALING OF THE WITHERED RIGHT HAND.

"*It came to pass also on another sabbath, that he entered into the synagogue, and taught; and there was a man whose right hand was withered. And the scribes and Pharisees watched him, whether he would heal on the sabbath day; that they might find an accusation against him. But he knew their thoughts, and said to the man which had the withered hand, Rise up, and stand forth in the midst. And he arose and stood forth. Then said Jesus unto them, I will ask you one thing; Is it lawful on the sabbath days to do good, or to do evil? to save life, or to destroy it? And looking round about upon them all, he said unto the man, Stretch forth thy hand. And he did so: and his hand was restored whole as the other. And they were filled with madness; and communed one with another what they might do to Jesus.*"—ST. LUKE vi. 6–11.

IT is not said, in this passage, *where* our Lord was on this particular occasion, but it seems by comparison of passages, that He was, most probably, in Capernaum, and that this was "**the synagogue**" of Capernaum, where such mighty deeds, so often, showed themselves forth in Him, and where there had occurred so many things of deeply touching interest. St. Luke tells us nothing with regard to the *time*, or place, when and where the circumstances recorded in the text, came to pass; but he relates them here, that he may bring them into close relation with our Lord's teaching concerning the observance of the Sabbath-day.

It does not follow, because the extreme in *one* direction is condemned, that we may fly off, like a pendulum, to the opposite extreme, and fall into the opposite error. *We* are not likely to fall into the opposite error, that of the Pharisees, in the present day. *Our* danger is likely to be in the other direction. *They* were for lading men with " heavy burdens grievous to be borne;" we are not in any danger of overburdening men with works of charity and goodness, nor yet with a hard ceremonialism, as they did. Our Lord refers to this, though it is not mentioned by St. Luke, as you may see by turning to Matt. xii. 11—" What man shall there be among you, that shall have one sheep, and if it fall into a pit on the sabbath day, will he not lay hold on it, and lift it out?"

The great point our Lord aims at here is this:—to show us these *two* truths.

I. That the sabbath was made *for man*, and not man for the sabbath.

II. That the Son of man is *Lord* even of the sabbath day.

However, it was this which led to the working of the miracle, the history of which I have now read to you. These Pharisees, whoever they were, and wherever they came from,—perhaps they had come from Jerusalem, perhaps they were of those spies, who were sent to dog His steps everywhere—were there to watch that they might find an occasion of fault in Him, concerning the Sabbath-day. You see, our Lord was like Daniel, only in a much higher degree; His enemies knew they could find no fault in *Him*, except "concerning the law of his God" (Dan. vi. 5), which was "read in the synagogues every sabbath day." (Acts xv. 21). These Pharisees were there, trusting by means of their human traditions, and with all their subtlety and enmity, to accuse Him of having transgressed the pure, simple ordinance of God. And that led to these circumstances.

"And it came to pass also on another sabbath, that He entered into the synagogue, and taught: and there was a man whose right hand was withered. And the scribes and Pharisees watched Him, whether He would heal on the sabbath day; that they might find an accusation against Him."

A man with an honest conscience, a man who is making "straight paths" for his feet, who is seeking to walk with God as Jesus Christ did on earth, need never fear scribes or Pharisees making their accusations against him. They may bring false witnesses, they may make false accusations, but it will all end in *their* utter confusion.

From this history we find (1) That Jesus Christ is *GOD*.

"He knew their thoughts."

They were standing there "in the synagogue"—a plain building, no doubt, it was; and Jesus Christ had been teaching there. And the Pharisees were sitting

amongst the rest, *watching* Him.   They saw something
lying in His path, they saw one who was likely to appeal
to His compassion, one whose eye was upon Jesus—a
poor stone-cutter, tradition says he was.   These men
saw *that*, and they saw that Jesus would, by-and-bye,
have either to *do* the act, or to *refuse* to do it.   But
though they saw all this, they thought they had kept
their secret quite close.   They kept it locked up in
their own mind, and they thought they were very *wise*,
very far-sighted, and that they were going to catch Him,
for they knew the man would appeal to that heart so
full of compassion, and that Jesus would never refuse
His help.   But Jesus "*knew* their thoughts"—knew
that they were seeking for somewhat to accuse Him of.

Now, we heard something about the Sabbath-day, in
our miracle last week.   But Jesus knew their *thoughts ;*
He knew the reasoning that was going on in their
minds. He knew they were not mere common thoughts,
but that they were subtle reasonings.   They thought
they knew how to prove, that an act of healing would
be an offence against the Fourth Commandment. They
were discussing in their minds, how to catch Him, if
He worked a miracle,—discussing how they could bring
Him into contact with the man, so that He could not
escape.   "*But*"—Jesus "knew their thoughts."

How many of us think to hide our thoughts, and our
feelings, and our reasonings quite close, but there is an
Eye that can look into the secret thoughts of the heart.
There is not a reasoning against Christ, or His truth,
or His holiness, there is not a reasoning against any-

thing that He enjoins, commands, or promises, there is not a thought that the wicked one inspires, that the Eye, which is "as a flame of fire," (Rev. i. 14), does not detect.

There these scribes and Pharisees sat, and imagined that they kept their countenances well, and that their secret was unknown. But Jesus could see right *into* their hearts. Oh! the *folly* of these men, who were afterwards "filled with" folly, as the text says. What folly to think that He could do these miracles of healing, and yet be ignorant of what they were thinking about!—to think that He *could* do such things, and yet have no *right* to do them!—to think that He could perform this work of matchless mercy to this poor man, and yet be open to their accusation and criticism! Oh! the folly of sin, and the folly of sinners! These Pharisees thought themselves wise, but they were *foolish*—they thought they could hide their counsel from Jesus, while they could not deny that He had power to heal the man.

"But He knew their thoughts, and said to the man which had the withered hand, Rise up, and stand forth in the midst."

Now, surely, we should imagine that this act of authority, and these words, would confound the gainsayers. Surely, if their consciences had not been seared and dead, they would have been struck with the thought— "He has found us out, He has detected our secret, He understands what we were reasoning in our hearts against Him,"—when they hear Him command the man

to " stand forth in the midst," with those words of
authority and power.

"And he arose and stood forth."

Here we have Jesus Christ before us.   We lose sight
for a moment of the Pharisees, and we look at this man
with his *right* hand (the Evangelist tells us) " withered"
—powerless ; all the life had gone out of it, it was perfectly useless, it could *do* nothing, it could *lift* nothing.
It was like a mere dead branch of a tree hanging there,
lifeless by his side.

"A man whose right hand was withered."

And Jesus says to the man—" Rise up, and stand forth
in the midst." You see that Jesus Christ commands this
man to do something that he *could* do ; he *could* rise
up and stand forth in the midst, he could make *that*
move, at any rate, towards restoration.   His right hand
was withered, but his *feet* were sound.   And he obeyed
—" he arose and stood forth."   The *first* act, the first
command of Christ to this man, is to bid him do something that he has power to do—" Rise up, and stand
forth in the midst."   And *he did what he could do*, and
was commanded to do.

Now, Jesus turns again, for a moment, to the Pharisees, and said unto them—**"I will ask you one thing: Is
it lawful on the sabbath days to do good, or to do evil?**
(that is, to *abstain* from doing good) **to save life, or to
destroy it ?"**

We notice here, that Jesus puts the point stronger
than it is seen in the case of the man before us.   " Is it
lawful to *save* life, or to leave it unsaved?"   Well,

surely, they must have been in a difficulty to answer that question. We do not see that they *tried* to reply. I do not see what answer they could make, except to their own confusion. "Is it lawful to do good on the sabbath day?" "*What* is the Sabbath *for?* *May* we save life, *may* we do good on the Sabbath-day?"

Our Lord waited not for an answer, but "**looking round about upon them all, He spake unto the man,**" who was standing forth, — a spectacle to all in the synagogue. Jesus Christ did not work His miracles in a corner; He wrought them, in order that the record of them might go forth to all times. He is now teaching a great lesson to these Pharisees. "Do ye not think it lawful to do such and such things?" God made Pharaoh to be lifted up, that all generations might see and be warned, and this miracle was *so* done, that all in the synagogue might see.

"**He said unto the man, Stretch forth thine hand,**" that we, too, eighteen hundred years after, might have perfect assurance that the thing was *done*, done in the presence of enemies, done in the presence of those who, if they could, would have confounded and destroyed Him.

Now we turn to the man still standing forth. Again Jesus speaks to him, and, as before He had told him to do what he *could* do, now He tells him to do something that he could *not* do—"Stretch forth thine HAND." When Jesus had said, "Rise up and stand forth," there was no need to hesitate, no need to falter. He had his feet to get upon and go, *they* were not "withered."

But now, he is told to do something that he *cannot* do; his hand hangs lifeless by his side, it is perfectly useless, he has never lifted it up since it has been withered, he could not. He knew it was impossible, yet we see Jesus, plainly telling him to do, what he could not do of his own power—what it was not in the power of that withered hand to do. He *had* done what he could, now he is told to do what he couldn't do—yet the moment he was told, it is said that *he did it.*

"**And he did so, and his hand was restored whole as the other.**"

First, you see, *at the bidding of Jesus*, he does what he can; and, then, *at the bidding of Jesus*, he does what, without the power of Jesus, he could not do,—"and his hand was restored." In all this, we have, not merely the record of a great work of Divine power, which was wrought to the confusion of the enemies—and for the confirmation of the faith of the followers—of Christ, but also, a simple parable in which two things are taught us.

I. We have the man, with his *right hand* withered. We know how utterly powerless a man is, without a *right* hand. We can spare our *left* hand. I mean, we can spare it, comparatively; but with a "right hand withered," we should be almost helpless. It was his right arm, not his feet. The right arm—the *best part* of the man, was dead; the best part of the man was powerless.

And, in all this, we have just a picture of our own fallen condition. Man is not actually powerless. He has *physical* power, and he can walk to church, if he likes ; he has *mental* power, with which to reason, if he chooses. He can use his body, *that* is not withered ; he can use his mind, *that* is not entirely withered. But the higher principle of the *soul*—which unites him to his Creator, which can enable him to love, and serve, and obey the great Lord of all—THAT *is dead.* All the other powers can be put into exercise for lower purposes, but the *right hand* is "withered." The BEST PART, that which can enjoy, and serve, and glorify the "Holy, Holy, Holy, Lord God of hosts"—*that* is "withered." "Man's chief end is to glorify God, and to enjoy Him for ever"—that is, as it were, with his right hand, the best and highest part of his nature ; but, to "glorify *GOD*," he is powerless ; to "enjoy" *GOD*, he is powerless—his *right* hand is withered. He can enjoy God's *works ;* he can use, as it were, his *left* hand ; he can enjoy this world, he can gaze on it, he can use it, he can delight in it. The lower part of him can act, move, think ; but the higher part—*that* is dead—*that* is withered.

And that is just the position, in which the Gospel of Christ finds sinners. It finds them, with their feet and left hand, able to enjoy things below, but it finds them all falling " short of the *glory of God,*" (Rom. iii. 23)— the right hand as withered as this man's, when he stood out in the synagogue. We are all as helpless, and all as withered, as this poor stone-mason's hand ;. and, if we have not " Christ in us, the hope of *glory,*" (Col. i. 27), if we have not the Spirit of Christ working in us, if we have not been brought unto God by Him, we are even now like this man with his "right hand withered."

II. Jesus Christ still addresses all who have their right hand—the higher nature—withered. He says, "This Gospel shall be preached to all men." He said, "Go ye into all the world, and preach the Gospel to every creature." (St. Mark xvi. 15). And he sends a *twofold* command to every creature.

(1.) His command is first, to tell sinners to do what all sinners *can* do if they like, they have the power to do it, —"**Stand forth in the midst.**" He will have them in the synagogue, and He will have them "stand forth" before *Him* in the synagogue. He will have them in the place of hearing, in the place of teaching, in the place where the Word of God is read every sabbath day, at the very least. "Stand forth"—*where?* In the place of gathering together, in the very presence of Jesus Christ, for "where two or three are gathered together in His Name, there is He in the midst of them." (St. Matt. xviii. 20). He says to every one, "HEAR," and they *can* hear. He says "Look"—and in vain is it that the sinner excuses himself, and says, "These eyeballs of mine are sightless."—"You can turn the sightless eyeballs to Me. If they have no light in them, you can hear the sound of My voice—turn your eyes to where the sound comes from—Stand forth in the midst."

This command has gone forth to all the world, and Jesus commands all sinners to do what they can; and, if the sinner *refuses* to give an attentive ear to this command, if he refuses to apply the power he possesses, in obedience to that command,—if he refuses to hear, if he refuses to apply those mental faculties, which he *does* possess, to the Word of God,—if he refuses to exercise his mind earnestly on his own state,—if he refuses, as a sinner, the word of Christ addressed to sinners, he must be responsible.

If that man had sat still, if he had said, "I won't," if he had just disregarded the word of Christ, you would say the man was *mad*—that he had lost his opportunity, and that he deserved that his hand should remain withered, and that he should beg his bread all his days. The man might have made many excuses, he might have said, "I don't like to be a spectacle." People tell us, they do not like to go to Church because of their clothes, and various things. *He* might have said—"There was once a time when I could earn my living, there was once a time when I could have stood forth respectably, but I don't like to be made a spectacle to all in the synagogue now; I will sit still here—if you like to come and heal me here, well and good; but I don't choose to stand out before all the synagogue. And there's *another* thing—I'd rather it was done quietly, and privately; don't you see these scrutinising Pharisees here? They can take away my chance of earning my daily bread, or of getting alms from the rich people's houses. If I allow you the chance of exercising your power, and it brings *me* into discredit, I must bear the consequences." He might have said that it was not *convenient*. He might have said, as

Naaman did, " May not I do so and so ?" But *he did
not* do so.   He did as it was told him ; he " stood forth
in the midst," because Jesus Christ told him to stand
forth.

Now, if a man refuses,—if he refuses to hear the
word, if he refuses to go over his own door-stone a few
yards, if he refuses to give attention to God's Word, to
God's command *by* His Word,—if he refuses to exercise his mind *on* that Word, when he is exercising it on
everything else,—if he does not exercise it on God and
eternity, on sin and the soul, on salvation and Christ—
if he refuses, so to speak, to " stand forth in the midst,"
and to do what he *can* do, surely he must answer for it.
Surely, if a man will not take down the Word of God
from the shelf, and read it, and ponder it, and use it,
and pray over it, but persists in neglecting it—if he
will not cry, " Open Thou my blind eyes, that I may
see "—if the man won't do what he *can* do, then,
indeed, he must not complain, if, at last, judgment falls
heavily upon him.

(2.) Now, look at the other truth. He has done what
he knew he could do, and what does he find ? He
finds that the commands of Jesus are going *higher*. He
had done what he could, and he had done it *at the
word of Jesus*, and he finds that it was a good thing, at
the word of Christ, to stand forth in the midst,—that it
is blessed, even in a little thing, to be obedient to
Christ. He finds his heart beginning to move, he finds
he is able to *trust* Him, Whose word made him stand
out there in the midst of that strange throng. He finds

already that Jesus Christ has *power* in Him, he finds the virtue of it coming into him, and giving him more confidence. He looks up in His face, and he cannot but trust Him. He has heard these mighty words of power, and he begins to feel that Jesus is worthy to be trusted. And then, he hears the word coming, not for the outward ear only, but going right down into his deepest and strongest feelings and affections—he feels the life circulating within *as* the word is spoken— **"Stretch forth thine hand."**

And he does not question it. There is power *with* the word; he has done what he could, and he goes on, step by step, and does what it would have been impossible for him to do, but at the word of Christ. He has put himself under the eye of Christ, he has looked up into the face of Christ, he has begun to trust in Christ, he has begun to hope in Christ. He thinks Christ will bring healing and strength to him, and the word comes —few words, very simple words—but *with the word* there is *life*. He holds out his hand— **"and his hand was restored whole as the other."**

And when a man places himself under the eye of Christ, when he takes the word of Christ, when he expects the blessing of Christ, not as a form or ceremony, and from no other motive but, simply and solely, because he *wants* Jesus Christ and His great salvation— the power comes. This man does, in a moment, almost without thinking, that which only Omnipotence could do. He did what he could, and doing what he could brought him into contact with the gracious Power, that

enabled him to do what, by nature, he could not do.
" And his hand was restored whole as the other."

Now we see the work of Christ on the one side, but
we never lose sight of this fact—" the carnal mind is
enmity against God."   You know what is said of these
Pharisees,—it is a remarkable word,

" And they were filled with madness"—

The Greek word here translated "madness" does
not mean furiousness, but MINDLESSNESS.   " They were
filled with *mindlessness*."   It shows this—it shows that,
while the man, who exercised the power *he* had, had
come into the presence of Jesus, and, coming into that
presence, got that which only Omnipotence could
give him—these men, who had been exercising *their
minds* that they might find occasion to "catch " Jesus,
find, all at once, that *they* are filled with " mind-*lessness*."
The mind, which had been exercised *against* Christ,
became utterly infatuated, and they do not know what
they do ; they go on headlong to perdition, and so they
**"communed one with another what they might do to
Jesus."**

There, in their mindlessness, they set themselves
against Him who had just proved Himself to be
Almighty ; and there, too, in their mindlessness, they
set themselves in opposition to the best Friend they
could ever have had.   They are filled with infatuation,
or folly, and set themselves to *get rid of Him,* who saves
sinners and blesses the lost.

Does not this teach us a great many lessons ?   Is it
not a good thing to stand forth in the presence of

Christ, and to look to Christ even though we have sightless eyeballs, and to turn the ear to Him even though we cannot hear,—praying to be brought into the presence of Christ, that He may speak the word to us, that shall make us sound, and whole, and for ever blessed?

We have before us, to-night, in the synagogue, a man who was a very pitiable object indeed, a poor, crippled man, unable to earn his living. And also, in that assembly, were the proud, lofty Pharisees with their broad phylacteries, making a god of their position.

Yet, at the close of the meeting, that poor, helpless cripple was turned into a blessed saint, his heart filled full with right thoughts of Jesus, and the Father, and eternity—and *they* go, in their infatuation, to put out (if they could) the light of the Sun—to stay the dew from Heaven—to destroy the only One who can ever bless the souls of men, or make "all things new."

XVI.

THE TEN LEPERS CLEANSED.

"And it came to pass, as he went to Jerusalem, that he passed through the midst of Samaria and Galilee. And as he entered into a certain village, there met him ten men that were lepers, which stood afar off; and they lifted up their voices, and said, Jesus, Master, have mercy on us. And when he saw them, he said unto them, Go shew yourselves unto the priests. And it came to pass, that, as they went, they were cleansed. And one of them, when he saw that he was healed, turned back, and with a loud voice glorified God, and fell down on his face at his feet, giving him thanks; and he was a Samaritan. And Jesus answering said, Were there not ten cleansed? but where are the nine? There are not found that returned to give glory to God, save this stranger. And he said unto him, Arise, go thy way; thy faith hath made thee whole."—ST. LUKE xvii. 11–19.

OUR Blessed Lord was now setting His face to go to Jerusalem; and on His way from Galilee to Jerusalem, you know, as we have seen several times, *Samaria* lay right in the midst. Just as a man, coming from Durham, would go through Birmingham, probably, to come to this place, so it was natural for travellers going to Jerusalem, to pass through Samaria. But it was not an easy thing, the Jews and the Samaritans were not on friendly terms—"the Jews had no dealings with the

Samaritans." (St. John iv. 9). And it was specially awkward, when passing up to Jerusalem to one of the three great feasts ; for the fact of people's going right up from Galilee to the Temple at *Jerusalem*, cast a slight, or slur, or reproach, on the opposition sectarian Temple on *Mount Gerizim*. Therefore it came to pass, that some travellers from Galilee would pass over the Jordan, and go down the eastern side, and pass over the Jordan again, when they had got below Samaria, rather than run the gauntlet, as it were, through the midst of Samaria.

Now, our Blessed Lord was going up to the Passover, and we find it said, that—

"He passed through the midst of Samaria and Galilee."

What is meant here? The natural thing to say, if Jesus was going direct to Jerusalem, would be that He passed through the midst of *Galilee* and Samaria ; but the Evangelist does not say so, but—" through the midst of *Samaria* and Galilee." That would be very much like, if, in order to get to London, we had to pass through the northern and midland counties, and we were to say, that to get to London, we must pass through the midland, and *then* through the northern counties.

The meaning was, evidently, that our Lord was not going through the *midst* of Samaria, but He took the border line to the East,—that He went skirting both countries, till He came to the Jordan ; and then, perhaps, He crossed the Jordan, and went on the other side, till, by and bye, He would cross it back again, and then, as you know, we find Him at Jericho.

And what does this teach us? It teaches us this, that, unless Jesus Christ had some very clear reason to go through Samaria, He did *not* go through Samaria. In one place, you know it is said, " He must *needs* go through Samaria," (St. John iv. 4), and you know what that " need " was,—a poor sinner needed Him to speak to her, and many poor sinners at her back needed Him to speak to them. But the feeling was such between the Jews and Samaritans, that, rather than excite their wrath, Jesus goes skirting the country for many a mile. What does this prove? It just proves the inextinguishable enmity that existed between the Jews and Samaritans. I do not mean, that this was in the heart of *Jesus,* but that the Samaritans felt so strongly the slight, that, in travelling, the Jews preferred passing right over the Jordan and back again, to passing through the country of Samaria. If that feeling was so strong, if the poor, outcast woman was so ready to allude to it, if the Jews had no dealings with the Samaritans, if, instead of travelling through one another's country, the Jews would rather go round about, far worse than our having to go to Swindon to get to London (which is indeed a very round-about way to get there),—it indicates a very sad state of feeling.

"**And as He entered into a certain village, there met Him ten men that were lepers, which stood afar off.**"

Now, as He was passing between the two countries,

avoiding Samaria, because of that embittered feeling, *what* does He meet with? He comes on a village, and a village with lepers herding together, living *together*, communing together, coming to Jesus together, all getting up one united cry. And who are these? Nine *Jews*, perhaps, and a *Samaritan*. We know that the feeling between the Jews and the Samaritans was such, as to keep them thoroughly *separate;* they would go miles out of the way, rather than pass through each other's country. But, here are ten men living in one house,— living together, crying out together—nine Jews and one Samaritan !

Does not this teach us a great lesson? That the suffering of leprosy, known and felt, obliterates all other distinctions. When these men find out that they are *lepers*, they can live *together*, talk together, and pray together. This mere fact—that they are all afflicted with what the soul loathes more than anything else—has brought them to this ; they can unite in the same prayer, and pour out the same lamentable supplication —" There met Him ten men that were lepers, **which stood afar off.**"

It was the leprosy, that kept them " afar off ;" they were bound by the law to stand afar off. If a man was a leper, though he were a king in Israel, he was bound to live in what was called a " several " house,—a house apart by itself. I need not dwell on leprosy, to-night, because we have had a case under our notice, already, this winter ; and we then saw that leprosy was a picture —a picture, in which God sets before us the loathsome-ness, the foulness, the uncleanness, of sin; but not only that—not only does the leprosy represent sin in its filthiness and wretchedness, but the leper represents a man who is perfectly *aware of the fact.*   I said, then, that no man could be a leper, without *knowing* that he was a leper.   He was not like many, who go and confess in Church that they are "miserable sinners," but who would be mightily offended, if anybody were to come and really bring the charge home, and prove them to *be* miserable sinners.   But they can say it in Church without ever meaning it, without ever sorrowing for it, without caring about it.   But a man with leprosy *hated* it, loathed it, wished to be rid of it, would have given anything on earth to be rid of it.   He looked on it as the greatest evil, as the greatest woe, as the greatest sorrow, that could befall a child of man.   The leper, then, is a picture; but a picture of sin hated, loathed, abhorred — of a man that is *convicted* of it, and who has been made by the Holy Spirit, to long for healing, —who longs, above all things in the world, to be delivered from it.

These ten men were *all* lepers; and the Jew did not point at the Samaritan, and say, "You're a Samaritan," and the Samaritan did not point at the Jew, "We have no dealings with the Jews."   No.   They had not the heart to do that, they had not the feeling left to do it, because they were all alike *lepers;* and the fact of their being lepers obliterated Samaritanism, and obliterated Judaism.   They were altogether, lamenting that they had this loathsome disease, and all, alike, eager and earnest to have that disease cleansed. They were not pointing one at another, and saying—"*You* are a leper;" not one of them said to another, "Stand by thyself, . . . I am holier than thou." (Isa. lxv. 5). But they say, "We all stand by ourselves, and we all stand 'afar off.'"

The law required this. The leper, as I said, in the law, was a type—a symbol—to teach the people; they had to cover their lips, and, as they went, to cry out, to cry out two words—one word, at least, twice over—that all the people might know a leper was coming, and stand apart. His mouth was "stopped"—his upper lip covered, and he had nothing to do but to cry, "Unclean, unclean." (Lev. xiii. 45). These men were not picking holes in one another, they were not throwing stones at one another, but they say, "We all stand on one platform."—And so they all stand together, "afar off,"—that "afar off" being an acknowledgment that they were not fit to approach the presence of holiness, and that they were "unclean."

"**And they lifted up their voices, and said, Jesus, Master, have mercy on us.**"

These men, you see, *acknowledge* Jesus, and they acknowledge Him to be their *Master.* Perhaps, all they had heard of Him was that He was a worker of great wonders. Perhaps the story had come to them, that once, when He had come down from a mountain, a man—who was a *leper*—had come to Him, and said, "If Thou wilt, Thou canst make me clean." That might have circulated, that might have come into the little company of these lepers dwelling together. And they

R

might have heard that He had healed the sick, and raised the dead, stilled the raging of the sea, and healed multitudes on multitudes.   They must have heard *something* of what He had done, for they evidently believed on Him, as they cried together—" Jesus, Master, have mercy on us."

Now just let us look, for a moment, and try to see why—we have seen it often enough—these men cry thus.   They cry out, they come to Jesus Christ, they all unite together ; they have but *one* petition, but one request, and that request they plead, and plead earnestly. *What* makes these men pray ?   What makes men, or women, or children cry out?   If these men had not had leprosy, if they had been perfectly sound in body, if they had been thoroughly well off, if they had been in comfortable circumstances in life, Jesus might have passed through without their crying after Him.   There were scores, perhaps, of villages that He went through, where not one came to Him.   There were, indeed, hundreds of thousands in the towns of Galilee, but we do not find others crying to Him, nor pressing on Him until He came down to Jericho ; but these men *do*. They felt they had a terrible, wasting, loathsome disease —a frightful disease, a disease that propagates itself—a disease hateful to themselves, and that separated them from the Temple and from the ordinances of God—that separated them from the ordinary avocations of men, and from all who were dearest to them—from wife, and children, and home, very likely.

And they knew *this*—that there was not another in

Immanuel's land who could help them.   They knew that nobody could cure that disease, that there was no one exercising Divine power in Immanuel's land, *but Jesus Christ;* and therefore they cry out to *Him.*   Why is it that lips are so prayerless?   Why is it that hearts are so prayerless?   Why is it. that prayer is the last thing people seem to think of—if they are not *driven* to it?   Why do not men cry to God?   Why are not all persons crying to Him now to-night?

Because they have not this knowledge.   These men knew something, and that something drove them to cry thus.   They had that disease, in their bodies, which symbolises, most clearly, what every child of man has in his *soul.*   Man has a disease in his soul that deadens it, that defiles it, that makes it morally loathsome; and why does he not cry—"Jesus, Master, have mercy on me?"   Because the leprosy in his soul is *hidden*, and requires the eye of the soul to be opened in order to see it.   These men, because the eyes of their body were open, could see their leprosy; but a man cannot see the leprosy in his soul, till the Holy Spirit comes to open and enlighten the blind eyes of the soul.

You remember Job,—I cannot recollect whether I spoke of him, the last time.   He lost his children, and his property, and his cattle.   The Sabeans came, and the Chaldeans came, and the wind from the wilderness came—he had calamity on calamity; and, at last, poor man, the Wicked one was allowed to touch even his flesh, and he sat down in the ashes—*a leper*—with leprosy all over him, so that he took a potsherd to scrape himself withal. And when his friends looked on his misery, they did not dare to open their lips for seven days, they did not dare to attempt to bring comfort, because of the greatness of that terrible misery. What was God teaching him by His marvellous ways and dealings? That the thing he had in his *soul*, was what that terrible disease in his *body* was a faint picture of; so that, at last, when God has taught him *that*, what does he say? "I have heard of Thee by the hearing of the ear; but now mine eye seeth Thee. Wherefore I abhor myself, and repent in dust and ashes." (Job xlii. 5, 6). So that, as his body had sat down in ashes, at the beginning, it ends by his *soul* going, as it were, to sit among ashes—" Behold, I am *vile.*" (Job xl. 4). What his friends saw in his body, at the beginning, that he sees in his soul, at the end—" I am vile." These lepers knew it, and therefore they cried out—" Jesus, Master, have mercy on us."

"And when He saw them, He said unto them, Go, shew yourselves unto the priests."

This reminds us very much of Elisha, when he said, " Go, and wash in Jordan seven times, and thy flesh shall come again to thee, and thou shalt be clean." (2 Kings v. 10). So Jesus says to these men, " Go shew yourselves unto the priests." Why is this? You remember, He said to the other leper, " I will; be thou clean. And immediately his leprosy was cleansed." (St. Matt. viii. 3). Why does He act differently now? He has different methods. He knew what these men were seeking after,—He knew what was in their mind, and He says—"Go shew yourselves unto the priests."

And they are a bright example to us *so far*. They obey the word, they do not get into a passion as Naaman did, because Elisha did not come and do certain things, but *they* took Christ at His word. That is what they did—they took Christ at His word, and *went.* That was all; but it was just what they ought to have done—we ought to believe that every word of Jesus Christ is a "faithful saying." And so they went on their way to get the blessing; and there is nobody who believes Christ's word, and who obeys Christ's word, but *will* get the blessing. To these men, coming now for the cleansing of their bodily disease, Jesus says— "Go shew yourselves unto the priests."

"And it came to pass that, as they went, they were cleansed."

Why? Because they just took Jesus at His word. Now, if Jesus Christ says, "Come unto Me, all ye that are weary and heavy-laden, and I will give you rest" (St. Matt. xi. 28)—that word is as much *worth* believing, as much worth trusting, as much worth obeying as this, "Go shew yourself unto the priests." Why is it that people do not get rest, and do not get pardon, and do not get Christ formed in them? Because they do not do what these men did. Jesus said "Go"—and they *went*, and their flesh came to them again "as the flesh of a little child."

Why should Jesus say, "Shew yourselves unto *the priests?*" I think I pointed out before, that the priest was the person appointed to determine whether a man had the leprosy or not,—when a man was suspected of having leprosy, he had to go and shew himself to the priest, and then the priest had to take certain measures, by which he could tell.   If it was *not* leprosy, the man was sent about his business ; if it *was* leprosy, he was subjected to all the restrictions and ceremonies appointed by the law.   Jesus said to them, "Go shew yourselves unto the priests."   He had nothing more to say to them,—He knew what He would do.   You know, that a man who has got the disease of leprosy, has only to lift up his hand in order to see the blotches and sores ; so these men went, each knowing "his own sore and his own grief."

Jesus knew what would happen *"as they went"* to the priests.   He does not touch them, but He tries them, to see if they can believe His Word.   And they *go ;* and as they take Christ at His word, so is it done to them— as far as their *body* was concerned.

" And one of them, when he saw that he was healed, turned back."

He did not go to the priest *then*.   He knew, without going to the priest, what had come to him ; he did not need to be *told* what had been done.   He knew it,—he saw it,—he *felt* that he was a new man.   Very likely, he was very ready afterwards, to go and offer the sacrifice appointed ; if he had not been, there would have been something wrong about him.   But he did not need to be *told* that he was healed,—he felt that his disease was gone, and he says, "Before I go to the priest, I must go somewhere else."—And he "**turned back, and with a loud voice glorified God.**"

"**And fell down on his face at His feet, giving Him thanks; and he was a Samaritan.**"

Yes; here is a man, who had come to Jesus in order to get a blessing for his *body*, and, in getting a blessing for his body, he finds he has got one for his mind, for his heart. A cord is drawn round his heart that brings him back to the feet of Him, Who had done these great things for him—he comes back, and glorifies God, and gives thanks to Jesus because he is healed. What a bright picture this is! He goes and just takes Jesus Christ at His word, and then comes back, and blesses Christ for His goodness!

"And he was *a Samaritan.*" There is something cheering in this—that this man was a Samaritan, belonging to an outcast race. He was as a Gentile, and *we* are Gentiles; therefore we ought to feel the more interest in this. We might have expected the children of Abraham, Isaac, and Jacob to come back,—but no —only a Samaritan.

"**And Jesus answering said, Were there not ten cleansed? but where are the nine?**"

In few words, let us try to see what lesson we are taught here. It is a very *serious* lesson,—*one* man comes back to Christ, but *nine* men who have got this mercy from Christ, never come back at all. Let us try to see what they were feeling. What had they come *for?* They had come to have their bodies healed, and they got it, — and then, what do they do? They hasten away, where to? To their wives and their children, to their business and their fellow-men. What had Christ done for them? He had given them *a passport* back again to society, back again to their business, back again to the world, and to their comfortable homes, and to the general concerns of life. They had been outcasts, they had had to dwell in separate houses, but Christ helps them back into the world, and business, and society—helps them to lay up treasure, and enables them to enjoy the good things of this life. They have got *this*, and away they go.

But one of their number wanted more than *that*, he wanted to be Christ's servant, to be Christ's friend. He was bound to Christ by cords of love; the love of Christ constrained him to come back. He did not run home and say, " I am a new creature; employ me. I have lost time enough, and now I must make up for it." But he goes back, and lays the first fruits of his new life, as it were, at the feet of Christ.

What do people want Christ for? To make them respectable, to set them going in the world. The profession of religion helps them on sometimes; they can get through the world better, they can get into better repute with it. Christ can do that—He can send back nine lepers to be respectable gentlemen, living in their homes, and attending to their business, and to their farms. Yes! Christ does *that*. But it is a very serious thing for people to use Christ *thus*. It is a very serious thing to make Christ a stepping-stone to worldly advancement, to worldly credit. These men get from

Christ what sets them up and makes them comfortable; but they never come back to His feet. They did not want *Christ;* all *they* wanted was clean flesh, in order to get rid of the ceremonial restraints laid upon them, and to get back again to the world. Very likely, this Samaritan could do his business better than any of them, when he set about it; but that was not the ruling principle in *his* mind. The ruling principle in *his* mind was this—"He has made me whole, I go back to give Him thanks, and to glorify God." He says, "Lord, Thou hast done this; do Thou take me, use me, command me; let me not run hither and thither, but only as Thou commandest me." He lays himself at Christ's feet; and no doubt Christ used him, enlisted him under His banner, made him His soldier. But oh! the other nine—

"There are not found that returned to give glory to God, save this stranger."

And so I have seen it, hundreds of times, and so have you. A man wants to get on in business, and he *takes up* religion, and religion helps him to get on in business; and then,—when his feet are firmly planted, *away* goes the religion, the religion that helped him to that! *That* was all he wanted,—he never wanted Christ Himself, and for His own sake. He only wanted the religion of Christ to help him into business—and then, it goes. I have seen it scores of times before my eyes— "Only cleanse us, and let us go back to our merchandise, to our home, to our farm, and we will be very much obliged to you, for enabling us to make the best of it. We have got all we want, and now we part company."

The Samaritan was the man for Christ. He says—" He healed me, I return to give thanks.

"And He said unto him, Arise, go thy way; thy faith hath made thee whole."

The other men were only *half-*" whole." They had been made whole in their *bodies*, but they carried the leprosy away in their *souls*. They were only half cleansed, because they had only come to be half cleansed. We know many, who have still leprosy in their soul, who have a very fair religious character—clean outside. But this Samaritan knew he had the evil deep down in his heart, and faith laid hold of *Christ*, and then the leprosy got its death-blow, and the man became the servant of Christ, "doing the will of God from the heart."

And so, we learn this—that we have, if we have not been cured—this deadly disease in our souls. Be sure, then, that you take Jesus Christ at His word; if He says, "Come to Me"—*Come.* Many people stand discussing and haggling about what He says, instead of hearing and doing it. These men were wise, they took Him at His word, and they got the blessing so far. But the Samaritan, when he had got the blessing, found it a string to draw his soul back again to Christ. That lays the man at Christ's feet, and makes him live upon Christ as his sustenance, day by day, and hour by hour—saying, "Thou art my portion, O Lord, I have promised to keep Thy Word."

XVII.

THE HEALING OF THE DAUGHTER OF A SYROPHŒNICIAN WOMAN.

" Then Jesus went thence, and departed into the coasts of Tyre and Sidon. And, behold, a woman of Canaan came out of the same coasts, and cried unto him, saying, Have mercy on me, O Lord, thou son of David ; my daughter is grievously vexed with a devil. But he answered her not a word. And his disciples came and besought him, saying, Send her away ; for she crieth after us. But he answered and said, I am not sent but unto the lost sheep of the house of Israel. Then came she and worshipped him, saying, Lord, help me. But he answered and said, It is not meet to take the children's bread, and to cast it to dogs. And she said, Truth, Lord ; yet the dogs eat of the crumbs which fall from their masters' table. Then Jesus answered and said unto her, O woman, great is thy faith ; be it unto thee even as thou wilt. And her daughter was made whole from that very hour."—ST. MATT. xv. 21–28.

WE are never told, that our Blessed Lord, when on earth — except on this occasion — went beyond the boundaries of the Holy Land. He came, as He says— " to the lost sheep of the house of *Israel*." Now, however, He had gone beyond the northern boundary of the Holy Land — across the boundary-line between Phœnicia and Palestine—" into the coasts of " Tyre and Sidon." He came, indeed, "to the lost sheep of the house of Israel;" but we find Him here, passing through these Gentile cities, which were inhabited by those who should have been destroyed, when Israel took possession of the land.

"**And, behold, a woman of Canaan.**"

She was not an Israelite, not a Galilæan, but a *Canaanite.* Centuries and centuries before, when Abram went into the country, "the Canaanite was then in the land," (Gen. xii. 6); when Joshua went over Jordan, the land was full of them, and their vile idolatry prevailed from Dan to Beersheba. The cup of their iniquity was full, and the punishment of their iniquity was to be ministered in God's righteous judgment. We do not find that our Lord, when He was here, put forth any invitation, any proclamation, to the Gentile world *as such.* He did not send His disciples on a mission to them, as, of old, Jonah had been sent to Nineveh; no invitation was addressed to them, they had no command to come to Jesus Christ at this time. They were left, as it were, without an invitation, without a sign; *but*—" behold, a woman of Canaan,"—she had never had an invitation, she had never had a message of mercy sent to her, she had never had the words of entreaty addressed to her; *but she came* to Jesus.

"**And cried unto Him, saying. Have mercy on me, O Lord, Thou son of David; my daughter is grievously vexed with a devil.**"

All she could ever have heard of Jesus was this,—

she might have heard of the many wonders, of the wonders of grace, that Jesus had done in the Holy Land. It may be, she had heard of what He had done in Cana of Galilee, of what He had done to the daughter of the ruler of the synagogue; she may have heard how He had healed the nobleman's son, and the centurion's servant. She had just heard, probably, what He had done for other people; and it appears, that she had carefully *reasoned* on it, and reasoned in a way that we may well take example from—for she had never been told that He would do this for *her*. She had never been told that He would heal *her* sick child; she had, positively, no encouragement to come to Jesus. But, under the pressure of great trouble, under the pressure of necessity, she had, probably, heard tidings that Jesus Christ had raised a dead child, had healed a sick servant, and restored a nobleman's son. Perhaps she had heard more—of what He had done in the towns of the thickly-populated Galilee. We must bear in mind this simple fact; but let us clearly understand all that led her to take this course.

She had a great, crushing necessity, and, in all probability, she felt that Jesus was the One, who could relieve her from such a crushing necessity. *And so she came,* without an invitation, without exhortation, without a promise. She had not been preached to twice on a Sunday, and exhorted, day after day, and hour after hour, that she would bring her trouble to the feet of Jesus. There was no need of that. She had just heard these things about the Good Physician, she had heard of One who was able to do these great things, when a terrible woe was eating all the joy and comfort out of her life, and making her home a dwelling-place next door to the bottomless pit. **"My daughter** is grievously vexed with a devil.   Have mercy on me, O Lord, thou son of David."   It was, as St. Mark has it, her *"young* daughter." (St. Mark vii. 25).

Now we must bear in mind, that, while these miracles are real facts, they are all intended to teach us *spiritual* things.   At that time, the Devil had great power over the *bodies* of men, and he was found dwelling in them, "tormenting" them, *possessing* them.   When Jesus Christ became Incarnate, and was manifested in the flesh, "the prince of the power of the air"—the ruler of the darkness of this world—was permitted to have a stronghold in the bodies of men.   He has, now, very greatly lost *that*, but he has not lost his hold on the *spiritual* nature of man; he rules still in the mind, and feelings, and principles, and heart of man.   If the *body* is not "vexed," the *mind* is "vexed," the *soul* is "vexed with the devil."   Therefore, this miracle has to teach us spiritual truth, while it is also a great *fact*.

This "woman of Canaan" came, because her "daughter was **grievously vexed with a devil.**"   This was her sorrow.   The sorrow was that her child was in the hands of the Wicked one; the Wicked one, then, showed himself in his true character—the child was *"grievously tormented."*   We know what happened, when the father brought his son to Jesus, and when He uttered the tender, touching words, which we have just

been singing—"Lord, I believe; help Thou mine unbelief,"—"when he saw Him, straightway the spirit tare
him, and he fell on the ground, and wallowed foaming."
Now this young girl—this daughter of a woman of
Canaan—was grievously tormented by a devil. That
was her sorrow, that was her trouble—that she had got
the *Devil* in the house, and that he was there—not as
"an angel of light," disguising himself, but letting out
what his true character is and what it will be—the
TORMENTOR,—not only "the accuser," not only the de-
ceiver, but the *tormentor*. He imagined that there he
had power, so that he *could not* be cast out; he
thought, perhaps, that he would not be found out—so
he shows himself in all his blackness of darkness, and
the woman cannot but see it. He was not present
there in a wily way, as now,—not as he came to our
first parents; though you may depend upon this—that
whenever he does come as "an angel of light," he is as
black as the "blackness of darkness," in reality. This
woman comes to JESUS, because the *Devil* has made
trouble in her house; and what trouble in the world is
there, that has not come from *him?* He is the beginning, and the end, and the middle, of trouble. He
brought the *first sorrow* into the world, he brought the
first sin into the world, he brought the *first death* into
the world. It was he who dug the *first grave*, it was he
who first stimulated man to feelings of envy and malice,
it was he who incited to the first act of murder. He is
the beginning, and the instigator, of all evil.

If we would have happiness in our hearts, and

in our homes, we must get rid of *him*.   This woman
had got him in the house; her misery was that she
had got him there, and got him in his *true* colours.
The mischief to us, often, is that he appears so different
to what he *really* is, that we do not realise the real,
crushing woe it is, to be in his power.   How many
homes does he live in ! · How many daughters does he
get hold of, to torment and destroy, and bring down to
the very misery of the bottomless pit !   How many
fathers and mothers, and brothers and sisters, does
he manage to get hold of, and lead captive, and do
with as he will !   This woman says—" my daughter is
grievously vexed with a devil."   The only gleam of
light in this, is *the suffering.   The suffering is the mercy.*
We know that it is just so in the body,—that when the
suffering has gone out of the diseased limb, it is *dead;*
the *suffering* is often the only good sign, often it is the
only hopeful sign.   Here, the Devil took so little care
to hide what he was about, that the woman found
him out.

Let us now turn away from the daughter, to look at
the mother herself ; we have seen her trouble, now let
us look at *her.*   If there is *any* part of the Gospel,
where we feel that we need to explain and defend the
conduct of Jesus Christ, it is here.   As we read this for
the first time, we ask, " Is this *Jesus ?*   Is this the
gracious, tender-hearted, loving Jesus ? "   Now look at
her conduct, and let us ask, in what spirit she came to
Jesus.   We just see this—the woman came to Jesus
with a certain feeling in her mind, which needed to be

driven out of her. *How* did she plead with Him? "Have mercy on me, O Lord, **Thou son of David.**" What had *she* to do with David? What *right* had she in David? She was not one of the chosen nation, she did not belong to the people of Israel; she had no part in David, she was a Canaanite, a Syro-phœnician—of Phœnicia bordering on Syria. She was "a Greek" in religion; that is, she was a poor heathen woman, dwelling in the coasts of Tyre and Sidon, and she had no claim on Jesus as being of His nation—no claim as a child of the promised seed. Yet she comes, and imagines, that the plea, as the "Son of David," will be more successful than any other plea.

It is natural that it should be so,—we find it so in almost every age. How did *Naaman* go to get his cure? The king said, "I will write a letter of recommendation." The only recommendation he needed was, that he was a leper. The letter was the worst recommendation he could have had; but he went with his eight or ten thousand pounds in gold, and some of the most precious and choice vestments made in those days, "changes of raiment." But the prophet did not come to the door, he did not hold any interview with Naaman, because he brought a quantity of goods and money to BUY his cure. Naaman thought that would be the best way, he thought that would be a recommendation; but *because* he has it, the prophet only sends a message to Naaman, saying, "Go, wash in Jordan seven times, and thy flesh shall come again to thee, and thou shalt be clean." But he was offended, and went away

S

"in a rage." (2 Kings v. 10, 12). He thought himself ill-treated. Perhaps, he thought he ought to have brought eighty thousand, instead of eight thousand pounds; but what he *did* bring was, really, the offence. But he thinks, that if only he can bring something to buy the cure, he will get it.

And is it not always so? Is not this the first thought,—" I have not been so very wicked, I have done this, and I have abstained from that"—as if that sort of thing could be a recommendation? Well, when you go to the doctor, you do not tell him how many sound places you have got, but, simply and solely, how many *un*sound places you have. He does not want you to tell him, that *this* is *not* a broken limb, and that you have not any disease *here*. It is *disease* that needs the doctor, not *health*. Jesus said, " They that are whole need not a physician, but they that are sick." (St. Luke v. 31.)

This woman, therefore, no doubt, thought that if she mentioned this name, as if she had an interest in Him, she would be sure to be heard. But no! Jesus had to teach her something ; He had to bring her down to her real position, to teach her *what* she was, and *where* she was. He had to drive out of her all desire of bringing some recommendation. Jesus Christ is the great Physician, and it is disease that He has to do with. It is the lost sheep, not the ninety and nine,—not those who fancy themselves whole and sound,—not those who tell of their soundness of wind and limb. He has nothing to do with those,—He is a Physician, and He looks for *disease*.

This woman comes, saying, "Jesus, Thou son of *David*, have mercy on me—my daughter is grievously vexed with a devil."

"But He answered her not a word."

Like that Pharisee, who "went up into the temple to pray," and said—"God, I thank thee, that I am not as other men, . . . or even as this publican," (St. Luke xviii. 10, 11)—but he went down *without a word;* he was not "justified" when he went down—"He answered *her* not a word." It is just so with Elisha. Naaman said—"I thought, He will surely come out to me, and stand, and call on the name of the Lord his God" (2 Kings v. 11)—"I thought he would have shown me some attention." But he was mistaken. If Naaman had come *as a beggar*, he would; but he came with his thousands. And so it is here. "He answered her not a word," because she pleaded A WRONG PLEA,—she had no business to have pleaded that, because she was not of David's seed. "He answered her not a word," and silence is sometimes the most painful of all things.

At length; the disciples, perhaps slightly touched by the woman's look and plea, and, more probably, because she was interfering with their purpose, said,

"Send her away; for she crieth after us."

It *looks* as if the disciples were more tender-hearted than the Lord; and there are some people who think that the saints are more tender-hearted than Jesus, and that it is safer to pray to the saints. It is a grand mistake. The disciples were never more tender than He was. The only difference is, that He knew, that He understood, what was in her heart, and what He had to teach her—what she was, and where she stood. "*He* answered her not a word." *They* say, "Do what you can to relieve her, and let us be alone, let us be quiet. Let us get the quiet that we need." *That* was not tenderness—that was not the tenderness of Jesus. He likes to have the weary and heavy-laden hanging, as it were, on to His garments. That is not real compassion which gives an alms to get rid of somebody, but does not enter into the case, and consider the circumstances, and intelligently administer relief. The disciples want *themselves* relieved ; there was more self-love in the disciples, than love for the woman and her daughter. But there was *love in Jesus*, and the purpose to teach her, and to teach all nations, how He will be approached before we can have salvation.

"He answered and said, I am not sent but unto the lost sheep of the house of Israel."

Why, this is worse ! "I have no commission to her —she is a Greek, a Syro-phœnician by nation." Had she not cried, "Thou son of *David ?*" Had she not, without a word of invitation, come and called Him the son of David ? Yes. He *had* come, as David's Lord, to David's people. If we go to Christ with the wrong plea, we shall not go away enriched. *She* went with a proud plea, she stood in a position that she had no business to stand in, she made a plea that she had no business to have pleaded. And, I believe, many do the same, and expect to get to Heaven ; they say, "I have done this and that ; I have been baptized, perhaps been even at the Communion, and I expect much because of all this." It is just, "We have Abraham to our father." (St. Matt. iv. 9). *She* expected much, because of the plea she used, and it would have been the right plea, if it had come from the lips of some *Israelite;* but she was taking a position, and making a claim, that she had no business to make. She made her plea, and she gets her answer,—but it is an answer that, apparently, shuts her out from hope. She had not come and said, "Thou Son of *God,* Thou Redeemer of all nations, Thou Ruler of the whole earth, have mercy on me, a poor Canaanite"—but she had pleaded as if she had belonged to the chosen seed of David, and, *therefore,* it shuts her out. What had David to do with Syro-phœnicia? What had David to do with a Canaanite?

Thus, you see, the wrongness of the plea. It is *a proud plea,* in reality. She is wrapping a garment about her, that she had no business with ;—in order to present a decent appearance, she had borrowed somebody's outside garment, and so she appears what she is not. You remember Bartimæus, and how he *" cast away his* garment." This woman borrowed a Jewish shawl, as it were, with which to cover over her Canaanitish origin. If she had come with a plea, that He would help those who had none to help them, who had no claim, who had nothing but misery and ruin, it would have been different.

If men go to God and say, "I have done this, and I have not done that; I'm an upright, honest man—I have a good name, I have dealt fairly and rightly with all; I have been respectable, I have kept church, and I have done what is right between man and man,"—if we make such a plea as that, then God will come and see, and examine if we *have* done it. You remember the man who came with his "do"— "What shall I *do* to inherit eternal life?" Jesus says, "If you mean to get eternal life in this way, you must keep the commandments," but that is a very serious matter. "Thou shalt love the Lord thy God with all thy heart, and with all thy soul, and with all thy strength, and with all thy mind, and thy neighbour as thyself." (St. Luke x. 26, 27). If any living man comes and says to me, "I have done that," then I say, "You have *not* done it for one hour. It must be done without spot and without flaw, not only sincerely, but *perfectly*. Have you broken it *once?* then you are condemned."

"Then came she and worshipped Him, saying, Lord, help me.

"But He answered and said, It is not meet (right) to take the children's bread, and to cast it to dogs."

What a hard word to come from the lips of Jesus Christ! You see, she had put in the plea that she was a *child*. She said—"Thou son of David"—"I come as a child." The Lord says, "No—I will teach you this, you come as a *dog*." It was not a bit too hard. *She* did not think it a bit too hard—she did not wince under it, for a moment—she did not reproach Him for calling her a *dog*—she had not a thought against Him, for using this terrible, crushing expression. He puts her in the right place. She pleads with Him as the

son of *David*,—He says, "What have you to do with
Me as the son of David? Why do you not go to your
own king, to your own priests? If you come and ask
Me, it must be as a poor dog—as a *heathen*, whose idol
is only a devil; and, knowing that a devil cannot cast
out a devil, you must say—'I come because THOU
canst save.'" He must teach her that—that she is a
dog, that she is a *Gentile*. We must realise our condition, we must know what we are, we must have the
right feelings, we must understand that we have no
right to sit at the table. "It is not meet to take the
children's bread, and to cast it unto *dogs*."

**"And she said, Truth, Lord: yet the dogs eat of the
crumbs which fall from their masters' table."**

Look at her answer, at her readiness, at her ingenuity. People are stupid, oftentimes, because their
hearts are not *in* what they are about. If the heart is
in the work, the head will do wonders that it never
could have been thought able to do. This woman feels
she cannot go home, to see her poor daughter still with
this grievous, tormenting devil. She is not going to be
discouraged, she is not going away without a blessing.
See how ready it makes her,—see how ingenious she is !
She does not contradict Jesus, she does not reproach
Him, she says it is quite true—quite true, but yet she
is *a dog in His house*, at any rate. She says even *the
dogs* are provided for. "To be a dog in His house, is
better than to be a king out of it ; it is better to be a
dog in the house of David, than to be a great prince of
Tyre and Sidon. I would like to live under the table

of Him Who can cast out devils." "Truth, Lord—but if you call me a dog, you give me a *right*, you give me a claim, you give me a privilege. You put me, it is true, *under* the table, but you *do* put me under *the table*. If I am a dog, let me be Thy dog,—if I am a dog, let me eat of Thy crumbs."

In those days, people used a piece of bread instead of a napkin, so that any particles that might adhere to the hands were removed by it, and then the bread was passed under the table to "the dogs." This woman says she is willing to be a dog, when once she is made to feel her right place. "Because thou sayest, I am rich, and increased with goods, and have need of nothing, and *knowest not* that thou art wretched, and miserable, and poor, and blind, and naked," (Rev. iii. 17)—that is the mischief—people *don't know* it. This woman *knows* the devil is in her daughter, and she wants to get rid of him. She comes, like Naaman, with her hands *full*—not saying, "Let the overflowing of Thy grace come unto the Gentiles, according to the Old Testament Scripture. Thou art the *Son of God*, as well as the Son of David; I am a poor, wicked, Gentile dog, extend some mercy to me."

But He has to bring her down. She came with a proud plea. There is enough pride in many a little hovel to ruin worlds; God has to bring us down, to teach us our real place. It is a great thing to be a sinner—I mean, to take the *place* of a sinner, to feel that you *are* a sinner, and nothing else. We all want to be righteous, and to plead something on our own behalf.

But to be brought to *that*—you remember, what work God had before He could bring old Job to that. He had to send this one and that one, but nothing did it, till God Himself spoke out of the whirlwind—and *then*, Job said—"Behold, I am vile. . . . . Wherefore, I abhor myself, and repent in dust and ashes." (Job xl. 4 ; xlii. 6).

Just so, this poor woman is brought down to the dust and ashes, and *then* she gets the blessing. First, then, we look at *the conduct of Jesus*—He has to bring her down, and to humble her, before He can bless her,—to teach her till she can say,

> " *Nothing* in my hand I bring,
>   Simply to Thy [feet] I cling."

And then, look at *the woman*—she was really one who knew Jesus could bless and save her. She believed it, and when she believed it, she held fast to it. She will "rise up in the judgment, and condemn" many. Some say this was very discouraging, but she rose over it all. If any of you find out that you are lost sinners, you will not rest until you have got the blessing. It is simply because sinners do not *know* and feel their wretched condition, that they do not come to Jesus Christ. There will be no difficulty that can hinder you from coming to Christ, when once you have found out your need of Him.

"Then Jesus answered and said unto her, O woman, great is thy faith; be it unto thee even as thou wilt. And her daughter was made whole from that very hour."

Where there is real earnestness of purpose, there will

be victory at last. She got the blessing she desired. Look at her, persevering in face of the obstacles which Jesus Himself put in the way, and see how she got the blessing,—because she just knew her own deep, deep wretchedness, and the power of Jesus to save her out of it all.

XVIII.

THE HEALING OF ONE DEAF AND DUMB.

" And again, departing from the coasts of Tyre and Sidon, he came
unto the sea of Galilee, through the midst of the coasts of Deca-
polis. And they bring unto him one that was deaf, and had an
impediment in his speech ; and they beseech him to put his hand
upon him. And he took him aside from the multitude, and put
his fingers into his ears, and he spit, and touched his tongue :
and, looking up to heaven, he sighed, and saith unto him, Eph-
phatha, that is, Be opened. And straightway his ears were
opened, and the string of his tongue was loosed, and he spake
plain. And he charged them that they should tell no man ; but
the more he charged them, so much the more a great deal they
published it ; and were beyond measure astonished, saying, He
hath done all things well ; he maketh both the deaf to hear, and
the dumb to speak."—ST. MARK vii. 31–37.

I SHOULD like just to read to you a verse or two from
St. Matthew's Gospel. You remember, that we were
speaking, last week, of the woman who came to Jesus
for her poor daughter. Now St. Matthew goes on, after
telling us of the driving of the devil out of her, in these
words—"And Jesus departed from thence, and came
nigh unto the sea of Galilee ; and went up into a mountain, and sat down there. And great multitudes came
unto Him, having with them those that were lame,

blind, dumb, maimed, and many others, and cast them down at Jesus' feet; and He healed them: insomuch that the multitude wondered, when they saw the dumb to speak, the maimed to be whole, the lame to walk, and the blind to see; and they glorified the God of Israel." (St. Matt. xv. 29-31).

Here it appears, that, after our Lord's interview with that poor "woman of Canaan," He went up into a mountain near the Sea of Galilee, and there, not *one*, but many—"great multitudes," came to Him, any one that had anything the matter—whether they were paralytic, or blind, or lame, or dumb—whatever calamity had befallen them in their bodily condition. Such was the reputation of Jesus, His fame had so gone abroad, that people were ready to bring their lame and maimed relations, and lay them at His feet. St. Matthew uses a strong word—he says, they "*cast them down* at Jesus' feet,"—as much as to say, that they did not mean to take them back again, till He had exercised His gracious power on them. "And He healed them . . . . and they glorified the God of Israel."

Now, you perceive, St. Mark takes one case out of that great category. There were many blind, and many deaf, and many lame. St. Matthew puts them all together—"Lord, we have brought them to Thee. There is no physician that can heal them; we cannot save them, we cannot heal them, but we have brought them, and cast them there at Thy feet, *and there we leave them.*" It is a very striking lesson. When we do not know what to do with those, whom we see afflicted with spiritual disease, with maladies which are here symbolised by bodily disease,—when we see nothing remaining that *we* can do, there is nothing for it but just to bring them, and " cast them down at Jesus' feet," just like those four men climbing up to the top of the house, and letting the man right down before Jesus. " None but Jesus can do" halt, and maimed, and " helpless sinners good."

Now we turn to St. Mark, and consider the one case, which he has selected out of all these. St. Matthew tells us of *all*, and St. Mark says, " I take *one*, and from that you can learn what all the rest were "—so he takes one case, and gives the details. St. Mark is very fond of doing that ; he is fond of giving us little, tiny particulars,—things that could not have been known by any but an eye-witness. For instance, he gives us the exact words that were spoken to the daughter of Jairus. And so here. It is all the Spirit of God; still, the Spirit of God used St. Mark for *one* thing, and St. Matthew for *another*. St. Matthew gives the great multitudinous account,—St. Mark, the account of one case out of that number. Then, we must *multiply* St. Mark by St. Matthew, for, from the one given by St. Mark, we learn what was done to *all*, who were cast down at Jesus' feet. In this way, we may learn many things, when we get one thought and work it out,—when we take one fact, and learn all the particulars about it.

This, then, is like St. Mark. If you study your Bibles—as I hope you do—you will be able to say— " St. Matthew says *that*, it's like him ; and St. Mark says *that*, it's like him." And this was, not only that out of the mouth of two witnesses every word might be established, but also, that we might have all the sides of the case before us. That is why we have *four* Gospels.

"And again, departing from the coasts of Tyre and Sidon, He came unto the Sea of Galilee, through the midst of the coasts of Decapolis. And they bring unto Him one that was deaf and had an impediment in his speech."

The real state of the case was this,—that the man did stammer to such an extent, that he could not bring out any particular sounds ; he could not *articulate* the words, as we say. Nobody could tell what he meant, but himself ; he was deaf and *dumb*, to all intents and purposes. Dumb people often make noises, very queer noises, but they have not the power of enunciating *words ;* people can tell what they mean by their *signs*, but they do not understand their *sounds*.

Well, this poor man was "deaf and dumb," and he was brought to Jesus for healing. It appears, that amongst all those who were laid at the feet of Jesus, all round about Him, very likely,—people were pressing through the crowd, and putting a paralytic woman here, and a lame man there, and a sick child there—all being brought before the great " Physician there " in Galilee, Who was ministering His " balm "' for the comfort of the distressed—amongst these, were some who were particularly zealous. Some are better able than others to shoulder their way through the crowd ; some find it very difficult, and others have the knack of managing to get along where they wish to go. When we really want anything, we are made ingenious ;—those four men, who were determined to get their friend to Jesus, were ingenious, and got up to the top of the house. So these people were very anxious about this man,—perhaps, his affliction affected many others. Afflictions do not affect only one, but other people suffer through the affliction of that one ; and this man's friends were very anxious, that Jesus' hand should be laid on him.

What do we see here? Persons very zealous, very determined, but not entirely enlightened—they seem to think that there must be personal contact between Jesus and the man, before he could be healed. They are not like the centurion, who said—"Speak the word only, and my servant shall be healed,"—but they are so eager, so determined to have the personal contact effected, that they bring the man to Jesus, and "beseech Him to *put His hand on him.*"

Now, I have often said it before, and I must say it again—these works of Jesus Christ, which were done on the *bodies* of men, were intended to teach us what He could do, and what He was fitted to do, for the *souls* of men. What are these miracles, but little types and pictures of what He can do for those, who are *spiritually* diseased? Let us see what this one teaches us. Here was a man *deaf and dumb ;* and what is the condition of multitudes? How many, *many* we know, who are both deaf and dumb,—many who have not got the string of their tongue loosed at the proper time, in the proper way, to bear testimony to the power and grace of this good Physician,—many who have not the ear of the heart open to hear all about Him, *so* to hear that it should move, affect, influence them, give them new feel-ings, make them new creatures ! Where is the deafness ? Where is the dumbness ?

How many deaf and dumb congregations have the Gospel preached to them ! They never *hear* it ! We preach to thousands, but they hear not. And why ? Because they are *deaf*. Look at the multitudes who go away ; do they go forth and tell their husband, their wife, their children, their friend ? No such thing. Why, they never *heard* it ! If they had heard it in their hearts, they would speak of it, "for, out of the abundance of the heart, the mouth speaketh." (St. Matt. xii. 34). If they did not speak with their tongue, they could make their very *life* speak. The proverb says—" He teacheth with his fingers "—(Prov. vi. 13), if a man had really heard the truth with his heart, he would teach it with his fingers ; if he did not teach it with his tongue, he would with his life, and walk, and conversation.

This poor man was **"deaf, and had an impediment in his speech."** Is he not a weak, poor, representation of the deafness and dumbness of multitudes of men, who never *hear* with their heart, who never *speak* with their lives ? Those, who brought him to Jesus, were very eager and earnest ; perhaps, *he* had some little inkling in his heart,—we cannot tell how they would communicate with him—but, perhaps, he had some idea that Jesus could do him some good. Consider what his condition was. In these days through the advance of an enlightened philanthropy, the deaf and dumb can be conversed with, and can converse together, and learn; and they are able to read, and to write, and so forth,—but it was not so *then*. The condition of a deaf and dumb man must have been a far more pitiable condition then, than it is, ordinarily, in these days.

They could only somehow, in some dim way, communicate to him that they were bringing him to Jesus; and perhaps, there would then arise some little desire, on his part, to aid them in bringing him to Jesus. But it was *they* who were bringing him; they could do little for him, but they felt they could do *that*—and so they brought him. It is often so with those we love and care for, they are "deaf" to all we say, they hear the Gospel with their outward ear, but with that only; they are "dumb," they never speak for Christ, they will not hear, they are not anxious—and there is nothing that we can do for them but what these men did, with sympathy and intelligence. Their whole interest was exercised about the man's unhappy condition, and they come, and *beseech* Jesus to lay His hand upon him.

This is an encouragement to intercession—an encouragement to *eager*, earnest intercession. These men shouldered their way through the crowd, they were determined to have the *hand* of Christ,—they do not ask for His word; perhaps, they had not light enough to see, that a *word* could do what they wanted. What did they imagine? They have led the man about by the touch, they are able to do nothing but by the *touch*,

T

and they have no idea of leading him about but in this way ; and they want to know, therefore, that Christ's *hand* is laid upon him.   They desire real, personal contact ; but perhaps there was something wanting— the knowledge that a look, a word, could heal the man. But earnestness and determination to reach Jesus Christ *never* fails.

"He took him aside from the multitude."

This is remarkable.   We do not read that Jesus did this often.   *Why* did He do this ?   What was it for ? Then, there was actual, personal contact between Jesus and the man.   We stop and ask, What is this action of our Lord's ?   St. Mark gives it very particularly.   They had broken through the crowd, and got him there ; and what does Jesus do ?   " He took him aside."   He leaves the maimed, and halt, and wondering multitude, and takes the man a little higher up the mountain— " *aside.*"   We have, here, a very significant action on the part of our Lord—in His taking aside this poor deaf and dumb man, in order to heal him.   You know, that, in the old time, God took Israel out of Egypt into the *wilderness*—" He led him about, He instructed him, He kept him as the apple of His eye." (Deut. xxxii. 10).   And so, it is said by the prophet—" I will allure her, and bring her into the *wilderness*, and speak *to her heart.*" (Hosea ii. 14, and margin).   And this miracle teaches us this great truth—that the healing process must be carried on where the voice of Jesus, *and that only*, can be heard.   Jesus takes the man away from the hands of those who had brought him ; they did not go, too. How glad they must have been when they saw Jesus take him aside! they knew, then, that the cure would be effected. They were blessed men, they brought him to Jesus, and left him there; and then, Jesus takes him aside, that He may have to do with him alone.

And so He acts, still. He takes one, perhaps, and lays him on a sickbed; another, He isolates *in spirit* from all others, perhaps in some deep heart-sorrow. When He would speak to our *heart*, He takes us into the *wilderness*, where no voice but that of the Lord can be heard. There must be the going "aside" with Jesus, before there can be real healing of our spiritual maladies.

"And put His fingers into his ears, and He spit, and touched his tongue."

Now, you perceive here, two very strange actions of Christ. First, He "put His fingers into his ears"—that was, in fact, *speaking* to him, because He put His finger on the diseased place. And then, "He spit and touched," by that which came forth from His own lips, the man's "tongue"—not for the healing virtue, but to bring the man into actual contact with Himself, with Him who is "the Life." (St. John xiv. 6). Here we see the finger of Christ put on the very disease—the deaf ear, and the dumb, silent tongue. The man finds out that a finger is put on the diseased part; and it is the finger of CHRIST that points out to him, for the first time in his life, what it was that was diseased. How could he know what was at fault? Nobody could make him understand, very likely, where the seat of his disorder was. But Christ puts His finger on the part, and then he learns where the disease is—he learns the root of the mischief, in that way. Christ puts His finger into his ears, and then the man knew that they were diseased.

You may depend upon this, none ever find out the spiritual malady under which they are suffering, unless Christ puts His finger on it. When Christ puts His finger on our pride, or our selfishness, or our self-righteousness, when He makes us feel it, feel there is a diseased spot on our soul,—when *He* directs our attention to it, then we find it out ; but not till then. So this man did not know, till he felt Christ's finger on the place, what was the matter. There was the poor, diseased man, and Christ comes and puts His finger on the place,—yes, and not only in order to point out the malady, but also to *remove* it. He must make *this* man *feel* his malady. He had no need to do that with the leper ; the leper had only to hold his hand up to his face, and he would see it. What is a leper a type of? Not only of a sinner, but of a sinner who sees, and knows, and *believes*, that he *is* a sinner. This was not the case here. The man was deaf, he could not *hear ;* he was dumb, he couldn't *speak ;* so he needs Christ's finger put on the evil, that he may know it. Christ will not heal the soul, till He has taught it its sickness—then, when it has found that out, He gives relief.

"And looking up to heaven, He sighed."
This is St. Mark, again. He was not there, but some one was there to note that sigh, and the Spirit of God

gives St. Mark that important peculiarity of mind, by which he teaches us these little things. **"He sighed"**—there was a sensible, audible something that came out of the very *heart* of Jesus. He put His fingers into the man's ears, and spit and touched his tongue, and then an audible sound of pain, of agony—came out of the very heart of Christ, at that moment. Perhaps, the very first sound that the man ever heard, was the heart of Jesus *sighing* because of him—the heart of Jesus sending forth that suppressed groan and sigh over a deaf and dumb world, over the deaf and dumb physically, and over those greater maladies which sin has brought into the world—the deafness and dumbness of the human soul.

"And looking up to heaven."

We have every little particular here. The man could now *see*,—he could see Christ's attitude, he could see His eyes as they looked up to heaven, not to call down Divine power from thence, but to show that Divine power was acting on the man, because Divine power was present in, and going forth from, Christ Himself. But He looks up to Heaven, because mercy comes thence,—" *I* came down *from heaven*, not to do Mine own will, but—to save the lost and to heal the sick." That deep sigh of Christ's went up, and was heard there. Therefore the man was taught so far—that suffering and sorrow brought groans even from Him, and that the only remedy for sorrow and for sin, was to be found there in Heaven above. " Looking up to heaven, He sighed"—

"And saith unto him, Ephphatha,"—

He said it in the old language; here St. Mark gives us the *exact* word again—"Ephphatha." What does that mean? **"That is, Be opened."**

"And straightway his ears were opened, and the string of his tongue was loosed, and he spake plain."

Now then, let us pick up the thread.

(1.) The finger of Christ must be put on the malady.

(2.) The man must feel his disease.

(3.) Heavenly help is to be looked for from Heaven itself.

(4.) The voice of Divine power must speak.

(5.) And then, there is the glorious result.

Let us, first, consider this as applied spiritually, and then see how full of blessing it is.

If Christ has come to you heretofore, or if He has come to any to-night, He does *this*—He, spiritually, puts His finger on your spiritual malady—He makes you feel it—He makes you feel, "*There* is my disease, *there*, in the depth of my heart. I know what I need a remedy for; I know it, and 'I abhor myself, and repent in dust and ashes.' I know where my malady lies." That is what Christ does, when He comes to any in order to heal them.

But I tell you this—the heart of Christ ever groans, ever sighs over the sins, as well as over the sorrows, of this world of ours—that heart, so holy and so heavenly, looks into the depths of our woe, and, perhaps, the first sound the awakened soul ever hears, is the sound that tells that the heart of Jesus feels for him, groans for him, was broken for him. He hears Jesus sigh, but he finds, too, that His help is Heavenly—Omnipotent—All-sufficient,—that we must look up to .the Mountains of "Gilead" sending down their "balm." We must look up to Heaven for help, and then we shall hear, and speak, and live.

"And He charged them that they should tell no man; but the more He charged them, so much the more a great deal they published it."

One cannot wonder at their going and publishing it. Jesus had His reasons for telling them not to do so; they were not to go and spread the news, to make it more difficult for Him to exercise His ministry, and so to interfere with the purpose He had in hand. And then they said, perhaps all unconscious of the deep, deep meaning of their words—

"He hath done all things well."

The words carry us back to the very beginning of the Creation of God, and to the old words which God had pronounced—"God saw everything that He had made, and behold, it was *very good*."

"He hath done all things well; He maketh both the deaf to hear, and the dumb to speak."

Now, this is the Jesus Christ whom *we* preach—the Jesus Christ who does all things "well." Let us learn a lesson from these men, who would have their friend in personal contact with Jesus. There must be the coming to Christ—there must be sensible knowledge of our malady, and, in some way or other, contact with the living voice, or the Divine touch of the Saviour. There can be no loosing of the stammering tongue, unless by being brought to Jesus, unless there is real coming to Him, unless there is real faith and trust wrought in the soul, a faith which rests on Him Who can heal the diseases of that soul.

And, in these days, when the world is getting Gospel-hardened, we need to dwell on this. People think that because Christ died on Calvary, all is well, and they are sure to be saved. But, unless we are born again—unless we feel the finger of Jesus, and have Him breathe into our heart His own life—unless we are truly healed by the Divine Physician Himself,—we cannot be saved. There *must* be the faith that lays hold of the Lamb, and unites the soul to Him, or there will be no part with Him in His kingdom and glory.

XIX.

THE TRANSFIGURATION OF CHRIST.

" And after six days Jesus taketh Peter, James, and John his bro-
ther, and bringeth them up into an high mountain apart, and
was transfigured before them ; and his face did shine as the sun,
and his raiment was white as the light. And, behold, there ap-
peared unto them Moses and Elias talking with him. Then
answered Peter, and said unto Jesus, Lord, it is good for us to
be here ; if thou wilt, let us make here three tabernacles ; one for
thee, and one for Moses, and one for Elias. While he yet
spake, behold, a bright cloud overshadowed them ; and behold
a voice out of the cloud, which said, This is my beloved Son, in
whom I am well pleased ; hear ye him. And when the disciples
heard it, they fell on their face, and were sore afraid. And Jesus
came and touched them, and said, Arise, and be not afraid.
And when they had lifted up their eyes, they saw no man, save
Jesus only."—ST. MATT. xvii. 1–8.

THE event, here recorded by St. Matthew, is recorded,
likewise, by St. Mark and St. Luke, and is, also, not
vaguely hinted at by St. John. It is recorded, also, in
striking terms, by St. Peter, one of the three witnesses
of the Transfiguration. It is an event that stands by
itself, amongst all the striking events chronicled in the
Gospel history. It is a bright gleam of heavenly glory
shining over that whole record. Like the mountain, on

which the event took place, overtopping all the rest—so this one event stands out, shining with heavenly and glorious brilliance. The event, itself, is known to us all by the term—the " Transfiguration of Christ."

Our Lord, as we are told in the previous chapter, had departed to the most northern part of Palestine that, in almost all His journeyings, He appears ever to have visited. We find, in the 13th verse of that chapter, that " Jesus came into the coasts of Cæsarea Philippi." He had, now, departed to the extreme northernmost point—to that great and beautiful city, which lay at the foot of Mount Hermon, and *there* the conversations, related in chapter xvi., were held. *There* Peter was led to make his great confession—*there*, after that confession, our Lord began to unfold to His disciples, in more full and striking terms, and in a more systematic manner than He had ever yet done, what would be the *end* of His ministry. He comes and antagonises the feeling prevalent, everywhere, in the Jewish mind ;—a glorious, conquering, triumphant Messiah was the only idea of Messiah, that the Jewish mind admitted to itself. That feeling, so deeply fixed and rooted in the Jewish mind, Jesus meets by the declaration, in the chapter that precedes the one from which my text is taken :—" From that time forth began Jesus to shew unto His disciples, how that He must go unto Jerusalem, and *suffer* many things of the elders and chief priests and scribes, and be killed, and be raised again the third day." (xvi. 21). Not one of these disciples could understand Him, not one of these disciples would believe Him. Peter, ever foremost, begins to rebuke Him, and says, "Be it far from Thee, Lord; this shall not be unto Thee." And *then*, the Lord unfolded to these wondering men a solemn, and, to them, an *awful* fact—that it must be as taking up the "cross," it must be as denying themselves, that *they* must enter into the kingdom of Heaven. But He adds, in precious words of mercy—"Verily I say unto you, There be some standing here, which shall not taste of death, till *they* see the Son of man coming in His kingdom." (xvi. 28).

We seem to recognise in this, that—so deeply rooted was the feeling, to which I have alluded, even in the minds of the disciples of Jesus—that the most merciful, the most striking, and the most effectual means have to be taken, that, from some minds at least, that idea might be eradicated. And then, still remaining in the coasts of Cæsarea Philippi—"**after six days**"—"about an eight days," says St. Luke (ix. 28)—the one inclusive, the other exclusive,—

"**Jesus taketh Peter, James, and John his brother, and bringeth them up into an high mountain apart.**"

I need not stop to speak of the mountain. A very current tradition fixed this as Mount TABOR. That view has, I believe, now long since been exploded by those who have carefully examined the scene, and by those, too, who have carefully examined the Scriptures. There are two things which seem to settle the question, that Mount HERMON—rather than Mount Tabor—was the scene of the Transfiguration. Both alike were to "rejoice in His Name," (Psalm lxxxix. 12), and why not

Hermon as well as Tabor? As I said, there are two proofs that Hermon, rather than Tabor, was the chosen spot.

(1.) Mount Tabor, as you all know, was quite at the S.W. of the Lake of Galilee, many miles from Cæsarea Philippi. It was as far from Cæsarea Philippi to Mount Tabor, as it was, in some parts of the Holy Land, from the Jordan to the Mediterranean; and we find no mark in the sacred records, indicating any change of place on the part of our Lord from the coasts of Cæsarea Philippi.

(2.) We have another proof from the fact—well known in history—that fifty years *before* the Transfiguration took place, Mount Tabor had, on its summit, a fortified town; and, twenty years *after* the Transfiguration, the fortified town was still there, and a great battle was fought between the Romans and the Jews, 20,000 of the latter being slain in the conflict. Whereas the whole history goes to show, that the scene of this all-glorious event was a " high mountain apart " by itself, a mountain where they would be undisturbed,—a mountain apart by itself, as they were apart by themselves; and where the bright, pure white of the snow was in fellowship, as it were, in sympathy with the bright, shining purity that surrounded our Blessed Lord and Master, on this occasion. And such would be " one of the lofty spurs of the snow-capped Hermon."

Here, then, we now find Him going apart with three of His disciples. And why *three?* That " in the mouth of two or three witnesses every word may be established." (St. Matt. xviii. 16). We find that the same three had, already, been taken into privileged nearness. These three had been taken into the chamber, when Jesus said to the daughter of Jairus—" Damsel, I say unto thee, Arise." (St. Mark v. 41). They had, already, seen their Master's power *over death;* they were to be witnesses, moreover, of a still more solemnly striking event,—they were to look on that countenance " marred more than any man," (Isa. lii. 14), to see it in the deepest grief, in the direst agony—they were to be with Him in the garden, when He should " sweat as it were great drops of blood falling down to the ground," (St. Luke xxii. 14),—they were to be with Him when He cried, " O my Father, if it be possible, let this cup pass from me." (St. Matt. xxvi. 39). And they,—for reasons that we, perhaps, may not inquire into, for reasons that, perhaps, we shall never perfectly ascertain, —these three chosen ones were taken also, to be the witnesses of the *glory* of Christ. They came with Him to the mountain, and when His prayer was over, they— roused from their sleep, (St. Luke ix. 32)—saw Jesus **"transfigured before them; and His face did shine as the sun, and His raiment was white as the light.**

"And, behold, there appeared unto them Moses and Elias talking with Him."

Here we have, at once, the Law and the Prophets, and the Fulfiller of both.

1. MOSES, who had never been permitted to enter the Holy Land, when he was alive, was here. He had died and been buried, *where—how*—no mortal knows ; " God buried him," (Deut. xxxiv. 6), God interred, with

His own hand, His dear servant whom He had chastened, whom He had forbidden to go over Jordan.   God
never left him, though He chastened him, though He
afflicted him, though He denied him the privilege of cross-
ing the river.   He left him not in his sorrow, but abode
tenderly by him, and buried him with His own hand.

2. And ELIJAH, who had been caught up to heaven in
a chariot of fire, was here.   He did not lay in the grave
his mortal body, but was " changed," " in the twinkling
of an eye," at the call of God.   The people of Jericho
sought him, thinking that " the Spirit of the Lord might
have cast him upon some mountain, or into some
valley," but they " found him not." (2 Kings ii. 16, 17).

How *Moses* comes to be possessed of a glorified body,
we know not.   We do know, that " the body of Moses "
was an object of interest to fallen spirits ; we know that
" Michael the archangel " contended " with the devil,"
for the possession of " the body of Moses," (Jude 9)—
perhaps, the Wicked one contended that, before the
time of the general resurrection, the body of Moses
could not be claimed back again from the grave.

We have, here, the one dead and buried, and the
other changed in a moment, and both appearing in
glory, and speaking with Jesus.   We have a glimpse,
here, into the unseen world ; we see the spirits of those,
who have long departed from the scene in which we
live, living, acting, thinking intelligently, deeply interested in what goes on in the earth.   They stand here,
recognised and recognising.   We know not how, but
the three disciples *recognised* that they were " Moses,"

the Lawgiver, " and Elias," the Reformer—the man who died and was buried in Mount Nebo, and the man who never had died, but had ascended. These were then present " in the Holy Mount," (2 Pet. i. 18), " talking with " Jesus. The disciples had just heard strange words from His lips, they had just heard Him say that He must *die*,—that He would be taken by wicked hands and be slain,—that in Jerusalem the chiefs of His own people would " kill " Him, and then, that He would *rise* again. And now, they see here, standing before their eyes—a *risen* man, " in glory." (St. Luke ix. 31).

Now we come to ask, *Why* this grand event of the Transfiguration of Christ? *Why* did Moses and Elias appear here, talking with Jesus? Men had been saying that *Christ* was Elias, and so it is said that, amongst other things, it was necessary to convince the disciples that Christ was *not* Elias,—but that is a small reason. There are other reasons, still more grave and more important than this. Jesus Christ was standing in the midst of His own people, in a very peculiar position. He was " a Hebrew of the Hebrews," and He claimed great authority, He claimed to be a greater reformer, than even Elias did ; but no one can read the history, cursorily, without seeing, that His teaching was in antagonism to everything that held sway in Jewish minds—in direct antagonism to the opinions and conduct, almost universally, prevalent amongst His people. Consequently, they said He had come to *destroy* the Law and the Prophets ; they said He was not a genuine Israelite ; they said, and truly, that He was in antagonism to *them* but then—*they* were not in accord with the Law.

Jesus Christ had said certain solemn things to His disciples—that the controversy would go on and on, till it would come to extremity,—they would *kill* Him, the authorities would kill Him by the hands of the conquerors of their people. Would He be righteously put to death? Would He be righteously condemned? Did *the Law* condemn Him? Did *the Prophets* condemn Him? He takes these three disciples up into the mountain, and the first thing that meets their eyes, is—*Jesus Christ in accord with the Law and the Prophets*, Jesus Christ conversing with *Moses*, conversing with *Elias.* Jesus, who was decried as a corrupter of their truth, as the breaker of the Law, as the antagonist of the Prophets, is seen in accord with Moses—He is seen in accord with Elias.

But Jesus had been saying other things to these disciples—He had been telling them to lay aside all their preconceived notions about their Messiah. He said, "You desire a crown—I give you a cross." They said, "We desire to triumph;" He said, "You must be willing to suffer." They said, "Give us thrones, and let us sit, one on Thy right hand, and the other on Thy left;" He said—"You must learn first to deny self, and to take up your Cross and to follow ME, even though I go to Jerusalem to *suffer* all these things."

Now, it was necessary that the disciples should understand the real truth of His position, and so they were taken up into the Holy Mount, as the Lord had said—"Verily I say unto you, There be some standing here, which shall not taste of death, till they see the Son of man coming in His kingdom." Yes,—though the Son of man shall embrace a Cross, He *hath a* "*kingdom*," and these shall see some glimpse of that kingdom ; yea, and now, in the full blaze of the glorious light that overshadowed all, they shall be led to ask what all this cross, all this self-denial, all this shame, all this ignominy was, compared with the glory, if this be, indeed, "the glory" which was "to be revealed." There was work, therefore, to be done in them in this respect,—they were not to see merely a part of Christ's mission ; they had seen *one* thing where they ought to have seen *two* things, which, had they seen, they would not have fallen into such serious error. There shall indeed be the cross, but there shall also be the kingdom ; and "I would," says the Lord, "have you 'reckon that the *sufferings* of this present time are not worthy to be compared with the *glory* which shall be revealed.'" (Rom. viii. 18).

This is one of God's remarkable ways of dealing with His people. He does not put the rough, and the difficult, and the suffering, before them, without putting also before them the exceeding and eternal great reward. He often cheers, He often strengthens and stimulates His people, by visions of *glory*, ere He calls them to *suffer*. He Himself will open the heavens, that they may see if it is worth while to walk with Christ suffering and bearing His cross, that they may ask, "Shall we care about the suffering, if we are indeed to be glorified together with Him?"

U

But there is another thing,—they needed a truer estimate of their Master's real character. Remember what the circumstances really were; they were following, as their Master, One Who was born in low estate, —they had heard the cry ring out again and again— "Can there any good thing come out of Nazareth?" (St. John i. 46). They knew that it was said of Him, "Is not this the carpenter?" (St. Mark vi. 3). "Is not this the carpenter's son?" (St. Matt. xiii. 55). They knew how the rulers looked on Him as mean and abject, and His many works of wonder did not dissipate the feelings of those who surrounded Him. Was it not needful that men, called to follow this mean, despised Master, should be taught,—it may be secretly, but *really*,—that though His was a lowly lot and walk upon earth, there was heavenly dignity and heavenly glory still hovering over Him? Did they not see, at a glance, that, untrue as ever the accusation was that He came to destroy what "Moses and the prophets" had "spoken," so was the charge of the meanness and the insignificance of His earthly life, His real earthly lot? They needed something beyond this—the knowledge that He *was* what He had *claimed* to be.

He had, already, in mysterious terms, but emphatically, unflinchingly, claimed to be that, which Israel had persistently denied that He was, in spite of the voice which came from the heavenly glory when He was baptized—"This is My beloved *Son.*" His claim to be the Eternal Son of God was, everywhere, and at all times, disallowed by unbelieving Israel. Now the effect of this, on those who were called to share His despised, troubled lot, must have been great. They could not, even now, withstand the public feeling everywhere against them, with constancy and success ; and, when they hear their Master say He is about to descend to *lower* depths, to go into *deeper* suffering, and that they cannot enter with Him into His kingdom, unless they share with Him His reproach, unless they share His despised and suffering portion—then, indeed, they do need what infinite grace bestows on them,—some new, striking assurance that He *is* what He claims to be.

So, "there came such a voice to Him from the excellent glory, This is My beloved Son, in whom I am well pleased,"—the Son of My love, (Col. i. 13, margin), the Son on whom My heart is fixed, the Son in whom My soul delighteth—"hear Him." "And this voice which came from heaven we heard, (says St. Peter), when we were with Him in the holy mount." (2 Peter i. 17, 18).

There is one more thing, in this part of our subject, that remains to be considered, and that is,—What sort of a reception the Lord's solemn declaration met at the hands of the Apostles ? When He had solemnly declared to them that He must go on to suffering—that He must go on to the *extremity* of suffering—that He must be killed in ignominy by the rulers of His people, how did they receive that ? how did they listen to that ? With unwilling ears, with hearts bereft of all sympathy, —in coldness—in unconcern—in unbelief. "Be it far from Thee, Lord ; this shall not be unto Thee." They listened with this feeling, and they would force their feeling even upon His mind, if they could—that the result could be avoided, that other means might be taken, by which such a dread result might be averted. " Be it far from Thee, Lord ; this *shall not* be unto Thee." "We have power, we have swords, we have a company of people devoted to Thy interest, we have ingenuity, we have wit, and we will take care and defend Thee—we will deliver Thee—' *This* shall not be unto Thee.' "

Nothing shows more clearly, than the conversation of the previous chapter, that they had not a single feeling of sympathy with their great Master, about the fact of His death. They did not realise the necessity of it, they did not realise the propriety of it, they had no conception of the meaning of it, they did not enter into the things concerning Messiah's mission. In spite of all that they had before them on the pages of the Old Testament, they did not see that all was being done scripturally, and for their sakes. They say—"It is a vain, weak fear of Thine. The enmity shown to you, you will outlive and overcome ; and if you do not overcome, we will rescue you." Not a single one of them had the mind of Christ, or could enter into the mind of Christ,—they were cold and dark from indifference and ignorance, they listened as to a mere idle tale, and looked on that which was nearest and dearest to His heart, without one spark of sympathy.

He had come from Heaven to earth, to fulfil every shadow of the old dispensation. Abel's lamb found *in*

Him its antitype—the Paschal Lamb found *in Him* its substance—all the wonders of the symbolic rites of the Temple and Tabernacle, found, in Jesus Christ, their true fulfilment ; yet the men, who gathered round Him and followed Him, had not the smallest conception of His mission. They were as dark and as blind on the question of Atonement, as multitudes now are ; and, as we see the ignorance around us now, we wonder less at that of the disciples who gathered round Him. When we find people saying that they believe in the New Testament, in the mission of Jesus Christ, and yet fail to see its essence and its substance,—we wonder less at the blindness of the olden time.

And so, the Son of man, whom God had made strong for His own self, looks round, and finds that there is not a human mind, however strong, however pure, however elevated, that understands HIS mission, or that will sit at His feet and hear His Word. He longed for one to anoint Him for His burial, but not a single spark of understanding of what He had come into the world to do, does He find in His own disciples,—not one is there who could go with Him in spirit, and converse with Him, feelingly, rationally, sympathisingly, " about His decease." They could see Him multiply loaves and be glad, they could see Him raise the dead, and cleanse the lepers, and rejoice therein,—but, of the greater work of the putting away of sin, of the great work of the redemption of man from sin to holiness, from Satan unto God,—they had no understanding. After all these months upon months of holy, glorious training, they have not a spark of sympathy, they are hard and cold ; and therefore, He takes three of them up into a mountain apart—and while He prays, they sleep!   And when they awake, they see the vision of glory—He "was transfigured before them, and His face did shine as the sun, and His raiment was white as the light ; and, behold, there appeared unto them Moses and Elias, talking with Him."

They speak to Him—not of restoring the kingdom to Israel, not of bringing forth Israel out of her temporal bondage, not of covering the hills with fertility and beauty, not of enriching His people with temporal things,—but—of His Exodus.   They "spake of His *decease* which He should accomplish at *Jerusalem*." (St. Luke ix. 31).

He had said, to His disciples, that He must go to *Jerusalem*, and suffer many things and be killed ; and *they* had said—" No, ' This shall not be unto Thee— That be far from Thee, Lord.'"   And now, the heavens are opened, and Moses and Elias, the Lawgiver and the great Prophet, come and speak with Him, and *they* say, " Yes, Lord ; Thou must go to *Jerusalem*,—Thy Exodus must be accomplished *there*.   Thy decease must be accomplished there—at Jerusalem."   Heaven has sympathy with Christ in His suffering, bleeding, dying Love, while earth is blind, hard, cold, and unconcerned.

This, as far as the Lord was concerned, was one of the leading necessities of this glorious vision.   Look at Him—perfect man, without spot or stain of sin, yet with every human weakness, partaker of all our weakness,—craving sympathy, and finding none. The one thought that filled His own mind was all alien from this earthly scene, and alien from the men who took His Name, who followed Him, who rejoiced in His works, who were proud of Him, and who even did really love Him, but who could not *understand* Him.

"**There appeared unto them Moses and Elias talking with Him,**" concerning His Exodus.

Surely this was most appropriate,—surely none, like Moses, could enter into the matter as yet, for he had been—not only the giver of the moral law, of the national law—not only the giver of that wonderful ceremonial law, every whit of which testified of Christ, every word of which pointed to Him—but He had been the great leader in the marvellous Exodus of the olden time ; and he knew that it was not by his own wisdom, or with the strength of his own arm, but in and through the slain Lamb and its sprinkled blood, that there was a real Exodus of Israel out of the great bondage. And he had come now, to speak to the true " Lamb of God," concerning *His* Exodus—*His* death of bleeding love, under whose shelter only can a sinner be safe.

Jesus finds sympathy, and finds rest, when the inhabitants of the heavenly places come, and show how intelligently, how feelingly, how thoroughly, they appreciate that Death, to which they owed their present place in the abode of bliss—that Death which they knew was to purchase, for all whom they had left in the unseen world, their salvation, their glory, and their eternal life. That Death, they knew, would be the only destroyer of sin, and the only means of redemption and remission. The heavenly inhabitants understand it; they feel it precious to converse together, and feelingly to speak of it. The Exodus of Jesus is the prominent thought in their mind, the deepest and mightiest power in their soul.

Now, look at the effect on the minds of these disciples. Peter immediately opens his mouth, and says, **"Lord, it is good for us to be here; if Thou wilt, let us make here three tabernacles; one for Thee, and one for Moses, and one for Elias."**

In this thought of Peter's, there is matter of suggestion on both sides of the question. Peter says, positively, " It *is* good." Now it might be good,—or it might not be good. Many things there might be good for them; that sacred solitude where they had been taken apart by themselves—taken out of the world with its confusion and its turmoil—taken apart even from the rest of the disciples—taken apart into that sacred solitude, with the light shining down upon them—yes, that might be good. Jesus had gone into a mountain apart to pray, —unlike the Israelites generally ; *He* did not pray standing at the corners of the streets, but went alone into a mountain, and it was " good " to be in solitude. It was a high mountain, standing apart by itself; and " it is good "—it *is* good to get into a high mountain, to get as near to the heavens above, as we can. " As an eagle stirreth up her nest, fluttereth over her young, spreadeth abroad her wings, taketh them, beareth them on her wings," (Deut. xxxii. 11), *near to the sun*, so " it is good " to be near to Heaven,—I mean, near Heaven in a spiritual sense—to be on a high spiritual mountain "is good." St. Peter calls this, afterwards, "the *holy* mount," (2 Pet. i. 18)—"it is good " to get into a place that is *sanctified*,—sanctified by the presence of Jesus, and by nearness to Heaven,—"it is good " *thus* to be there—to be in the place of holiness, to be in the place that is consecrated to Jesus Christ.

It was good to be there, because *Moses* was there. Surely it must be good to be with Moses, if we understand Moses aright.

It was good to be there with *Elias*. It will ever be good to be with Elias, if we understand Elias aright.

But—it was good, most of all, to be there because JESUS was there. There cannot be anything but what is good for us, when we are near to Jesus.

It was good to be with them all there *together*—the Law, and the Prophets,—and the Saviour, the Fulfiller of them all. It was good to have them all together—not separate one from the other, but all combined—not one opposed to the other, but all together. Yes, it *was* good to have Moses, and the Prophets, and Jesus, in the mountain *together !* Men will take the old " penknife," and cut out Moses,—and they will cut out Christ, when they have got so far. "It is good " to have them *all*, —and to have them *all together.* So far, thus far, Peter was right when he said, " Lord, it is *good* for us to be here."

But, I doubt much, whether he said these things rightly. It is sometimes very dangerous to be in high places; there is a danger lest the spirit should be lifted up—a danger that, unless the spirit be very lowly, it should meet a fall.   Some say, "It is good for us to be *here*, amongst these lofty thoughts, here amongst these high glorious speculations,—it is good to soar aloft, and to think and to investigate, and to ponder, and to get up into high, glorious things, out of sight of other men." It is dangerous, sometimes, to get up into the clefts of a lofty rock, unless it be "in the cleft" of the ONE ROCK.   There are some things for a Christian to do, some duties for the disciples of Christ to do, that are to be found in a *lowly* place—in a true humility, in a lowly walk, and in the diligent labour, and the constant toil of an affectionate love.   Some would have their life completely spent in a high mountain, but that is not a life granted to the pardoned sinner here on earth.   No! it must be the lowly, practical, loving, consistent walk of holy obedience, and ready submission, yea, even to a suffering, needy lot, if our Lord and Master requires.

It was very fine for Peter to make tents *there*,—out of the reach of conflict, out of the reach of toil, out of the reach of labour, and to bask there in the sunshine, and quietly refuse to work, quietly get rid of the Cross, quietly to set aside all the life of obedience on the plain and in the valley of humiliation, to which his Master had called him.   Yes—it is good, often, for the "bright clouds" to vanish.   I think, we shall find, if we ever reach Heaven, that we shall thank God *most* thankfully for many of our darkest days, for our deepest sorrows, and our sorest afflictions—that we shall thank Him more that we have been in the raging of the tempest, more that we have been in the plain, in the valley of humiliation, than that we have been on the peaks of the high mountain. We shall thank Him that we have been afflicted, and say—almost in the language of Peter, but really in the language of another saint—"*It is good* for me that I have been afflicted. . . . Before I was afflicted, I went astray." (Ps. cxix. 71, 67). We know that it is good for us to come down here, and feel the toil, and pressure, and want, and necessity, and to meet the enemies and the conflict. We cannot abide ever on the bright mountain of glory; the spirit must be braced and made brave in the lowly walk of conflict, and it would be far from "good for us" to be without chastisement. I know it is pleasant and delightful to have the "mountain so strong," that a man imagines he cannot be "moved,"—but that man needs many a time to be made to feel the hiding of God's face, and then, indeed, he is "troubled." (Ps. xxx.)

Peter says—"**If Thou wilt only let us make here three tabernacles, one for Thee, and one for Moses, and one for Elias.**"

It is a great mercy that St. Luke has put in a word—"not knowing what he said." (ix. 33). But he said it; and *what* was he saying, at that moment? He who, a few days before, had said—"Thou art the Christ, the Son of the living God"—lifts Moses and Elias up *to a level* with his Master! "Let us make three dwelling-places for the Shekinah, one for Thee, one for Moses, and one for Elias." Peter would give Moses a tabernacle covered with glory, and Elias a tabernacle covered with glory, and Jesus one, too! What an unworthy thought! The very Romans would have allowed the image of Christ in their Pantheon; they would have put Him *on a level* with the best of their gods. Yes! and it is the old thought in Peter—he would give Jesus a tabernacle, but he puts Moses and Elias on the same level, he would give *them* the Shekinah, too.

And then, at *that* moment, when this weak foolish man, so blind, so forgetful, so dark, says this,—there comes down on the mountain's peak, settling over all, the *real* SHEKINAH—the real dwelling-place of Jehovah, that which rested on and over the Mercy-seat; and, in the dazzling brightness, Moses and Elias vanish out of sight, and a voice comes " out of the excellent glory" —the others were gone,—" THIS—*this* is My beloved *Son*, in whom I am well pleased," " hear ye HIM." The voice came from the Father, and it came to the servants who had degraded their Lord—came to them in tender, solemn, heavenly rebuke—"*Hear* ye HIM." Moses is not,—Elias is not,—hear ye *Him*. As Moses himself had said—" The Lord thy God will raise up unto thee a Prophet from the midst of thee, of thy brethren, like unto me, *unto* HIM shall ye *hearken*." (Deut. xviii. 15). Moses did not wish to be listened to —he wished to " decrease." Elias had nothing now to say. Let Christ be heard—let the voice be heard which had spoken, in outward signs and types, before, let it now be heard in the glorious Gospel—" This is

My beloved Son, in whom I am well pleased, hear ye Him." That is God's voice; that voice comes from Heaven, and it puts "Moses and the Prophets" in their right place, as in after days—" Beginning at *Moses* and all the *prophets*, He expounded unto them in all the Scriptures the things *concerning* HIMSELF." (St. Luke xxiv. 27). " Hear *Him*."

In conclusion, let me leave two thoughts with you. Let us never lose sight of this—if the glorified spirits in Heaven have their deepest, their most constant, their highest thoughts, concerning the *Death of Jesus Christ,* surely, we upon earth ought ever to put that in the fore-ground. If they could converse with Jesus concerning His Death, then let us speak to Him on the same subject. What are our prayers, too often, but ignorant petitions for temporal things, for some mental or spiritual good ? But do we seek to converse with our *risen* Lord now, in the heavenly mountain, in spirit, about that which lies so near to His heart—" His decease "—which is as near to His heart now, when He pleads it at the Throne of grace, as when, upon Mount Hermon, He looked forward to its accomplishment? He seeks where He may have fellowship, and the saints ought to have fellowship in Christ's sufferings—to go with Him in spirit again to Calvary, and to ponder, with the love and sympathy of loving hearts, that Exodus which He "accomplished at Jerusalem," when He said, "It is finished."

And there is, still, another thought—it is this :—they who have fellowship truly with Jesus thus, shall be with

Him on the mountain, and shall see the overshadowing glory—" Father, I will that they also, whom Thou hast given Me, be with Me where I am ; that they may behold MY GLORY. (St. John xvii. 24). " Father (perhaps, He had said in the mountain), Father, I will that Moses and Elias come down to this Mount, and see, and sympathise with, the feeling of My heart concerning My Exodus."

Now, He says,—" Father, I will that they also, who rest in My Atoning work, and wash in the Fountain of My precious Blood, and are cleansed thereby from all sin,—go up into the mountain, and see My glory, which Thou hast given Me." And *then* they shall say, without possibility of a mistake, without a qualification—" Lord, it is good for us to be *here*,—in our Father's house, where there are many mansions."

XX.

THE CURING OF THE LUNATIC CHILD.

" *And when he came to his disciples, he saw a great multitude about them, and the scribes questioning with them. And straightway all the people, when they beheld him, were greatly amazed, and running to him saluted him. And he asked the scribes, What question ye with them? And one of the multitude answered and said, Master, I have brought unto thee my son, which hath a dumb spirit; and wheresoever he taketh him, he teareth him; and he foameth, and gnasheth with his teeth, and pineth away; and I spake to thy disciples that they should cast him out; and they could not. He answereth him, and saith, O faithless generation, how long shall I be with you? how long shall I suffer you? bring him unto me. And they brought him unto him; and when he saw him, straightway the spirit tare him; and he fell on the ground, and wallowed foaming. And he asked his father, How long is it ago since this came unto him? And he said, Of a child. And ofttimes it hath cast him into the fire, and into the waters, to destroy him; but if thou canst do any thing, have compassion on us, and help us. Jesus said unto him, If thou canst believe, all things are possible to him that believeth. And straightway the father of the child cried out, and said with tears, Lord, I believe; help thou mine unbelief. When Jesus saw that the people came running together, he rebuked the foul spirit, saying unto him, Thou dumb and deaf spirit, I charge thee, come out of him, and enter no more into him. And the spirit cried, and rent him sore, and came out of him; and he was as one dead; insomuch that many said, He is dead.*

But Jesus took him by the hand, and lifted him up; and he arose. And when he was come into the house, his disciples asked him privately, Why could not we cast him out? And he said unto them, This kind can come forth by nothing, but by prayer and fasting."—ST. MARK ix. 14–29.

PERHAPS you will recognise ât once, that it was after our Blessed Lord had been up in the Mount where He was transfigured, and when He was coming down from that Mount of Transfiguration, that He found these circumstances existing which are recorded in these verses. He had been up there in " the holy mount," and Moses and Elias had appeared to Him there, in " the excellent glory;" and we find that when He came down, and these multitudes beheld Him, there was still, as it were, the halo of heavenly glory round Him, for they were attracted to His presence. There was something attractive in His appearance, for

"straightway all the people, when they beheld Him, were greatly amazed, and running to Him saluted Him."

What a striking contrast it must have been to Jesus —coming down from " the excellent glory" in which He had been on the Mount,—coming down from converse with Moses and Elias, who had been speaking, in sympathetic and intelligent tones, about the decease He was to accomplish at Jerusalem ; and then, when He comes down from that society to the level of earth again, to find nothing but reproach, nothing but difficulty, nothing but conflict, nothing but turmoil, nothing but sin !

"**When He came to His disciples, He saw a great multitude about them, and the scribes questioning with them.**"

Jesus had left His nine disciples below,—you know that He took only three with Him up into the mountain; and when He came back, there were these proud scribes and Pharisees, cavilling and saying, " *We* have you; we've found you out. This is a fair test that has been given you, to see if you *have* the power you say you have to work miracles; *and you have failed.* You *can't* do it." Here had this father brought his child to the nine disciples; he had heard that Jesus had given them power to heal diseases, and to do many wonderful works, and so he brought his child possessed with a foul spirit, and asked them to cast out the foul spirit; and they could not do it. And, inasmuch as they could not do it, these proud, lofty Pharisees triumph over them. They care more for their own victory, than for the suffering of their fellow-men. If only they could confound the disciples, the poor child might go on suffering. The Devil might go on tormenting the bodies of men, and their miseries be unalleviated, if they, in their great pride, could only get the victory over the disciples of Christ. The father had brought his child to them, and the nine disciples could not cast out the unclean spirit, and the scribes and Pharisees had their short-lived triumph. For all that these nine disciples could do, the poor child might have gone on suffering for ever, in a state next door to hell. The finger of scorn was pointed at them, and, *through them*, at their Master, be-

X

cause the poor child was still there unhealed. But—the Master comes.

Is there nothing like this on earth now? Is there nothing like the triumph of the scribes and Pharisees? Is there nothing like this young child, held fast in cruel bondage? As we go through our streets, we see proofs, on every side, that there *are* devils,—devils with various characters, various names, various powers and uncleannesses, who hold a mighty power over, and right down in, the souls, and in the homes too, of men. And is there no finger of scorn? Are we not taunted—we, who are disciples and ministers of Christ—by hearing men say, "If you are the disciples and ministers of Christ, *why* are not these devils cast out? These devils of profanity, of drunkenness, of licentiousness, which are desolating the homes of our town, and of our country—nay, of the world, and wearing out human lives, *why* are they not cast out?"—There are many "questionings" because of it.

But these disciples had a Master, and He, Who had been up in the Mount, comes down to them, and says to the scribes—

"What question ye with them?"—
They do not pretend to do anything in their *own* power. And now, Jesus comes and says, "Look *Me* in the face. Let your questionings be addressed to *Me*. Let your cavillings fall on My ears." Their Master is here now. They bungle, and make mistakes, and are weak as children in their hearts, but their Master is come, at length. People do taunt, people do cavil, because the disciples

of Christ are found unequal to cast out *all* devils ; but, if they go on cavilling, they must be content some day to answer the Master—they must be content to hear what the *Master* has to say to them. Why, the Lord saw, at once, that these questioners were very hollow-hearted indeed. He saw that they cared for the triumph of their sect, more than for the delivery, from almost infinite misery, of this poor child and his father,—He saw that they had *no heart* to feel for the suffering world,—He saw that they put forth no hand of love to alleviate its calamities, to rid it of its grievous load of woe. They only cared to ask, as scoffers ask now, "Why has not Christianity done this? Why have not the disciples of Christ done that? Why has not the Church driven all wickedness out of the world?" But they must be contented to have their whole heart, and mind, and understanding, investigated by the disciples' Master.

The father of the poor child leaves the disciples no time to say anything, because he is so very eager himself to have the first word, as soon as he sees the Lord. He had come to the disciples, and asked *them* to rid his house of this misery, to rid his child of this devil ; and he sees how weak the disciples are, without their Master. And now that he catches a glimpse of the Master, he goes to *Him*, and says—

"**Master, I have brought unto Thee my son, which hath a dumb spirit**"—(he was possessed by a devil, that rendered him incapable of articulate speech), " I have brought him to *Thee.*" And he tells Jesus what the condition of his son is ; he says he is possessed of a devil—a devil of *silence.* We saw something, the other day, about a deaf and dumb spirit; and we saw Jesus Christ putting His finger, in that case, on the diseased spot, before He healed the man.

"And wheresoever he taketh him, he teareth him; and he foameth, and gnasheth with his teeth, and pineth away."

Here we see what the Devil is. The Devil here was honest, in *his* way; he let it be seen what he was. He did not clothe himself as "an angel of light," but he said—"I'm strong enough to go forth, and show myself *as I am."* And he went forth, to show what a *cruel* Devil he is. He is not ashamed to show how cruel he is, but he lets us see what devils are, and what they can do, when they have power. It is said—"Wheresoever he taketh him, he teareth him; and he foameth, and gnasheth with his teeth and pineth away." *That* was what this dumb devil did to that poor child; and, if the Devil had greater power over the bodies of men, when Jesus was Incarnate on earth, than he has now,— if he has lost something of his power over the *bodies* of men, he has not lost his power over human *hearts.* If he does not tear the bodies of men, as he tore the body of this poor boy, yet he does tear man's spiritual nature, that ought to soar up to high and heavenly things, and causes it to pine away in sorrow, shame and woe. What is the state of the spiritual nature of most of those whom I address, to-night? Is it not torn by the Devil? I do not mean, that the life of God is naturally within us; but I speak simply of the soul, with its capacities of knowing God, and of loving God, and of being like God. *Are* we like, do we *look* like God? Do we know God? Do we think God's thoughts, and desire God's desires? And are we longing to be perfectly like Him?

We see, in this case, what the Devil did, and if he is cast out of the *bodies* of men, he clings faster and faster to the *souls* of men, wherever he has the power; and he has the power wherever Jesus Christ is not found, by the Holy Spirit, dwelling in the heart. But he is not always an honest Devil where he has power; he does not always appear in his true character. He comes to some very often, in such a way, that they would not know him to *be* a Devil, if his character had not been exactly drawn, by the Holy Spirit, in the Word of God. He makes his appearance clear, bright, and lofty in thought often. But here we see truly, what he *was*, and what he could *do*.

Jesus Christ had given His disciples power over unclean spirits, He had given them power to cast out devils; and yet, there is a devil here that beats them. They come face to face with it, and they cannot manage it; they *cannot* cast it out. Though their Master had given them power to cast out devils, yet armed with that power as they were, there is a devil that they cannot cast out.

"I spake to Thy disciples that they should cast him out; and they could not."

Then Jesus speaks some words here, that require some thought, in order to see to *whom* He was speaking.

"O faithless generation, how long shall I be with you? how long shall I suffer you? bring him unto Me."

Now, when you come to read this verse, you are very likely to be very much puzzled. The question is, *Whom* was the Lord speaking to? *Who* is this wicked generation? Was it the disciples, who could not cast out the devil? or was it the multitudes gathered around them, who did not believe? Or, was it *both* of them? It would seem, as if our Lord did speak to them *all.* You know what He says, afterwards, to the disciples about "faith;" and it would seem that, when He was speaking of a "*faithless* generation," He spoke of all who were gathered round Him, and who were interested in the recovery of this poor child.

Now, what did He mean by this? "How long shall I be with you? How long shall I suffer you?" Well, let us look at the facts. This man, in consequence of what he saw, had brought his boy to the disciples, and had asked *them* to cast out the dumb spirit from his son; and he had expected that they *would* do it, that they *could* do it. And, very likely, he looked no higher than those nine disciples; and, very likely, the multitude around thought of nobody but the disciples doing it, and of their being armed with wonderful power, to rid the body of this poor boy of this frightfully wicked and unclean spirit. If that was *all* that they felt, we cannot call it *faith.* The disciples had no power over the Devil, except as that power was *derived* from Him, who was "manifested that He might destroy the works of the Devil." (1 John iii. 8). No one could destroy the works of the Devil, but He who met the Devil first in the wilderness, and then bruised him on the Cross. *He,* and

He *alone*, came to destroy *all* the works of the Devil; therefore, if the eye of these people looked no higher than those disciples, and imagined that no power, higher than theirs, was needed to subdue the power of the Wicked one, and looked not to the Source of power over the Wicked one—in Him, who came to take "the truth of our nature," and, as the second Adam, to overcome in that nature,—they had no real faith. No,—no more than when people think to get their soul saved by ministers and ordinances, and stop short of the grace in the heart of Jesus Christ on His Father's throne. There is no *faith* in believing in ministers, there is no *faith* in believing in ordinances, if we do not rise, above and through them, to the great living Head, Jesus Christ. There, and there alone, *true faith* has its exercise.

"Bring him unto ME."

"Do you not know that yet? It is but a stream that flows, as it were, through My disciples." He points out to them *where* faith must rest. This work requires *Divine* power—"Bring him unto *Me*." That answers it. That was where the mischief was, at first. There was the unbelief—expecting, apart from the Master, to get the blessing from His disciples. If they had come and expected, at the hands of the disciples, the exercise of power in Christ's name, and as coming alone from Him, that would have been something like true faith, however weak. But He has to teach them the lesson, in another way.

"And they brought him unto Him; and when he saw Him, straightway the spirit tare him; and he fell on the ground, and wallowed foaming."

Now, St. Mark, as I told you the other day, is very particular in his descriptions. We can fancy all this passing before our eyes—"he wallowed foaming." And Jesus asked the father, as his child lay there—

"How long is it ago since this came unto him?"
He would have the thought fixed on the poor, suffering child there, and He would have it all out. Was it since yesterday, or was it a week, or a month, or a year ago? Has he been suffering like this only a short time? *How long* is it ago?

"And he said, Of a child."
Now, just look at what Jesus gets out of this man. What *sort* of a devil is this? Is it a devil that has compassion, tormenting only for a little while, for a few days? No—"Of a child." Then we see that the Devil will take possession of a *child*, that he does not disdain to fix his fangs in a tender infant. Yes: he had fixed them in the child, and it had lived on thus through childhood to youth. The Devil had held him fast. No power had been able to extricate him from the hands of the Wicked one; and here, in his youth, he is still the subject of that dread, wicked spirit.

"And ofttimes it hath cast him into the fire, and into the waters, to destroy him."
Oh! see what the works of the Devil are! See how he will drive his subjects anywhere,—see how he will drive them into bad society, into evil practices, into dens of iniquity,—see how he will land them in the fire, or in the water—anywhere, to drown them in destruction! *This* is the work of *the Devil.*

" But if Thou canst do anything, have compassion on us, and help us."

When we look round about us everywhere, we see just *this*—the great work of the Devil going on, and we see men and women and children *loving* it,—helping it forward,—doing all they can for the Devil ! ! . . . . Surely there should be—but there is not—a great universal voice going up to the throne in Heaven—" have compassion on us, and help us." " The whole world lieth in the Wicked one," (1 John v. 19), and there is none to have compassion but this One—Christ Jesus. But how *careless* we are about Him ! Why are we not like this poor father, crying for our friends, for our children, for our fellow townspeople, for all around us—" Have compassion on us, and help us ? "

Look at this man. You see how weak his faith was —he says, " *If* Thou canst do anything." But what was it that made that man say " *If* " ? Was it unbelief ? It was unbelief, very likely, and he is rebuked presently for it ; but we should be very glad sometimes to hear this " if," rather than what we *do* hear. It was because of the deep, terrible, awful sense he had of the power before his face : and he says, " Look at that *power*, look at what this evil spirit does to my child ; look at its fearful malignity, month after month, year after year. Is there any power in the Universe that can—no *ordinary* power can—destroy the works of this Devil ? " Ah ! and is there *any power*,—we may well say—in the Universe, that can come into the heart, and uproot those cherished sins by which he holds his power over his slaves ?"—I know it *was* unbelief ; but it was that kind of unbelief, which real knowledge of the Devil's power over the soul brings. When a soul *knows* what power the Devil has over it, and how full of sin it is, then it asks, Is there any power in the Universe that can cleanse me from this ? " If Thou canst do *anything*, have compassion on us, and help us." It is a grand, noble prayer, from a broken heart—" I am a piece of my child, and my child is a piece of me, and I ask Thee to have compassion on *us*, and to help *us*."

" Jesus said unto him, If thou canst believe."

I said just now that his unbelief had to be rebuked ; and it is rebuked with another " *if*." You will always find that Christ answers in that way. If a man comes to Christ with an " if," he will get an " if " back again. If we come like the centurion, " I am not worthy that Thou shouldest come, but speak the word only, and my servant shall be healed"—the answer will be—" *As* thou hast believed, *so* be it done unto thee." (St. Matt. viii.). This man is so overwhelmed with the sense of the power and might of the Devil, that he comes with an " if," and gets an " if" back again. " *If* Thou canst do anything," says the man : " *if* thou canst believe," says Jesus.

" All things are possible to him that believeth."

" Who do you think that I am ? Do you think I am like one of My nine disciples—a mere man, who may fail in anything I undertake ? Or do you look to Me and trust Me, as One who has power over the spirits of darkness, and can order all things as the Lord of the

Universe? 'If thou canst believe.' *What* trust do you place in Me? Do you look to Me as the Lord of all? Do you look to Me as the Ruler of all? Do you look to Me as the Redeemer, as the One who has *come to* DESTROY *the works of the Devil?* Can you surrender your child into My hands? can you give him to Me? can you trust him to Me? can you cast him at My feet?" The man is challenged here by Jesus Christ— "*Can you believe?*" There is a great deal in that. Is he willing to give up his child to Jesus, and to say, "Do unto him even as Thou wilt?"

"And straightway the father of the child cried out, and said with tears, Lord, I believe; help Thou mine unbelief."

Now, there is faith, and there is wisdom, and there is humility. Where there is strong faith, there is almost always *some* unbelief. Where there is the most exalted confidence, there is also a deep sense of the need of help still in the human heart.

"When Jesus saw that the people came running together, He rebuked the foul spirit, saying unto him, Thou dumb and deaf spirit, I charge thee, come out of him, and enter no more into him."

If we could but just grasp this grand idea about Jesus Christ! We hear Him say, "Let there be light, and there *is* light," and we know that His Almighty power is ever in the world; but if we could only grasp this—Jesus says "I CHARGE THEE, come out of him, and enter no more into him!" If we could but realise that He is *ours*, if we believed in Him as our Saviour, if we walked with Him as our Master,—if we could but realise that He is our Husband, and Shepherd, and Friend—and that He has power, as the Shepherd of His flock, over every wolf that would come to destroy, that He has power over the mighty spirits of darkness and death!   Ponder this word—" *I charge thee.*"

If any one of us is under the power of the Wicked one, if any one here present is the slave, in his soul, in his life, in his home, of the spirit of darkness, it is because he has not been brought to Jesus, to hear Him say, "I charge thee, come out of him, and enter no more into him."   *This* was one of those devils that was wont to go back again.   One devil, when he had been cast out, said, " I will go back again ; " but he thinks it may be difficult to go back, and therefore he goes and fetches other devils of this kind," more wicked than himself "—and " they all enter in and dwell there ; and the last state of that man is worse than the first." (St. Luke xi. 26).   Look, then, at this spirit as it comes out,—

" And the spirit cried, and rent him sore, and came out of him ; and he was as one dead : insomuch that many said, He is dead."

Just as an old writer says, in his quaint way,—" Like a bad, unprincipled tenant, who does as much mischief as he can to the tenement he is being turned out of, so this foul spirit rends the poor child, ere it leaves him." See what the Devil *is*—see how *cruel*, how *merciless* he is ! so merciless that he will rend a child in pieces,— that he will cast him down as one dead,—that he will

" cast him into the fire and into the waters to destroy him.". And yet, perhaps, I am speaking to those who love the Devil, to those who love the Devil more than they love God,—nay, who do not love *God* at all, but who do love the Devil, and would rather be under *his* control, than under the sweet and gentle control of Jesus Christ,—to those who like to have the Devil in their homes, who like to frequent places where the Devil is, and where he holds his high festivals. They would rather live all their days as the friend of the Devil, than as the friend of Jesus Christ. The Devil, who is so loved, so obeyed everywhere, is seen truly here,—you see *what* he is, and you see *what*, if you are in love with him, you may expect from him, and what he will do with you.

"But Jesus took him by the hand, and lifted him up : and he arose."

It is Jesus who lifts him up again, and takes him by the hand. It is *Jesus* who brings help, and comfort, and strength, and gentleness, and kindness, and life-giving. It is *the Devil* who rends, and casts down, and tears, and causes to foam. It is *Jesus*, in His infinite gentleness, Who comforts and raises up the poor stricken ones ; and yet — JESUS is *rejected*, and the Devil is loved, cherished, served, obeyed ! The Devil can tell people to go, and they go ; the Devil can tell people to go and ruin *themselves*, and they go and ruin themselves. He can tell them to go and ruin their *children*, and they go and ruin their children,—he tells them to go and ruin their *friends* and their *relations*, and they go and do it.   He tells them to ruin their *bodies*, and they go and ruin their bodies ; he tells them to ruin their SOULS, and they go and ruin their souls.   He tells them to go and ruin their *fortunes*, and they go and ruin their fortunes —he tells them to go and ruin themselves for *time*, and they do it,—he tells them to ruin themselves for *eternity*, and *he is obeyed*.   He stalks about everywhere ; and if it were not for man's submission to him, and love of him, what happiness, what peace, what comfort there would be in families and human hearts !

But the Devil is strong, and *these* are his " works," And *this* is certain,—only serve him well, and he will pay you your wages, and deal infinitely worse with you, than he did with this child, because the duration of his power will be for ever, and his opportunities will be for ever.   He will do this, because he will do it in a world where there will be no restraining power.

"And when He was come into the house, His disciples asked Him privately, Why could not we cast him out ? "

I think it is a great lesson.   I am not so very sorry that these disciples had this downfall, and that they were made to feel how weak and helpless they were.   It is a great lesson to the Church in all ages,—to you and to me.

"And He said unto them, This kind can come forth by nothing but by prayer and fasting."

So that there are *different kinds*, different degrees *of devils*—one above another, one mightier than another, one more subtle than another, one more cruel than another.   There are various orders of them, and they rise up in their power; and here we see one of the worst, one of the mightiest, one of the cruellest—"*this kind.*"

Remember, there are weak kinds—timid devils that can be, apparently or really, overcome with comparative ease; but they have at their beck "legions," who are ready to help—"veterans" in sin—deep-stained, well-practised, experienced spirits of darkness. And we may not go to cast them out by ourselves, without a deep sense of our own weakness—"By prayer and fasting." We must get that deep sense of our own unworthiness, and of our Master's power, and only by that Master's power can they be driven out.

Our time is more than gone, because our subject is longer to-night. Let us gather, at any rate, these two lessons—

1. What the *Devil* is.

2. What *Jesus* is.

And then, "Choose you this day whom ye will serve."

XXI.

THE RAISING OF LAZARUS.

" Then when Jesus came, he found that he had lain in the grave four days already. Now Bethany was nigh unto Jerusalem, about fifteen furlongs off; and many of the Jews came to Martha and Mary, to comfort them concerning their brother. Then Martha, as soon as she heard that Jesus was coming, went and met him; but Mary sat still in the house. Then said Martha unto Jesus, Lord, if thou hadst been here, my brother had not died. But I know, that even now, whatsoever thou wilt ask of God, God will give it thee. Jesus saith unto her, Thy brother shall rise again. Martha saith unto him, I know that he shall rise again in the resurrection at the last day. Jesus said unto her, I am the resurrection, and the life; he that believeth in me, though he were dead, yet shall he live; and whosoever liveth and believeth in me shall never die. Believest thou this? She saith unto him, Yea, Lord; I believe that thou art the Christ, the Son of God, which should come into the world. And when she had so said, she went her way, and called Mary her sister secretly, saying, The-Master is come, and calleth for thee. As soon as she heard that, she arose quickly, and came unto him."—ST. JOHN xi. 17–29.

THE first thing we meet with, in this passage, is the Divine wisdom shining forth in our Blessed Lord and Master. We see how wisely He times His coming to Bethany. We see Him, in the previous verses, tarrying where He was, but not tarrying one moment beyond the *right* time ; and now, we see Him arriving at Bethany, at the *right* moment. He comes at a time, when many Jews from Jerusalem are gathered together at Bethany, —He comes at a time, when there can be no doubt in the minds of any that Lazarus is actually *dead*,—at a time when the sorrow is fresh and deep,—at a time when there had been no opportunity as yet, for other thoughts, for other feelings, for reviving joys, to soothe the memory of this great bereavement. The wound is still sore, it is still very deep ; Lazarus is certainly, un-mistakably, undeniably—*dead*.

We see also, in the previous verses, what must have been in our Lord's mind, and what His purpose was, with regard to His disciples. He was going to take them to the side of this grave, to confirm their faith, and to prepare them for a greater bereavement—for that trial of faith when they should see Him, their own Lord and Master, give up the ghost, and be laid in the tomb. We must not fail to note, in this account of the raising of Lazarus, the fact in the 17th verse,—

"When Jesus came, He found that he had lain in the grave four days already."

There is a difference—a strange difference—between Lazarus and the other two who had, previously, been raised by the word of Jesus. Our Lord comes to Bethany, at a moment when Lazarus "had lain in the grave *four days already*,"—at a moment when the Jews are still remaining, to do their best to comfort Martha and Mary. It would be interesting, if we could lift up the veil, and ascertain by what arguments,—by what

Y

statements, by what words, these Jews sought to pour comfort into these broken hearts. It is interesting to recall the custom of the Jews under such circumstances, — to remember that, when they assembled round the mourners, they placed one of their number as the special Comforter. It would be interesting to speculate, as to how these particular Jews would fulfil that office. No doubt, they were Pharisees, and therefore believers in the doctrine of the Resurrection ; and that truth must have been one element in any real, effectual consolation, that they would attempt to pour into the hearts of the bereaved sisters.

God, we know, had a purpose to fulfil—" This sickness is not unto death, but for the glory of God, that the Son of God might be glorified thereby," (ver. 4). We cannot suppose that these men—perhaps, not any of them—were real friends of Christ. Perhaps, it was some mere earthly relationship, some mere earthly connection, some mere earthly acquaintanceship, that brought them, from motives of mere human kindness and benevolence, to do their best under these trying circumstances. We have seen and heard, over and over again, the attempts of men like these to pour balm into wounded hearts, and we have seen how utterly fruitless have been their best efforts.

"**Now Bethany was nigh unto Jerusalem, about fifteen furlongs off,**" says the sacred historian, to account for the presence of these men. It is an important statement, it is an important fact, that there were witnesses from Jerusalem itself,—that the raising of Lazarus

was not done in a corner,—that it was not wrought only
in the presence of the immediate household of the de-
ceased man, and of the mere villagers of Bethany; but
Jerusalem was two miles from Bethany, and inhabitants
of Jerusalem heard of the decease of Lazarus. They
were near enough to be acquainted with the fact, they
heard of it somehow, there was a channel of communication between the two places—the news travelled,
and brought kind men from Jerusalem to Bethany at
this time. The resurrection of Lazarus was a thing,
which must be well authenticated *in Jerusalem*, as well
as in Bethany. The comforters of Mary and Martha,
we thus see, came from the Holy City.

**"Then Martha, as soon as she heard that Jesus was
coming, went and met Him; but Mary sat still in the
house."**

It would appear that our Lord halted. He knew
perfectly well what was going on in the house of Martha
and Mary, and He appears to have remained with His
disciples, at a little distance. A messenger goes and
reports His coming; He tarries there, and as soon as
Martha hears that Jesus is coming, she sets out at
once. There is, apparently, no feeling of anger or
bitterness in the mind of this woman, because of the
grievous disappointment she had undergone. All this
seems to have had no place in her generous heart,—
immediately, she went out to meet Him. The passage
I have read for us to meditate upon, to-night, is a
passage that shows the various weaknesses, and the
varied strength, of weak believers. There is something

remarkably touching in this woman's having sent the
message to Jesus, and being grievously disappointed at
His not coming—that feeling she thoroughly lays bare,
subsequently,—yet, when she hears that He is within
reach, that moment she bounds off.

"But Mary sat still in the house."

The position of this sister is equally interesting, but
scarcely so commendable.　Hers seems to be the position of one grievously overwhelmed.　She was one who
had sat at His feet and heard His word,—one who was,
presently, able to anoint Him for His Burial,—yet, when
the crushing trial came home to her, it proved to be
crushing indeed.　*Martha*, then, was first at the feet of
Jesus ; she seems to remind us of St. Peter in this
respect.　And she said,—

**"Lord, if Thou hadst been here, my brother had not
died."**

Now she lets out all that is in her heart, at once.
We see just by these few words, as clear as the sun at
noonday, the position of this holy woman,—" Lord, if
Thou hadst been here."　" *Why* wast Thou not here ?
Surely it was not kind.　If Thou hadst been here, this
evil might have been averted ; therefore why wast Thou
not here ?"

Here we see, at once, distrust,—we see a tendency
in her heart to believe that she knows better where
her Lord ought to have been, than He knew Himself.
" Lord, if Thou hadst been *here*."　But more than
that—while in her secret heart she discredits the wisdom, and discredits the kindness of Jesus, she discredits

His power, likewise. There was enough in the history of His going about "doing good," with which she must have been well acquainted, to have taught her a great lesson, in this respect. She must have heard of the centurion who said—"Lord, I am not worthy that Thou shouldest come under my roof, but speak the word only, and my servant shall be healed," when Jesus said, "I have not found so great faith, no, not in Israel;" no, not in Bethany—no, not in the house of Martha and her sister Mary. She can only say, "Lord, *if* Thou hadst been *here.*" Thus we see, all at once, the ignorance and unbelief coming out. She cannot believe that He has been kind, that He has been wise; she cannot believe that He has all power in His hands, and that He could have said when beyond Jordan,—"Thy brother liveth."

And truly, there are a great many things that do not enter into our minds when the pressure is on us, that *ought* to enter,—and that do enter when the pressure is *not* on us,—and that would greatly strengthen and comfort us if they did present themselves, when the pressure *is* on us. This woman had seen her brother languishing—dying—buried,—and he had been "in the grave four days already;" and she knew that Jesus had been told, several days ago, of this sickness, and He had never come—and was that *like* Him?—"Lord, if Thou hadst been here, my brother had not died." And when we listen to the talk of the Christian Church, we hear almost this identical sentence, almost the same words—'If I could hear Jesus call with His voice, if I could look up into His face, if He would walk here as He did in Palestine,—if I could come to Him as the Centurion came, as the Leper came,—*then* I could trust." " Lord, if Thou hadst been here."

O what thorough ignorance there is in all this of the real nature of Jesus,—as to *Who* He is, and as to *what* He is,—as if He were not GOD, always at hand, and One Who can see into all hearts and circumstances, and Who is as able to save from beyond Jordan as if He were on this side of it, and as able to save from the Throne of His Father, as when He was sojourning here below. " Lord, if Thou hadst been here, if we had had Thy bodily presence, we should not have had trouble."

How did she know that ? *How* did she know that, if He had been there, Lazarus would not have died ? If it was right and wise and good for it to happen, when He was at a distance, would it not have been right and wise and good for it to happen, when He was near at hand ? How often we say, " *This* would not have happened—*that* would not have happened,—we should not have had this trial, we should not have had this bereavement—Lord, if Thou hadst been here."

We see, then, this good, excellent, confiding, generous woman, who loved the Lord and was loved of Him, darkly ignorant as to His real nature. We see, that when trouble and affliction come heavily upon her, her faith fails, her fancied knowledge of the Lord passes away ; if He is not *on the spot*, if He has not love enough to *come*, she thinks He has not power enough to

save, " Lord, if Thou hadst been here, my brother had
not died."

We might illustrate this sentence in a variety of ways,
did time permit.   The only thing I desire to show you,
to-night, is the thorough misapprehension of our Lord's
character, person, and power, and of His heart, too, by
Martha, that required to be set right.   The same misapprehension, I fear, lives still, and we say—" The
Lord tarries long, He has not put forth His hand, He
has forgotten to be gracious,"—whereas, if we thoroughly
knew and understood Him, we should know that He is
always near, *always* kind, *always* wise, *always* powerful.

**"But I know, that even now, whatsoever Thou
wilt ask of God, God will give it Thee."**

And so we see her, with all this misapprehension,
still clinging to her Lord.   She has nothing else to
cling to.   He has failed her, she thinks ; He has
not done what He might,—yet she has nobody else,
and she cannot help, to some extent, believing.   " I
know, that *even now*, whatsoever Thou wilt ask of God,
God will give it Thee."   All her hopes are not buried.
She cannot look up into the face of her Lord, she cannot realise any portion of His work, without believing
that He is the hope of Israel, and her hope.   " I know,
that even now, *whatsoever* Thou wilt ask of God, God
will give it Thee."

So far, so good ; but it is far from being enough.
What kind of idea was there in this woman's mind con-
cerning Jesus Christ?   What conception had she of
Him?   We could with calmness consider this subject,

if it were not for the sad conviction that, with greater light, with greater opportunities of knowledge, there are many Marthas still,—that many, who are called Christians, are no further than this—" I know that whatsoever Thou wilt *ask* of God, God will give it Thee."   I know there is a great truth in all this ; Jesus "ever liveth to make intercession," as the Mediator of Redemption for His people.   But was that *all?*   We are speaking now of raising the dead, we are speaking now of *life given back again;* and Martha sets aside Him Who is standing before her, and speaks to Him as if He were only some good, holy, superior being, who had power with God, as Elias, to open and shut heaven.   This is all, that, at this moment, she sees.   " Thou hast failed, but go to God for me—I know that, whatsoever Thou wilt ask of God, God will give it Thee."   It is little better, apparently, than a prayer addressed to a saint.

"**Jesus saith unto her, Thy brother shall rise again.**"

There is something very tender, in the way the Lord asserts His own glory,—there is something very touching, in His way of dealing with unbelieving and erring saints.   " Thy brother shall rise again."   There is a Divine wisdom in this ; the Lord would exercise this woman's mind, He would awaken her interest.   He gives her first a promise, not *how*, or *when*, or by *whom*, but—" Thy brother SHALL rise again,"—that the word may come into her heart, and revive her strength and hope.   He leads her upward, and directs her thoughts, not to the grave where Lazarus lay, but to the resurrection. How—when—by what means,—that is another thing; but there is the promise of the *fact*—"thy brother *shall rise* again.

You will remember, that she had no promise to warrant her thought of his not dying. It was never promised that he should not die. Now the great promise is given—he shall *rise again,* but her mind is to be exercised concerning that fact. How is it to be? when is it to be? by whom is it to be?

"**I know that he shall rise again in the resurrection at the last day.**"

"I know"—as if she had said, "I know that my Redeemer liveth." This was an Article of Confession in the believing Jews' Creed—"I believe in the Resurrection of the Body." Here she had got hold of a great truth, but that truth had been no strength, no comfort to her. She had got hold of it, she said it, she believed it; but how little intelligence was there in her mind concerning it! "I know that he shall rise again in the resurrection at the last day." And we believe that, multitudes believe it, and have just as little intelligent perception of it, as Martha had.

"**Jesus said unto her, I am the Resurrection and the Life; he that believeth on Me, though he were dead,** (and buried, like Lazarus), **yet shall he live. And whosoever liveth** (like Martha and Mary), **and believeth in Me shall never die,**"—shall "not die eternally."

Now then, this woman had the privilege of receiving this great announcement. She believed unintelligently

about the Resurrection at the last day; she had no idea
of the mode of the Resurrection, or by whom it was
actually to be accomplished—whether it would be by
an act of mere power, just as the work of Creation.
But the work of Resurrection is a very different thing, to
the work of Creation. The work of Resurrection comes
through perfect Redemption.

"I am the Resurrection."

She had never seen *that;* she had never apprehended,
thoroughly, the simple truth, that the corn of wheat must
fall into the ground, and die, and then rise, bearing
much fruit. (St. John xii. 24). She had never understood this one thing—that the Resurrection of the Head
includes in it the Resurrection of the whole body,—that,
in the Resurrection of Jesus Christ, *life* was redeemed
back for sinners who had forfeited it—a life in which
they might live for ever. " I AM the Resurrection,"—

"And the Life."

But *how* is Jesus Christ the Life? By *redeeming* life,
—by bringing it out of death; not by creating it anew,
not by performing a mere act of creative power, but by
taking that life, and laying that life down in death, and
coming out of death as a Conqueror,—bringing it back
again from the power of death. This presents us, at
once, with the great fact that there is no life, no living
eternally in glory, but in connection with Jesus Christ.
All else is but *Death.* He is Life, and in Him is the
Life of sinners. " I am the Resurrection and the Life;
he that believeth in Me, though he were dead, yet shall
he live," and if you believe, you shall never die. One-

ness with Christ, and oneness *in* Christ, is life eternal ; so that it is not real death—" Our friend Lazarus *sleepeth*."

" Believest thou this ?"

" Believest thou *this ?* Thou dost believe in the Resurrection at the last day, but dost thou believe that *I* am the Resurrection, and that *I* am the Life ?"

We have here an instance of grievous want of perception, yet, at the same time, of strong faith mixed with much ignorance, darkness, and unbelief. **" She saith unto Him, Yea, Lord ;"** and then goes on to another subject, and presents us with a confession of her faith,— a remarkable confession it was, as being beside the present point, and remarkable also in its fulness.

" I believe that Thou art the Christ, the Son of God, which should come into the world."

She says, " I cannot take in all this, Lord,—all this about the Resurrection and the Life, about the dead living, and the living continuing to live. I cannot apprehend that, but I do know *one* thing—I believe that Thou art the Christ, the Son of God, which should come into the world"—and then she is happy about all the rest. If only she has got hold of this, she can leave everything ; if only she has got Him, all things else will come right. " I am very ignorant (she seems to say), I am very unbelieving, I cannot grasp all this marvellous truth,—but I lay hold of *Thee.* ' Thou art the Christ.' Whatever unbelieving thoughts I have had of Thee, whatever hard thoughts, whatever mistrust, when Thou didst not come,—though there seemed to be shadows on Thy face, and I began to think, and to think wrongly about Thee,—yet, 'Lord, to whom else can I go? Thou hast the words of eternal life,'—'I believe, help Thou mine unbelief.' I do not pretend to give a full confession of faith concerning all these things, but I *will* say this—I believe that Thou art THE CHRIST. I believe that if there is hope for sinners living, like me, it is in *Thee,*—and that if there is resurrection for believers who are dead like Lazarus, it is in *Thee.* I believe that if the prophets gave promise of One who was to come, it is *Thou.* If there is life for the dead, it is in *Thee.* Then, having got hold of *that,* I leave everything else."

There is such a thing as sitting at the feet of Christ, learning all He has to teach,—and that gives strength, and intelligence, and faith, and hope; and there is such a thing as great ignorance about many things in the Divine plan, and in the Divine truth, but yet a simple clinging and cleaving to Him, who is "the Way, and the Truth, and the Life." (St. John xiv. 6). Martha seems to say—"I am but a little child, I can only do this—cling to Thee. I am but very weak, very blind, very sinful; I know but very little, but I know THEE; and I put all things into Thy hands." This woman needed teaching, she needed guidance, she needed great and long instruction; but she had got hold of the fundamental verity—*she had got hold of Christ.* When she heard of His coming, she ran to meet Him; when He is come, she has no hope but in Him. Dark as her views were, weak as her faith was, unable as she was to apprehend other mysteries, she could apprehend this,—"Thou art the Christ, the Son of God."

So, let the weak in faith take courage; do not stop there, but go and sit at Jesus' feet. But when we see mysteries that we cannot fathom,—when we feel the darkness which we cannot see through,—when burdens oppress us that we can scarcely bear,—when trials come that try us to the quick,—when, like this tempest-tossed woman, we are getting into difficulties in things temporal and in things spiritual, let us take care to cling to this as our sheet-anchor—"Thou art the Christ; I cling to Thee. I let the mysteries go, I let the darkness go,— Thou art the Christ, I will go with Thee. Though my precious and beloved one lies in the grave, Thou art near the grave, and Thou art the Christ; there is no darkness in which I cannot be comforted by the touch of Thine hand,—no circumstances in which I cannot feel hope, while I am leaning on Thee." "*I know,*" she says,—"I believe that Thou art the Christ, the Son of God, which should come into the world."

And look, again, at the practical tone of her mind. We need practical Christianity; and this woman, whatever else she may have been, was thoroughly practical. We see it in these little things.

"When she had so said, she went her way, and called Mary her sister secretly, saying, The Master is come, and calleth for thee."

That was a very sisterly thing to do. She might, very naturally, have stopped and done something else; she might have asked questions, perhaps puzzling questions about what manner of man Lazarus would be in the resurrection; but "she went her way, and called Mary her sister,"—a very sisterly act. Whatever we may think of her, when she went to the Master and asked Him to bid Mary help her,—*here* she is a real, true sister; she would not be at the feet of Jesus without her sister,—"The Master is come, and calleth for thee." It is a beautiful and touching incident, and it is worthy of all imitation. It was done with a Divine simplicity,—"She went her way, and called Mary her sister *secretly*, saying, The Master is come, and calleth for thee." They are but few words, yet they are words that must live for ever—and an example that must live for ever — *Martha calling her sister to the Master's feet.*

And there is another lesson to be learnt from them,— how little we can tell who will be our helpers, how little we know on whom we may lean some day. When we saw Martha "cumbered about much serving," and Mary at the feet of Jesus hearing His word, and shooting on ahead, as it were, ever so much, we should have said— "Mary will always be first." But the moment comes in the life of the more advanced in faith, when one, whom we may have considered weak, is the one to lend a helping hand, and to go with the word of comfort and admonition—"*The Master is come*, and calleth for *thee*." The strong, oftentimes, are helped by the weak; those are often last, who were very much first. The Master uses Martha to help Mary; and He can use very weak instruments to help those who appear to be strong.

"**As soon as she heard that, she arose quickly, and came unto Him.**"

We would have the example of *Martha* followed ; we would have the example of *Mary* followed. Here we see the two sisters, in great affliction, and what do they do ? As soon as Martha hears of Jesus, she arises and comes to Him, and then she fetches her sister—where to ? To the feet of Christ, that, in the time of sorrow, when others had comforted perhaps in vain, the two *together* in their woe, might be *together* at the feet of Jesus. "As soon as she heard that, she arose quickly, and came unto Him."

And, you may depend upon this, no sorrow can befall us in which we cannot find comfort *there*,—and a great additional comfort it is when all the sufferers are *together*, heart joined to heart, as it were, gathered round the feet, and looking up into the face of Jesus. There we shall be in rest,—there we shall be in peace.

XXII.

THE RAISING OF LAZARUS.

(*Continued.*)

"*Now Jesus was not yet come into the town, but was in that place where Martha met him. The Jews then which were with her in the house, and comforted her, when they saw Mary, that she rose up hastily and went out, followed her, saying, She goeth unto the grave to weep there. Then when Mary was come where Jesus was, and saw him, she fell down at his feet, saying unto him, Lord, if thou hadst been here, my brother had not died. When Jesus therefore saw her weeping, and the Jews also weeping which came with her, he groaned in the spirit, and was troubled, and said, Where have ye laid him? They said unto him, Lord, come and see. Jesus wept. Then said the Jews, Behold how he loved him! And some of them said, Could not this man, which opened the eyes of the blind, have caused that even this man should not have died?*"—St. JOHN xi. 30—37.

LAST week, we broke off the consideration of this narrative, at the point where Mary, having received, from her sister, the information of the Lord's coming, had arisen quickly and gone forth to meet Him. Our subject, this evening, opens with the declaration that our Lord, for wise and necessary purposes, had abstained from coming into the village of Bethany, or near to the house of Martha and Mary, but had remained outside the village. He abode still **"in that place where Martha met Him."**

To this place Mary resorts; she goes out "quickly," at the first intimation of His approach. She rushes at once to the feet of her Master—into the presence of her Lord, and comes to Him in the very same spot where Martha had met Him.

We have, then, before us, at the present moment, the conduct of Jesus in this matter, the conduct of Mary, and the conduct of Martha.

A meeting had been effected between the longed-for Lord, and these two longing spirits. How they had waited for Him, as they that watch for the morning! How they had watched, how they had longed, how they had prayed, and how impatient they had been at that long delay! We must not pass by this part of the subject, without attempting somewhat to realise the feelings, with which they found themselves again in the presence of the Lord. He had never disappointed them *before*,—He had never failed, before, to justify their loftiest conception of His character and of His work,—He had never, before, been wanting in any single thing; but *now* He has disappointed them. It appears as if He had failed now,—it appears as if something had happened which He either *would* not, or *could* not, grapple with. They have asked Him to do something, and He has not done it; they have asked Him to bear their burden, and, apparently, He has not borne it,—yet " Jesus loved Martha, and her sister, and Lazarus," and Lazarus, and Martha, and her sister loved Jesus. But a new feeling has crept into the hearts of these women, since last they saw Him,—nevertheless,

z

they love Him still, and there is some indescribable, irresistible influence drawing them to His feet, as the dearest place on earth. They came to the place where Martha had met Him, where He was waiting for them. *Why* did He wait? Was He conscious that He had disappointed them? Was He unwilling to enter the house, to which He had delayed to come until it was too late?

Let us, however, now proceed, at once, to consider the Jews who had come from Jerusalem as comforters to the bereaved sisters.

" The Jews then which were with her in the house, and comforted her, when they saw Mary, that she rose up hastily and went out, followed her, saying, She goeth unto the grave to weep there."

We have to look at the conduct of these people. They were come to *comfort* their friends, they were there for that only purpose. Martha, however, had gone out, and, apparently, they had not noticed it. Now Mary goes out, and the moment " they saw *Mary*, that she rose up hastily and went out"—we know not where Martha was at this time—they " followed her, saying, She goeth unto the grave to weep there." Their one thought was,—Lazarus is gone, he is lost; theirs is nothing, for the present, but a hopeless, uncomforted sorrow. If these men had, any of them, been Sadducees, or had had any infection of Sadducism in them, their conception of the present subject would be darker and gloomier still. Their one thought and feeling is that of a hopeless, crushing sorrow in the heart of these women, and that the place where they can best express it, is at the graveside. "She goeth unto *the grave* to weep *there*," and they follow.

There was nothing wrong in Mary's going to the grave to weep, there was nothing wrong in her going to the grave to ponder, there was nothing wrong in her going to the grave that she might stir up her faith to look, through the gate and grave of death, to the life that is beyond it. But there was, evidently, in those who gathered round her, a feeling such, perhaps, as that which we see in the Jews now, who come to a certain spot under the Temple wall, for the express purpose of weeping and wailing. There is a " Jews' wailing place." These men were, evidently, very poor comforters ; their intentions were good, but their powers were small. " She goeth to the grave to *weep* there,"—and they will go and manifest their sorrow there, too ; they are there almost as professional weepers round the grave. What hopelessness ! What desolateness of heart ! Their sorrow is unmitigated, unredeemed—Lazarus is lost, and the world is desolate, and dark gloom and shadows settle on it. Nature is cut and halved, and there is little beyond nature to be seen,—the grave and tears, and that is just all. " She goeth unto the grave to weep there."

Yet, at that very moment, when they see nothing but darkness, sorrow, tears and the grave, there was the Eternal Life within a few yards of them. Like the woman in the wilderness, hiding herself from her own flesh lest she should see its death, while there was a spring of water close at hand, if only her eyes had been opened to see it,—so these men see the Grave and the great hopeless sorrow, and yet there is, within reach, a spring of living water, "springing up into everlasting life." (St. John iv. 14).   There is close at hand One Who could say, "O death, I will be thy plagues : O grave, I will be thy destruction ; repentance shall be hid from Mine eyes." (Hosea xiii. 14).   They saw sorrow—they saw woe, and they saw death ; but they could not see Him, Who was "THE LIFE."

"Then when Mary was come where Jesus was, and saw Him, she fell down at His feet."

Here we find Mary again at the feet of Jesus.   We have seen her there, on a former occasion, sitting at His feet, and learning His words.   Yes ! she *did* learn them, she did drink in the meaning of His teaching— of His words ; they did sink into her heart, they found a "good ground," and sank deep.   And you may depend upon this, whenever the words of Jesus do, in truth, sink into the hearts of people, they will not only be there for real edification, and as blessed knowledge,—but they will have to be tried and put to the test, how far they have been really learned, how far they have been really trusted, how far they have been precious to the soul, so that it can, in truth, live upon them, lean upon them, rest upon them, in the dark, dark day !   Mary had learned enough from her Lord, to lead her to anoint Him for His *Burying*, while the whole College of the Apostles remained ignorant, and unbelieving, about the fact of the Lord's approaching Death.

We must not imagine, because of the present circumstances, that all her sitting at His feet, and hearing His words, had been unfruitful. It was just because she *had* learned, that her faith was so put to the test, to see if she had got it for her very own—to see if she had grasped His words, and leaned on them—to see if she had learned the lesson—" Let not your heart be troubled; believe in God, believe also in Me,"—whether she had so learnt the fact of His coming to be death's conqueror, that she can in peace see the grave open, and know that her brother will not be *left* under the power of death, but that he shall rise again to glory and everlasting life.

" Then when Mary was come where Jesus was, **and saw Him**."—" Sir," said some, " we would *see* Jesus." (St. John xii. 21). They only really know Him, who by faith have seen Him, who have seen by faith " the glory of God " shining " in the face of Jesus Christ," and who are able to say, " One thing have I desired of the Lord, that will I seek after; that I may dwell in the house of the Lord all the days of my life, to behold the beauty of the Lord, and to enquire in His temple." (Ps. xxvii. 4).

When Mary " saw Him, **she fell down at His feet**."

We read in the book of Revelation, of this Evangelist St. John—" when I saw Him, I fell at His feet as dead," (Rev. i. 17); and so Mary, when *she* saw Him, fell at His feet. I do not think this is to be put down to mere human weakness, nor do I think it was an act of worship. It seems to be just this—whoever truly sees

Christ, does fall at His feet—is laid low in deep humility—is made to feel that his or her place is at the *feet* of the Master. "She fell down at His *feet.*" Where could she be better? What happier place could there be for her than at the feet of her Lord? Where else could she get peace, comfort, and blessing?

When we look on all these poor, well-intentioned Jews—with their good motives, and their excellent intentions, and their effort and willingness to sacrifice themselves—coming to comfort her, we ask, what could they do? They had not cast a single ray of comfort into her heart, they had not wiped away a single tear, they could not lift up her disconsolate heart for one moment. She goes out from their presence—they think, to the grave, but really—to the feet of her Master, and *there*, there is peace, and *there*, there is happiness. Whatever may be our philosophy, whatever may be the efforts of our own mind, whatever power we may have to bring in all the world has to give, there are times and seasons when not one, or all, of these can cast a ray of light into the heart—when they cannot give rest for a single hour to the troubled spirit—when there is not a place in the whole Universe where the weary one can rest, but only at the feet of Jesus, "When she saw Jesus, she fell down at His feet." Happy is the sight of this woman as we see her now, looking up into the face of her Lord, and seeing what He is, and then laid low at His feet!

Well, they who lie at the feet of Jesus often have manifold imperfections of faith, hope, and knowledge.

We find it so even with Mary here.   She had seen His love beaming forth in His face, inspiring confidence and trust as she looked upon it—that face beautified with beauty above the sons of men, yet so soon to be " marred more than any man " (Isa. lii. 14)—and her confidence all comes back again ; she sees what she can implicitly, unhesitatingly trust.   She trusts Him, but yet she says,—

" Lord, if Thou hadst been here, my brother had not died."

She takes her sister's words, no ! not quite her sister's words—they are the same in our translation, but they are not quite the same as they were originally uttered. There is only a slight difference—but a shade, and it is hard to catch the difference, but there *is* one.   " Lord, if Thou hadst been here, my brother had not *lain there dead*," says MARTHA.   " Lord, if Thou hadst been here, *death had never come near my brother*," says MARY.   That shows a slight difference in these two women's minds, in their perception of Jesus.

But Mary could not go further,—it is " Lord, if Thou hadst *been here*," still.   It is this,—while He is away, while He is not seen fulfilling His words, and giving tangible proofs of His love,—while He is not sending messages, nor hastening to the spot, she doubts ; but, when she looks up into His face, she sees that which her heart must trust—she *must* trust Him.   Blessed are they that see and believe, but *more* " blessed are they that have not seen, and yet have believed." (St. John xx. 29).   She looks, she sees, and she trusts ; but she cannot trust at a distance, she does not know Him afar off as being all that she wants—she has to learn that lesson painfully. We like to look at people as perfection—we like to look at Christians as perfection, but they are all imperfection. We have little else to do here, but to learn how imperfect we are, and to learn the glory of the Lord. There was that in Mary which was very blessed—she " saw," and then she could not but confide in her Lord ; but she trusted only *when* she saw.

Now we have to try and look into the heart of Jesus. **"When Jesus therefore saw her weeping, and the Jews also weeping which came with her, He groaned in the spirit, and was troubled."**

There was a very Bochim round about Him—a valley of tears. He saw the tears flowing from all this variety of characters ; the death of Lazarus, and the sorrow of the household, had moved these Jews to tears. Perhaps, some of them could weep without much feeling, others may have wept from deep feeling, and Martha and Mary for their deep, deep woe. And Jesus stood there in this valley of Bochim—stood there amidst the tears. What a picture it is ! Jesus Christ, the Incarnate Son of God, standing amidst the tears, and sorrow, and woe, and seeing them all weeping ! We endeavour to look into the heart of Jesus, and we find that—"He groaned in the spirit, and was troubled" in the spirit; He stirred up all the trouble of which His great, tender heart was capable.

Now, I say, we try to look into the heart of Jesus,—

it is not an easy thing; it is a very solemn scene this,
and not without things to warn us to be very careful,
how we try to interpret what was in the heart of our
Lord, at this time. There was pain in His heart, there
was trouble in His heart, there was sorrow in His heart
—whence came it? What caused it? *Why* did He
stand there amongst those tears, groaning and troubling
His own heart?

There is something mysterious in it. He knew what
He would do—He knew what He could do—He
knew for what purpose Lazarus was laid in the grave—
He knew what He could effect in one minute—that He
could say to the dead—"Arise," and so fill the hearts
of these weeping ones with joy and gladness. But He
does not hasten to do it at the first moment; He stays
—He, Who holds the power of giving back life, and
restoring Lazarus to his sisters, and making a scene of
joy out of that Bochim—HE delays there, stirring up the
trouble of His heart, groaning in the spirit.

We cannot look on this without rightly fearing, lest
we should go beyond propriety in our thoughts concerning it; but if we only get *that* lesson, we shall have
gained something,—in these days of deep irreverence
and impatience—in days when the human mind so dis-
putes the works of God,—it is well *to stop short*, and
to see in all this a picture, a symbol, a foreshadowing,
of something very solemn. We have seen the Lord
tarrying beyond Jordan; then He had stayed two days
ere He comes to the village of Bethany. Now the
mourners are at His feet, weeping—and *again* He stops,

"groaning in the spirit," and "troubled"—as if He could do nothing, as if He could not help them, as if He could only shed tears, like the Jews, in sympathy with the sisters,—" He *groaned.*" There is a time for all God's works; there is a time for His Providence to act. There is a right moment for each thing to be done, and there is something to be learned here, in what takes place before Jesus will come to the grave.

Let us never, *never* forget this in all our sorrows, that Jesus stood in the midst of a Bochim—that He saw the sorrow and heard the weeping, and that He was moved by it—that His very heart " groaned " at the sight of all He saw. The tears were being wrung out of breaking hearts, yet He did not hasten—He delayed, tarried, waited, as the groaning but sympathising, as the troubled but tender Lord of Life. He does not at once tell them what is to happen, but He stands " groaning in the spirit,—

"**And said, Where have ye laid him?**"

There is to be, manifestly, no collusion between the Lord and these two sisters. " *Where* have ye laid him?" The Lord knew everything ; He knew that Lazarus had been sick, He knew that Lazarus had died, and *He knew*, of course, where they had laid him ; but He will be guided, He will be led by those weepers to the place of death. Just as God called Adam—"Where art thou?" (Gen. iii. 9). He would have him come and show himself in all his nakedness, ruin, and rebellion,—so Jesus would have others to guide His feet to the side of the grave.

There is something very touching in all this,—the Saviour asking *mortal* men to guide HIM to the place of *death*,—Jesus asking that the Lord of *Life* may be taken, by those who have the seeds of *death* working in them, to the *tomb*. "Where have ye laid him?" It is a touching sight to see Jesus being guided to the tomb of Lazarus—to see Him going to the grave; there is in it something beyond what at first sight appears. How blessed is it that we can go and tell Jesus "where" we have "laid" our dead—where we have laid them, "in sure and certain hope of the Resurrection to eternal life." It is a sacred spot where the "dead in Christ" rest. It is very comforting to see that there is One, with all power, and tenderness, and compassion, and love, Who will permit himself to be guided to the place where the dead lie. "Where have ye laid him?"

We have heard another cry,—"Come, see the place *where* THE LORD *lay*." (St. Matt. xxviii. 6). Now, we have the Lord going to the place where the *dead* lay. We have seen Mary coming and sitting at Jesus' feet; it is blessed to see the living go to the feet of the living God. Now, we see the same feet going to the *tomb* of Lazarus.

"They said unto Him, Lord, come and see."

Unconsciously, perhaps, uttering the prayer which has been given to the Church to use in all ages. Alas! how she forgets it! "Lord, come and see. Come and see where the dead in Christ are sleeping, come and see the graves of earth so filled, these sepulchres so sated. Come and see." It is a grand, glorious prayer

to be poured into the ear of Him, Who said—"I am
THE LIFE"—"Come and see the place of *Death*"—to
bring the Lord of Life to His real work, to bring Him
to fulfil His promise, "O *death*, I will be thy plagues,"
(Hosea xiii. 14),—to hasten the day, when "shall be
brought to pass the saying that is written, *Death* is
swallowed up in victory." (1 Cor. xv. 54). "Lord,
come and see."

There is no prayer but this that we may rightly pray
for the dead, and for the dead we *may* pray *this* prayer,
—"Lord, come and see." We may pray for the dead
thus, in the petition, "Come and see," that the dead in
Christ may arise. And,—

"Jesus wept."

These words defy all exposition; they warn us that
we are on holy ground. What *can* we say of them?
Remember, this word is not the same word that is used
of the weeping of Mary, and of the Jews. The word in
the 35th verse—"Jesus *wept*," is "Jesus *shed tears*."
The other is a demonstrative weeping—to cry—to
weep; but *this* was a *silent* weeping. The word used is
intended to convey the idea of tears silently flowing
down—no crying—no noise—no exclamation—no de-
monstration; but the silent pouring out of tears down
the cheek of the Saviour, as He stood there,—the fountain opened, as it were, and the tears silently falling
down. "Jesus *wept*."

We hear of His weeping "with *strong crying* and
tears." (Heb. v. 7). We hear of His weeping over
Jerusalem with strong lamentation; but *here* it was in

absolute silence. "Jesus wept." I repeat,—these words defy exposition. It is just the heart of Jesus pouring itself out.

"Then said the Jews, Behold how He loved him!"

Now I have not attempted, this evening, to explain difficulties. I have rather felt that there is some danger in attempting it; we may be easily led into unprofitable speculation. What was it that caused this groaning and troubling, and these tears? Was it the hard-heartedness of the Jews? Was it the sorrow of Martha and Mary? Or was it for Lazarus laid in the grave? *What* was it?

I have not attempted to meet these inquiring thoughts. Jesus had come into the scene of sorrow, weeping, and bereavement, and "Jesus wept." Were the tears shed because of death—death which symbolised the utmost of the ruin, that sin has brought into the world? Was it that He saw its ravages, saw the evil all around? Was it for *this* that He wept? When these Jews saw Him weeping, they interpreted it, saying, "Behold how He *loved* him!"

"Behold how *He* loved him!"—There is something very striking in these words. Who were those that spake them? Some of the Jews who had come to comfort Martha and Mary; and they see One so quiet, yet withal so full of tenderness, so full of compassion, so full of love—His heart silently manifesting its sorrow, —and they, who perhaps respected Him, see signs and tokens of something deeper than they themselves felt— "Behold *how* He loved him!"

And yet, these words mean more than they who

spake them knew.   Had they any conception of the
love which Christ bore to Lazarus?   They look at the
tears on His cheeks; had they any conception of the
great love, that would pour out Its very life-blood for
the man, over whose tomb He now wept?   Had they
any idea of the love that brought Him down from His
Father's throne, and that would carry Him up to the
accursed tree?   No.   We talk of the sympathy of
Christ, and we look at Christ's goodness, and at all that
He has done ; but do we not, very often, see little more
than these Jews when they said—" Behold, how He
loved him ? "   Are *we* able to look deeper, and deeper,
and to realise all that was in the Saviour's heart?
Whilst they looked at Him weeping beside Lazarus'
grave, did they think of the tears that were to be wept
in Gethsemane, and of the Blood that was to be shed
on Calvary, ere He could be the Victor of death?
They little knew.   They did not " know the love of
Christ, which passeth knowledge," (Eph. iii. 19);
they could only interpret His heart by the tears they
saw on His cheeks.   But still, there was something even
in that ; it was something, if only they could be brought
to see, in this small way, the love of Jesus.   Contrast it
with what follows.

**" And some of them said, Could not this man, which
opened the eyes of the blind, have caused that even
this man should not have died ? "**

Then they admit—these men do,—that He *had*
" opened the eyes of the blind."   Unbelief, very often,
over-reaches itself.   These unbelieving Jews are, evi-

dently, unconscious how much they are admitting. It is a great miracle to open the eyes of the blind; but they admit it only to dishonour Him—"He could do *that*, He has not done *this;* then what is He? Who is He? What is His power and His claim, if He could not cause that even this man should not have died?"

Yes,—there is the voice of unbelief there—a voice speaking through ten thousand tongues, in ages long after—"Why could He not have done this? He has done all these other things, why could He not do something more? He made the world, could He not have kept evil out of it? He has caused the planets to move in their courses, and made all fair, and glorious, and beautiful, but was there not something too hard for Him? Was there some power that He could not grapple with? He opened the eyes of the blind, why then could He not cause that Lazarus should not die? Who is He? What are His claims to be the Messiah worth, if He could not do this,—to save the man He seems to love so much?"

I leave it there. It is just the voice that speaks, and that has spoken, in all ages. God says He has done all these things, and He claims to be the Sovereign Lord of all; yet we look at the world, at trouble, at suffering, and the ages of woe that go on, and the world is still full of sorrow—could He not have caused these things to be different? Just as these men cavil at Christ, so the carnal mind cavils at a God, in Whose ways it will not walk, and Whose authority it will not acknowledge. There was a time, when Jesus vindicated Himself from that reproach ; there will be a time, when the Living God will vindicate Himself, from all the charges brought against His love and goodness. But alas ! the world does not see it. These very men go to the Pharisees, (verse 46), their hearts still unchanged by grace, and impenitent before God.

"**Could not this man have caused that even this man should not have died ?**"

Yes ! He *could* have done it, if indeed it had been right, if it had been wise, if it had not been for greater blessing, honour and glory. How little they knew ! what fools they were ! how utterly unwise ! And how utterly unwise are *we*, when we look at things as they are, and ask, Why,—Why,—Why? O that dreadful *why !* If God does not see fit to answer, and man cannot answer, we may ask it, and ask it, and ask, till it is too late to seek for our salvation. God has all things in His own hand,—He knows *when* He will do it,— He knows *how* He will do it ; and, at last, the great chorus shall celebrate His praise—for that " He hath done *all things* well."

Let us beware of asking this question ; let us take care that we trust Him Who can do all things, and Who will make "all things work together for good to them that love" Him, (Rom. viii. 28), so shall we find peace and rest in our darkest day.

XXIII.

THE RAISING OF LAZARUS.

(Continued.)

" Jesus therefore again groaning in himself cometh to the grave. It was a cave, and a stone lay upon it. Jesus said, Take ye away the stone. Martha, the sister of him that was dead, saith unto him, Lord, by this time he stinketh: for he hath been dead four days. Jesus saith unto her, Said I not unto thee, that, if thou wouldest believe, thou shouldest see the glory of God? Then they took away the stone from the place where the dead was laid. And Jesus lifted up his eyes, and said, Father, I thank thee that thou hast heard me. And I knew that thou hearest me always; but because of the people which stand by I said it, that they may believe that thou hast sent me. And when he thus had spoken, he cried with a loud voice, Lazarus, come forth. And he that was dead came forth, bound hand and foot with graveclothes: and his face was bound about with a napkin. Jesus saith unto them, Loose him, and let him go. Then many of the Jews which came to Mary, and had seen the things which Jesus did, believed on him. But some of them went their ways to the Pharisees, and told them what things Jesus had done."—ST. JOHN xi. 38–46.

WE closed our meditation, last week, by a consideration of the state of mind of several, perhaps many, of those who had come to Martha and Mary to comfort them, and who, now, seeing the Lord Jesus come into the midst, and weep by the side of the grave of Lazarus, said—

" Could not this man, which opened the eyes of the blind, have caused that even this man should not have died ? "

Now, it may be in connection with this state of mind in these people, or it may be because of other thoughts swelling up in the heart of Jesus, all of them considerations of sorrow,—for it is sorrow that causes Him to groan—all of them either considerations of sin, or of the effects of sin, for it was because of sin and the effects of sin, that this great groaning came from the deep heart of Jesus, that—

" Jesus therefore again groaning in Himself cometh to the grave."

It was in this attitude, with these feelings, with this deep heart-sorrow swelling up within Him, that He came and stood by the grave-side.   And it is not only a solemn, but a most deeply interesting, and a most affecting sight, to see Him, Who said when He came—" I am the Life," (St. John xiv. 6)—the Life of men,—Who had come that men " might have life, and that they might have it more abundantly," (St. John x. 10)—it is a most deeply interesting and affecting sight to see Him, Who is " the Resurrection and the Life "—not only the Life but the *Resurrection*—not only One Who could say, Let there be Life, and life was—not only One Who could create, but One Who could *re-*create—Who could raise out of the power and bring again out of the dominion of *death*, those who had fallen under it,—to see HIM coming to " *the grave.*"   The grave is our enemy ; death is our enemy.   When any human mind contemplates either the one or the other, it must necessarily shrink from it,—I mean, when it considers death in itself, in its own nature, and the circumstances belonging to it. It is possible to close our eyes against the thoughts of death and the grave; it is possible to close our eyes and our ears against all these solemn considerations, and to live carelessly, thoughtlessly, heedlessly. But he is a miserable man of whom it can be said, that there is anything in human life,—in the present or in the future,—that he cannot, that he dare not, look in the face, and that he cannot bear to contemplate and examine into his own relation thereto.

The grave is a solemn subject of consideration; it is that from which the human mind naturally shrinks— shrinks appalled. And it is to the side of the grave that we now see Him, in whom is the Life of men, draw near; and, as He draws near, He comes groaning in spirit. No well-instructed, no truly enlightened spirit, no believing heart of man, draws near to the grave without thoughts of sadness, without feelings rising and swelling up into painful emotion. "Jesus therefore again *groaning* in Himself cometh to the grave." We must not look even at the work of Christ and all its glorious effects, the putting away of sin, the renewal of soul into the image of God, the bringing unto everlasting glory them that believe, the doing away of sin's effects,—we must not look even at these things, without remembering that there never was a sin, that there never was a sorrow, that did not

"cost His heart a groan."

Jesus Christ went to the grave-side to conquer—to conquer death, and He went "groaning." It is a solemn world in which we live, and all its circumstances are deeply solemn. "Fools" may "make a mock at sin," (Prov. xiv. 9), and blind their eyes to sin and its effects, but those who are wise and thoughtful, those who are truly taught of God, know what devastation sin has wrought, and see, in the opening graves in all the wide world, what deep sorrow and heart-breaking affliction it has brought—and when He, Who said, "O death, I will be thy plagues; O grave, I will be thy destruction," (Hosea xiii. 14), was brought to the side of the grave, let us never forget that He came with deep groaning. "Jesus groaning in Himself cometh to the grave."

"**It was a cave** (says St. John), **and a stone lay upon it.**"

Very probably, it was one of the stone sepulchres going down obliquely, as it were, into the earth. It was not a cave in the side of a rock, as our Blessed Lord's sepulchre was. *There* the stone was *against* it, and had to be "rolled away." (St. Luke xxiv. 2). *Here* the stone was "*upon* it," and had to be lifted up. This was one of the three kinds of sepulchres common in the East—"a cave, and a stone lay upon it." And when the Blessed Master came to that grave-side, He said,—

"**Take ye away the stone.**"

These words have been often commented upon; they speak for themselves. They are touching words, nevertheless. All our Lord's actions in this most solemn and momentous scene, are actions of deep importance—His actions are all teaching actions. As all the things that He *said*, so all the things that He *did*, have a deep, solemn significance. So, no doubt, it was here. We have seen, already, that it was for a set purpose, for a great glorious end, that this miracle was to be wrought. It is the grand rehearsal scene of a greater miracle which was to follow it, and—in the presence of those who denied His mission, denied His authority, denied His power—in the presence of those who, possibly, would imagine that, by keeping away from the sick-bed of Lazarus, Jesus had only given proof of the natural weakness that was in Him,—in the presence of all these—the miracle was to be wrought. It was not to be done in a corner, but *so* done, as to be a voice speaking into the very heart of the Jews, as we see it did—*so* done as to be a public, manifest declaration of His claim to have authority over " death " and the " grave."

It was well known that He had not been near to Bethany —that He had only just arrived—that kind and friendly hands had tenderly committed the body of Lazarus to the grave, four days ago. They would not have bound the napkin about his face, which would close every inlet of air—and have laid him there in the cave, and rolled the stone upon it,—if friendliness and care had not come to the conclusion, on the very best evidence, that death had *actually* taken place. Jesus will not draw near to the sepulchre, He will not touch the stone that covered the sepulchre, He will not be in close proximity to it ; but He stands at a little distance, and commands that the hands of those, who carried the body of Lazarus to the cave and deposited it there, shall *open* the cave. They themselves had *closed* it; He now commands those who had closed the mouth of the cave to come near, to be witnesses that it had been closed, and that everything was found in order, just as when their hands had deposited the dead body of their friend in that sacred spot.

But there are other conclusions to be drawn from these words—conclusions which are deeply interesting, and well-founded; for the actions of Jesus do not teach us one lesson only,—they teach many lessons. Like all His words, they will bear turning round, and every act has a voice of wisdom, and a voice of love. Just as every one of His precious Names "is as ointment poured forth," (Song i. 3), so His acts speak many lessons.

Oh! how they needed to be taught, and impressed with, this lesson! and how we still require to be taught, that Omnipotence will only do the work, which nothing short of Omnipotence can do—but when anything short of Omnipotence *can* do the work, *that* is not the work of Omnipotence! Here was something that these men *could* do, here was something that it was proper they should do. The same power that was to be put forth, presently, could have caused the stone to be taken away; angels from heaven might have been sent—as afterwards—to roll away the stone from the sepulchre, and have been there as heavenly witnesses. But no! there was something that these men could do; *they* could do it, there was nothing in it that required a heavenly agency—though, for another great purpose, and to teach a deeper lesson, angels did come at *the Lord's* Resurrection.

"**Take ye away the stone.**" That is the lesson for all of us; the lesson teaches us *our* duty. It is not given to any man to quicken the soul, any more than the body; that is "not of blood . . . . nor of the will of man, but of God." (St. John i. 13). But here was a work, which man is endued with power that he may do, —"take *ye* away the stone." "Omnipotence shall do the work that belongs to it, but you can take away the stone." Angels from Heaven might have been sent to preach the Gospel; we can even stretch our imagination so far, as to think that it *would* be a Divine work, and *only* a Divine work—to proclaim the Divine Gospel. But there is a part of it that man can do—a part of it that the believing man can do; when he *believes*, then he can *speak*. Men were to be endued with gifts to carry that Gospel to the length and breadth of the earth. "We have this treasure in earthen vessels"— (2 Cor. iv. 7); if earthen vessels *can* carry the treasure, then it is the *business* of earthen vessels to carry the treasure. If there is a part of the work of God that feeble man can perform, then man is responsible for the performance of it.

"*Take* ye *away* the stone." We cannot give life, we cannot convert souls, but we *can* "take away the stone." Alas! has it not been the case, and is it not the case still, that multitudes who are called Christians, instead

of *taking away* stones, place stones of stumbling in the
way, and at the very feet, of men—of the young, of the
ignorant, of the foolish—" stumbling stones "—stones
of " stumbling," and stones of " offence "?   It is the
business of the Church of God,—it is the business of all
believers, of ministers, of parents, of Christian friends,
to "·take away *the stone*"—everything that hinders—
everything that impedes—everything that is an obstacle
—everything that may cause stumbling.   There is responsibility—" take *ye* away the stone."   Jesus will not
do what it is the business of these men to do ; their
hands had *put* the stone on the cave—their hands
should *take away*, and lift up, the stone.

"**Martha, the sister of him that was dead, saith
unto Him, Lord, by this time he stinketh : for he
hath been dead four days.**"

Now here we see the exact picture of Martha.   It is
Martha's idiosyncrasy coming out again,—it is just the
thing that she might almost, of a certainty, have been
predicted to do.   It is just one of those practical things
that would never, probably, have entered into Mary's
head ; but Martha's tendency was to be " careful "—
to be " troubled "—to be exercised by things that do
trouble.   What would be *the consequence* of taking away
that stone ?   Her brother had been " dead four days,"
—and we know what that, in an Eastern clime, really
means.   We see the practical mind of Martha express-
ing its thought, and she prays, " Lord, let it alone ;
what is the use of it ?   Not only is there no use in it,
but it may cause annoyance,—' by this time he *stinketh*.'"

It is just her practical turn of mind that comes out here. And, while we thank God for practical minds, and practical turns of mind,—while we thank Him for all the great and good works which practical people do in their practical way,—this very practicalness has in it danger. The practical mind is prone to unbelief— prone to let thoughts, which naturally arise about natural things, and the use of means, and so forth, cumber it. Practicalness is very often "cumbered;" it is apt, I say, to end in being cumbered, and to let go that which is of infinite importance. Martha could not see *why* the stone should be put away; the very moment that the thought comes into her mind, it banishes all the promises and words of Jesus,—what He had said to the messenger beyond Jordan—what He had said to her, "Thy brother shall rise again. I am the Resurrection."

"**Jesus saith unto her, Said I not unto thee, that, if thou wouldest believe, thou shouldest see the glory of God?**"

But now, that practical character looks only at the inconvenience that would arise—looks at a mere paltry matter—and the great promise, the great expectation, the great love, and the real character of her Lord is all gone—gone before a little practical thing! Let us not be *less* practical, but let us take care that we are *more* believing. Let our practical thoughts, and our practical arrangements, our devotedness and all, spring out of a true and living *faith*—a realising faith in the word and promise of our Blessed Lord. "Jesus saith unto her, Said I not unto thee, that, if thou wouldest *believe*, thou shouldest see the glory of God ? "

This is a very tender, but a very searching, rebuke; and is it not a rebuke that comes home to every one of us —" Said I not unto *thee?*" Is there not ground for applying it, in every hour of our forgetfulness of His power and love,—when trouble crushes us, when sorrow overwhelms us, when we are inclined to say, "I shall now perish one day by the hand of Saul," (1 Sam. xxvii. 11)—when we really say—"All is over, it is hopeless—'by this time he stinketh, for he hath been dead four days'—this can never be remedied, what is the use of moving the stone?"—and when faith grows weak and faint, and we lose sight of the Saviour's great power and love—oh! "*said I not* unto thee?" Has He not "said" to us what is suited to our every need, in every time of need, in every circumstance of need? And when we forget all this, do we not deserve the rebuke—"*Said I not unto thee?*"

I think, these words are words of solemn rebuke for all believers ; and they will be the bitter worm that never dies to the *un*believer—"Said I not unto thee, then, that, if thou wouldest *believe*, thou shouldest see the glory of God?" "Did I not say to thee, O sinner, did I not say, tenderly and lovingly, in the days of thy life, and strength, and buoyancy,—did I not say that if thou wouldest *believe*, thou shouldest *see* the glory of God? Did I lay on thee any hard thing? Did I set thee any overwhelming task? Did I call thee to any hard, unendurable penance? Did I not say that if

thou wouldest *only believe?*" "O my father, if the prophet had bid thee do some *great* thing, wouldest thou
not have done it? how much rather, when he saith to
thee, Wash, and be clean?" (2 Kings v. 13). "Said I
not unto thee, that if thou wouldest only *believe?*"

To the believer and to the unbeliever, alike, Christ
declares the result—"**thou shouldest see the glory of
God.**" Believing must come before seeing. God gives
us His Word, and bids us trust His promise, and lean
upon it; He comes to us, and, "because He could
swear by no greater, He sware by Himself. . . . That
by two immutable things, in which it was impossible for
God to lie, we might have a strong consolation." (Heb.
vi. 13, 18). "Said I not unto thee?" O let it ring in
our ears, let it ring in our hearts, when we are talking
of things as hopeless—when our sorrows are not to be
endured—when men are still going on in impenitence
and unbelief—"Said I not unto thee?" Yes, there was
a voice that once "spake on earth," and now there is a
voice speaking "from heaven. See that ye refuse not
Him that speaketh." (Heb. xii. 25.) What a knell will
it be in the ears of the perishing soul—"Said I not unto
thee?" as he cries—"The harvest is past, the summer
is ended, and I am not saved!" (Jer. viii. 20.) It will
be in vain, then, to say—"I heard other voices; I
heard a voice that told me I might continue in sin, that
I might follow the imagination of my own heart. I
heard the voice of a false philosophy—the voice of a
dark superstition, and, all the while, I had that which
satisfied me, that appeased my conscience, and left me

careless—left me loving my sin? The voice of Him Who is "the Truth," Who spake amid all the voices of earth, will answer then—"Said I not unto thee, that if thou wouldest 'only' believe, thou shouldest"—not be in the blackness of darkness, but—"see the glory of God?"

"**Then**"—then, that tender heart-searching rebuke spoken—Martha's interference, and the hindrance she had caused, all obviated, "**then they took away the stone from the place where the dead was laid.**" And then we have Jesus, not in mere contact with the grave, but with the *dead*,—"**And Jesus lifted up His eyes,**" —He hastens not, "he that believeth shall not make haste,"—(Isa. xxviii. 16.) He "lifted up His eyes" first, "**and said**"—showing us at once that it is Almighty power that must deal with *death*—"**Father, I thank Thee that Thou hast heard Me.**"

We come here into a subject that is deep—difficult —mysterious; we come upon the fact of our Lord's mediation, and the communion which He, the God-man, the Surety, had with the Eternal Father "in the days of His flesh." Whatever the Father gave Him to say, He said; whatever the Father gave Him to do, He did; but all was done in that close, intimate, inconceivable fellowship and communion. All was of the Father, and all was of the Son; the Son did "nothing of Himself but what He saw the Father do, for what things soever He doeth, these also doeth the Son likewise." (St. John v. 19.) There was not a thought in the mind of the Mediator, which was not also a thought in the mind of the Eternal Father. We see here that close fellowship—the Eternal love and communion—"Father, I thank Thee that Thou hast heard Me,—it is not My work in opposition to Thee." It is not a loving Son in opposition to an unloving Father, but it is the Son in communion with the Father, coming to make war in death's domains.

"And I knew that Thou hearest Me always."

Yes! in every hour, in every moment, of that wondrous life, which He lived out on the soil of Palestine. There was never a moment in which—if I may say it without irreverence, and if I may be understood while I say it—there was never a moment in which the Father was out of the hearing of the Son, or the Son out of the hearing of the Father. Jesus was ever in close communion with the Father—"I knew that Thou hearest Me *always.*" The very beating of the heart of the Son is heard in the ear of the Father.

"But because of the people which stand by I said it, that they may believe that Thou hast sent Me."

Yes, they were to learn the lesson—the deep, mysterious lesson, of that Mediator's close intimacy with the Father in Heaven, and how everything He did, and everything He said, had the sanction, the *imprimatur*, of the Father on it. There was nothing in the Son, which was not in the Father also—there was not a thought of love to man in the Son, which was not in the Father, too—there was not a purpose of grace to a dead world in the heart of the Son, which was not also in the heart of the Father. But He says, "I want these men to understand it, and all the millions of men who shall come (as we, to-night), and gather round the grave of Lazarus.   For *their* sakes I said it."

Can we grasp this thought—that when we are near to *Jesus*, we are close to *the Father*—that when we are at the feet of Jesus, we are at the feet of the Father— that when our hearts are beating out their confessions of sin and sorrow at the feet and on the bosom of Jesus, that sound is heard, and reverberates in the heart of the Eternal Father? " Thou hearest ME always."   *Through* the Son *to* the Father, every sound is heard, every prayer, every sigh, every tear.   It is "for their sakes."   We have this Mediator to bring us to God, and when we are near to Him, we are near to the Eternal Fountain— the Lord and Life of men.

"And when He had thus spoken, He cried with a loud voice, Lazarus, come forth."

These words, as I have said about some others, defy exposition.   We have just to consider our Lord standing in such a position, as to render it absolutely certain to the minds of all, that He was speaking *so as to effect* its being done—that there was nothing but His word of command intervening.

"Lazarus, come forth."

This shows us, at once, that He is the One Who had the power over death.   There was one who had brought death, and who had "the power of death" in his hand—he had power to *inflict* it, and he has inflicted it on a world of sinners ; but there is Another, Who has come into the world, Who has power over death to

destroy it, and to bring life out of death, and to say—
"Lazarus, come forth." We must die, we must be laid
in the tomb—unless the Lord shall come again in our
time,—and, as we lay our heads down to die, what are
our thoughts? Do we fall before the tyranny of
a conqueror, insatiable and cruel? or will it be the
conviction of our hearts, that he is no longer a conqueror, but that we are in the hands of Death's Conqueror—in the hands of One Who can remove all its
terrors—of One Who can give Life,—yea even bring it
out of Death—of One Who can say, though our tomb be
closely sealed—"Come forth,"—"I say unto thee, Arise?"

Is He our Friend? is He our Lord? is He our Husband? is He our Brother? is He our Saviour—so that
we have nothing to fear? Can we look death in the
face, and *so* look it in the face as to smile on it? Can
we look at it undismayed, feeling that we are in the
hands of Him Who has dealt with it and will deal with
it, and that the spirit renewed, justified, purified, ransomed, cannot be touched by it, any more than the
body of Jesus was touched by the hands of wicked men,
after He had said, "It is finished"? Though death
has a little power over the body, it is not for long; for
" the hour is coming, and now is, when the dead shall
hear the voice of the Son of God; and they that hear
shall live." Yes—but He has power over all *flesh* as
He has over all *spirit*—they "shall come forth; they that
have done good, unto the resurrection of life;" but
" they that have done evil, unto the resurrection of
damnation." (St. John v. 25, 29.)

We see our Master, then, standing by the grave, and dealing with the dead—" Lazarus, *come forth.*"   Well might Jesus have said to these sisters, in words that were afterwards spoken — " Let not your heart be troubled : *believe* in GOD, *believe* also in ME." (St. John xiv. 1).   If they had *believed*, they would not have been " troubled "—for it is *un*belief that is the great troubler of the hearts of men.

" And he that was dead came forth, bound hand and foot with grave-clothes ; and his face was bound about with a napkin."

Here, then, we have the trappings of death, sure signs and tokens of death.   Lazarus could not—after being *four days* bound round about the face with a napkin—have been a living man.   Here, however, the living man rises up at the words of Him, Who is " The Life "—the breath comes again into his body, and the slain one is seen struggling to come forth, still fast bound, scarcely able to see or to move—wondering at the life coming back, marvelling as he again becomes subject to the original condition of his body, after all that he has seen in the third heaven, as a disembodied spirit.   We dwell not on the traditions of his future state ; yet we cannot but marvel at the thoughts, which would swell up in his heart, as he was now raised up again from the dead to live a life of comparative silence, —to live a life of wondering, grateful, adoring affection —to live there as a strong, marvellous token of the power of Him, Who was, presently, to lay down His own life.   " He that was dead came forth, bound hand

and foot with grave-clothes; and his face was bound about with a napkin." And here, again, we see how marvellously the Lord teaches lessons of wisdom.

" Jesus saith unto them, Loose him, and let him go."

He had done one thing—one thing that stands by itself—that *was* to stand by itself—He had given *Life* to that dead man. It was not for *Him* to " loose him, and let him go;" He had done the one act that was to stand alone, and *by itself.* He does not move away the stone, nor remove the bandages; men could do *that*, and it was good for " *them* " to do it—for those who were gathered round wondering at the sight. Here was a mission for them—to open his eyes that he might see, to loose his bands that he might walk, to remove whatever hindered his coming forth right out of the cave— there was a mission and work for them. The Church of God has such a work to do; when the Spirit of life begins to stir in the soul, there are things to be loosed, to be removed. When any sign of spiritual life is manifested in the soul, then there is a mission for the Church of God—it wants to see, it wants to know; and the Church's office is to edify the soul, to remove the stones of stumbling, and to take off bandages. " Jesus saith unto *them*, Loose him, and let him go."

" Then many of the Jews which came to Mary, and had seen the things which Jesus did, believed on Him."

"But some of them went their ways to the Phari- sees, and told them what things Jesus had done."

There are two thoughts in connection with this :—

2 B

these men and women were gathered round our Lord, they heard these words, and saw this great sight; and *some* believed, and *some* believed not.   There were men there—men, perhaps, of tender heart,—who had come to comfort the sorrowful, they had come in honest sincerity, and when they saw Jesus, they candidly looked on His works, and thoughtfully and earnestly pondered His words, and conviction laid fast hold of them.   They admitted Him to be the Messiah, and that none could do the works He did but the Messiah; they acted on the words—acted on them as reasonable men.

But *others* "went their ways to the Pharisees, and told them what things Jesus had done."   It might have been said of them, for they seemed determined to take the very position of those, of whom it was said by Him Whom they were about to betray—"If they hear not Moses and the prophets, neither will they be persuaded, though one rose from the dead." (St. Luke xvi. 31.) They went and told the Pharisees "what things Jesus had done."   Yes! they saw the things that were done, but they did *not* "believe."

We may well tremble at this great sight—tremble more at the hardness of men's hearts, than at the mighty strange miracle.   We may well tremble when we think of the havoc sin has made of the heart, when we behold acts of Infinite power and Infinite tenderness, wrought before men's eyes as a testimony to His Divine mission, and yet the heart remains full of enmity and full of hardness.   We tremble when we think of the judgment that must fall on the impenitent, who harden themselves in their pride and will, at length, call on the rocks and the hills to cover them, to hide them from the sight of that tenderness and compassion of Him Who said—" If thou wouldest *believe*, thou shouldest see *glory of God.*"

May God grant that we all may learn these lessons, and that the Church of Christ amongst us may learn the lessons taught here; and if there are any amongst us who believe not—oh ! may this voice speak from this grave, and still speak from yonder heaven—" If thou wilt believe, thou shalt see the glory of God." May they *believe*, and then they shall *see !*

And let us look at one thing more, it is this :—the comforting, consoling thought that He, Who is our Lord, our Life, our Saviour, has power over death and over the grave, and that if He is our "Shepherd" we cannot "want." He will make us "to lie down in green pastures," and when we pass "through the valley of the *shadow* of death," (the *substance* being gone), we need "fear no evil," if He is "with" us; we may well lie content under the green sod, or in the dark tomb, till we hear the footfall of the Lord of life, and His voice, as "the voice of many waters," saying, "Come forth— come forth at length to 'see the glory of God.'"

XXIV.

THE WITHERING OF THE FIG TREE.

" Now in the morning as he returned into the city, he hungered. And when he saw a fig tree in the way, he came to it, and found nothing thereon, but leaves only, and said unto it, Let no fruit grow on thee henceforward for ever. And presently the fig tree withered away. And when the disciples saw it, they marvelled, saying, How soon is the fig tree withered away! Jesus answered and said unto them, Verily I say unto you, If ye have faith, and doubt not, ye shall not only do this which is done to the fig tree, but also if ye shall say unto this mountain, Be thou removed, and be thou cast into the sea ; it shall be done. And all things, whatsoever ye shall ask in prayer, believing, ye shall receive."— St. MATT. xxi. 18–22.

IT is necessary to point out, perhaps, that St. Matthew is not careful about the chronological order of his statements. He is more concerned to bring things so together, that the great lesson may be at once presented to the reader's mind ; and if you compare this passage which I have now read, with the corresponding passage in St. Mark's Gospel, you will have a striking illustration of the different methods adopted by the Evangelists. St. Matthew is not concerned to state on what particular day the facts, which he records, took place, nor when they were noticed. St. Mark, on the other hand, is careful to note the point of time, and tells us exactly when the facts occurred, and also when they were noticed by the disciples. The fact is, that the circumstances, recorded in the first words of my text, took place *before* the cleansing of the Temple, which is recorded in the previous verses of the chapter. It was on the Monday morning that Jesus returned into the city, and on His way, He noticed the fig-tree, and pronounced on it this condemnation. He *then* proceeded to the Temple, and cast out the money-changers and the buyers and sellers. Having returned to Bethany in the evening of that day, on Tuesday morning we find Him coming again into the city, and *then*, Peter and the rest of the Apostles call His attention to the fact, that the fig-tree, upon which He had, the previous morning, pronounced condemnation, had "withered away"—had—as St. Mark, in one of his beautiful touches, says—"dried up from the roots." (St. Mark xi. 20). The circumstances, recorded in our passage to-night, occurred on the *Monday* morning in Passion Week. The reference to the withering away was made on the *Tuesday* morning, when also the Lord sought to impress on the minds of His disciples the great lesson, which that judgment gested.

Various difficulties have been started with regard to this act of our Lord, but they would not be worth much attention, if it were not that they have been made so much of. It is a suspicious thing when facts of paramount importance are, to a great extent, lost sight of, and trifles made into mountains of difficulty.   These will occur to us as we go through the miracle.

On Sunday evening, after our Lord's triumphal entrance into the city, St. Mark tells us that " when He had looked round about upon all things, and now the eventide was come, He went out unto Bethany." (xi. 11). There is something very touching in that, but also something awfully solemn.   Here we have the great King, here we have Messiah, here we have " the Lord . . . come to His temple " (Mal. iii. 1),—and He looks round about upon all.   That all-seeing and all-searching Eye, which is " as a flame of fire," looked on all things in that House of God—saw what was wanting—saw what ought to have been, but was not,—saw into the hearts of those men—regarded all their will-worship, and estimated rightly the exact position which that House of God held, and how all its ceremonies were being carried out.   " He looked round about upon all things," and the mind—yes ! the human mind, of Jesus " looked " on every single particular of what had occurred, and of what was occurring, on the motives, actions, and intentions of all who were connected with the administration of the House of His Father ; and, " having looked upon all,"—with this in His mind, " He went out unto Bethany."   How He spent that night is not revealed ; that He spent it in the house of Martha and Mary seems improbable, from the little circumstance mentioned in the text.   Yet He may have done so, and then, rising up a great while before day, have retired to some secluded spot in the neighbourhood, there to commune with His Father, before He entered on the sorrowful proceedings of the ever memorable *third* day in Passion Week.

"In the morning, as He returned into the city, He hungered."

We have brought before us here, by the Evangelist, when he is about to record the manifestations of the Divine power of our Blessed Redeemer, a fact which sets forth His true and real Humanity. He shows us how the weaknesses, that pertain to these bodies of ours, were all shared by Him. He could not pass through that night, after He had "looked round about on all things" in the Temple, and enter fasting on the morrow, without suffering in the same way that any other human being would have suffered under the circumstances. "In the morning, as He returned into the city, *He hungered.*" We see here the actual Humanity of Jesus Christ, and you will always find, that, when we are going to have the great flashes of His Eternal Deity shining forth in all grandeur and power, we are ever, at the same time, reminded that "in all things" He was "made like unto His brethren." (Heb. ii. 17). He came forth from Bethany, to enter upon that solemn day of renewed labour and sorrow, and when He came forth, "He hungered." It is a fact that our Redeemer suffered as we suffer, fainted as we faint, hungered as we hunger.

"And when He saw a fig tree in the way, He came to it, and found nothing thereon."

St. Mark tells us, strikingly, that He saw it "afar off"

(xi. 13); that is, it could be seen at a distance—it was no little puny thing springing just out of the earth, but a great, noble tree that could be seen from the far distance by our Lord, as he was coming into the city. "He saw a fig tree in the way," growing as fig trees do, and as they did, by the wayside; and "He came to it, and found nothing thereon,"—

"But leaves only."

We find our Lord here face to face with a great, pretentious, promising, professing fig tree; we find Him drawn aside from His journey by the promise it held forth. There is a striking word in one of the old prophets,—" I found Israel like grapes in the wilderness; I saw your fathers as the firstripe in the fig tree at her first time." (Hosea ix. 10). This was what Israel was like, even in the *wilderness*. God says that, when He looked for fruit, Israel was as "grapes in the wilderness"—that He found there "the firstripe, in the fig tree"—the luscious, pleasant fruit—"the firstripe in the fig tree at her first time." Those were the days of Israel's prosperity, she was "grapes" to the Seeker of fruits, "as the firstripe in the fig tree at her first time," in the days of her wandering and sorrow. And now, here is something that promises to be as Israel in the wilderness, as Israel in the days of old— something that seemed to say, "I symbolise that which, of old, ancient Israel was unto Him who sought fruit from her;" and Jesus, naturally, turns aside, and tests the profession.

The discussions as to whether our Lord was deceived,

as to whether He knew or pretended not to know—are all vain, worthless notions ; and they ought not to enter into the consideration of this subject. Our Lord was man as well as God, and if He knew—as He *did* know —that it bore only leaves, there was no deception in what He did.   He was about to *act* a parable ; He was about to do something solemnly symbolical, and, in turning aside, our Lord did what *any* man would, naturally, have done under the circumstances.   We know what is said respecting Him, when He joined the two disciples going to Emmaus—" He made as though he would have gone further "—(St. Luke xxiv. 28)—not to deceive them, but He *would* " have gone further," if they had not besought Him to stay.   He went on in order to draw out what was in the hearts of these men ; as they confessed afterwards—" Did not our hearts burn within us by the way ? "   So He would bring out of the burning heart, the prayer, " Abide with us, for it is toward evening, and the day is far spent." (29).   Neither here have we anything but what is perfectly natural under the circumstances, and the man *must* be eager to find difficulties, when he can find one here.

" A fig tree . . . and nothing thereon, but leaves only."   There is something very striking in this, from the fact that our first parents, when they saw themselves condemned, when they saw their nakedness, and nothingness, and unpardoned sin, sought to cover that emptiness of good, that loss of good, by sewing " fig-leaves together," to make to themselves garments. (Gen. iii. 7).   And, as in Paradise, so now—

when the scenes of this great week were being enacted, the fig-tree is again on the scene, fig-leaves again, in wondrous profusion, but now, as then, they covered only emptiness, barrenness, and worthlessness.   We find the fig-tree doing what our first parents had done—covering thus its nakedness and want of fruit.   Jesus came, seeking fruit upon the fig-tree, and "found nothing thereon but leaves only."

Now, difficulties are made here.   *Ought* there to have been fruit on the tree?   If, as St. Mark tells us, that, "the time of figs was not yet," (xi. 13), and there was no reason why our Lord should have expected to find fruit at the end of March, *why* was the tree condemned for not bearing fruit, when the *time* for bearing fruit had not yet come?   This is thought by some to be a great difficulty.

We are told this, that there are *three* times of figs in the year.   The *first* was in the case of the winter figs, which sprouted during the autumn, and lay dormant in the winter, and ripened as the genial spring came.   Subsequently, the fig-tree bore again ; and then later on, in August, was the final ingathering of figs—the best ingathering.   If this is so, and if, as the spring opened, the winter figs were to be found, as travellers tell us they are now, why was it unreasonable that our Lord should expect to find them on this tree ?   But this fact is well known—the real, genuine fruit comes, as fruit ought *always* to come, *before* the leaves,—and this being so, whether it was the time of winter figs or not, there ought to have been fruit upon the fig-tree, *before* it put forth a leaf. Therefore, we see, that the tree to which our Lord came, challenged attention, invited Him by the leaves it had put forth ; it said, as it were, "I am a fig-tree in full process of bearing fruit." It is the nature of the fig-tree to put forth first fruit, *then* leaves ; therefore you may be sure if you see leaves, to find underneath those leaves—*fruit.*

Well, the Lord saw it, and He came to it, seeking fruit. Many difficulties are raised here, by people who, probably, do not like the lesson which this miracle teaches. This was a solemn act, and the Lord, *by* that act, was speaking a solemn parable. This fig tree invited the attention of the passer-by, invited the passer-by to come and examine, whether the profession and the practice agreed one with another. Remember, our Lord had been in the Temple the night before, and, as I said, Israel had been of old "as grapes in the wilderness," and He had the right when He had come in the morning, and the Temple doors were opened, to ask the question—"Is Israel as the firstripe in the fig tree at her first time? Is Israel as a fruitful field? Shall I find this?" And He—the hungering, longing Seeker after fruit comes to this tree, and makes it a great parable of Israel's condition and Israel's destiny. He was more an hungred, infinitely, to find fruit in Israel, than to find fruit, for the supply of His natural wants, on that fig tree. He brings His disciples there, and shows them, in a living symbol, the sad reality which would presently be unfolded.

Israel—what was her condition? The condition of

this fig tree.   This fig tree was there with all its green leaves, while others had not yet put forth a leaf—all appeared still in their winter dress—dry, not a leaf—nothing yet in promise.   And what was Israel?   She was standing pretentiously among the nations of the earth.   All these were dry, apparently, in their winter garb ; and *she, only*, attracted the attention of the passer-by, by her green leaves, saying, "Come and examine me, and see whether I am not unlike the nations round about, which bear no fruit unto God." And Jesus Christ was coming to examine Israel ; her leaves were indeed fair, but her fruit was not much,—nay, there was nothing thereon but fig-leaves only.   She had her great sacrifices, her incense streamed heavenwards, her priests were still clad in garments "of glory and beauty"—her Temple, in its great and Divine magnificence, was still in her midst—there was everything of pretence, everything of profession, everything of promise.   Israel said—"That God Whom I worship is the true and only God, I keep the fire burning on His altar, I send the incense up to His throne, I bear His Name, and I only am holy."   And Jesus was coming to examine into the reality.   And when "He had looked round about upon all things," "He found nothing thereon but leaves only"—that was just the condition of Israel,—

"**And said unto it, Let no fruit grow on thee henceforward for ever.   And presently the fig tree withered away.**"

He, the great Seeker, had come—He had come to

Israel, hungering, and Israel had nothing to give Him. He could say of her, in truth, " I was an hungred, and ye gave me no meat." (St. Matt. xxv. 42). There was promise, there was profession, there was everything to entice the weary wayfarer—but " I was an hungred, and she gave me no meat "—there was nothing to satisfy the hunger of the great Husbandman, who had planted the " vineyard in a very fruitful hill," (Isa. v. 1)—and so He says, " Let no fruit grow on *thee* henceforward for ever."

Remember, this was done in the presence of His disciples; it was a forecasting of what was to come. Jesus had " wept over the city," and said—" The things which belong to thy peace . . . are now hid from thine eyes." (St. Luke xix. 41, 42.) There was no hope left for Jerusalem, she was not to be tried any longer. No! the trial was over, and our Lord says to Jerusalem, " Let no fruit grow on *thee* henceforward." All those fig leaves were to be swept away, all that ceremonial was to pass away, all those joyous services were to come to an end, and the Temple, and the city, and Jerusalem's children within her, to be laid " even with the ground." And so saith Jesus, " Learn this ' other ' parable of the fig tree."

One almost shrinks from even a passing allusion to those, who speak of our Lord here as guilty of *cruelty* to a fig tree—as if a fig tree had feeling—as if a fig tree had senses ! No! when our Blessed Lord did works of *mercy*, He did them on *men ;* but when He would speak a parable of *judgment*, He did it on an *un*feeling object.

He is here in His solemn acts speaking judgment ; and there is a feeling latent in man that would not have Him judge at all, and therefore it would not have Him judge even a fig tree.   Though man will cut down a tree, and cast it into the fire to warm himself any day of his life, yet he finds here ground for casting a stone at our Blessed Redeemer.   "And on the morrow," (St. Mark xi. 12), on the Tuesday morning,—

"When the disciples saw it, they marvelled, saying, How soon is the fig-tree withered away!"

They were solemnised by the fact, they were startled by it.   They see that their Lord, Who had cured the paralytic, cleansed the lepers, and raised the dead, is a God of judgment as well as a God of love ; and they say, "How soon is the fig tree withered away!"   And how soon might He have withered up His enemies in Jerusalem who were waiting for His life—but no ! He speaks His parable by this tree,—that tree, incapable of actual suffering, answers His end.

"Jesus answered and said unto them, Verily I say unto you, If ye have faith, and doubt not, ye shall not only do that which is done to the fig tree, but also if ye shall say unto this mountain, Be thou removed, and be thou cast into the sea ; it shall be done."

What did the Lord mean ?   He had been performing *a miracle of judgment*, and the question is a question of miracle—it is not a question of the Divine life—it is not a question of daily bread—it is not a question of the soul's need—but it is a question of *miracle*.   Remember, these men had seen the Lord do this, and they themselves were to be workers of miracles—by power from Him they were to work great wonders, and He says to them, "Learn, from this—*What* withered that tree? My Word; but My Word would not have withered it, if my Divine power had not gone forth. The Divine power which withered the fig-tree with a word, made the world, and will execute judgment on a wicked world."

"**Verily I say unto you, If ye have faith.**"

What is Faith? Faith is the hand that lays hold of Omnipotence; faith is that which brings God into everything; and if these men are to go forth and work miracles, they must "have faith." They cannot do it of themselves—they must have the hand that lays hold of the Divine power, and brings that Divine power into the circumstances, whatever the circumstances may be, in which the miracle is to be wrought.

Now, remember, the power of working miracles is not given to any man to be exercised at any time, on any thing, in any way he likes. Samson, as you know—and so it is with all—could not work a miracle in the olden time, but by special instigation—"*The Spirit of the Lord* began to move him *at times* in the camp of Dan." (Judges xiii. 25). So with regard to all merely human workers of miracles—they could not do them except as the Spirit moved them, in that particular instance there before their eyes. They must know that the Lord was guiding them; whether it were to open the eyes of a blind man, to heal a lame or palsied man, or to strike a man with blindness, they could not effect it, unless the Spirit of the Lord guided them to that. "If ye have faith,"—

"And doubt not."

The worker of a miracle must have the faith that clings stedfastly to Omnipotence—that never looks *down*, but ever looks *up*. You remember what Peter said—Peter saw the Lord on the water, and he said, "Lord, if it be Thou, bid me come to Thee on the water." "And He said, Come." (St. Matt. xiv. 28, 29). "*Come.*" There was a miracle. The Lord walked on the sea, *that* was a miracle—and Peter walked on the sea—*that* was a miracle ; *but*—Peter could not *go through* the miracle, because he had not the faith that looked constantly on the face of Jesus "the Mighty God"— nor the hand that held stedfastly by Jesus Christ. Therefore Jesus said unto him, "O thou of *little* faith, wherefore didst thou *doubt?*" **"Doubt not,"** says our text. Peter had not the faith that doubts not, therefore He could not go through the miracle; he doubted— and so the Lord says, "*Wherefore* didst thou doubt?" It is not for us to answer that "Wherefore"—but we know that he ceased to look to the Lord's Omnipotence, and to rely on the promise implied in the word of command, "Come—come to Me on the water."—"He saw the wind boisterous, and he was afraid," and so doubted in his heart. "If ye have faith, and doubt not, ye shall not only do this which is done to the fig-tree, but also if ye shall say to this mountain"—this Mount of Olives— "Be thou removed, and be thou cast into the sea,"

—yea, into yonder Mediterranean — "it shall be done."

"**And all things, whatsoever ye shall ask in prayer, believing, ye shall receive.**"

I believe, the Lord is here still speaking on the same subject, and still speaking of it to these disciples, on that solemn morning, as He was going again to the devoted city,—He is pointing to the time when they should be hated of all men, and be brought into circumstances of great anxiety; of supreme difficulty; and then, in *that* hour, whatever the Spirit of God should move them to ask, believing, they should receive, for they should have that faith which unites to the Omnipotent. And St. Mark tells us what St. Matthew leaves out—he cuts it short, but St. Mark adds that He charged them, that, whatever they did by this power, was to be done in the spirit of love—" When ye stand praying, forgive if ye have ought against any," (xi. 25)—that is to say, when they were going to bring Omnipotence into the affairs of the world, whether it was in the case of Ananias, or of Æneas, or any case in the times when the Spirit of the Lord should lead them to see that Omnipotence *was* to come in—I say, if they were seeking to bring Omnipotence into the affairs of the world, it was not to be used for vindictive purposes, it was to be used in a forgiving, loving spirit. They would not be able to use it for selfish or vindictive ends, for the Heavenly Father would not even *hear* them, if they did not forgive. They would see in the withering up of the fig tree, an act of judgment, and some of those now standing there had

2 C

said—" Lord, wilt Thou that we command fire to come down from heaven?" (St. Luke ix. 54). And St. Mark tells us how the Lord here settles that question—" No; ye are not to have the spirit that would call down fire from heaven, but the lowly, meek, gentle, and forgiving spirit. I have done this work of judgment to foretell and to warn; but you have seen from the works of *mercy* which I have done how ' I delight' and am 'rich in mercy.' Take heed ' what manner of spirit ye are of.' "

May I just, in conclusion, lay before you one thing more—we are thinking of John and Peter and the rest, and this poor, pretentious, professing fig-tree—we are thinking of the Pharisees, and of the men who stood and thanked God they were " not as other men,"—but there is a principle running through all this applying to them, which is capable of being applied to every one of us. What profession do *we* make by the wayside, or in the House of God ? What profession do we make as we open our Bible, or come to worship, or as we kneel round the Table of the Lord ? There are the fig leaves ; and the Lord comes—He is ever coming— and He lifts up the leaves, to see if they cover anything worth His notice. Is there fruit under the leaves ? There ought to be fruit *before* leaves ; is there fruit *with* the leaves ? Is there found there " love, joy, peace, long-suffering, gentleness, goodness, faith, meekness, temperance " — " courage " added to " faith," and " knowledge " to courage, and " temperance " to know-ledge, and so forth even to the end, so that he who has the leaves is also " neither barren nor unfruitful in the knowledge of our Lord Jesus Christ"? (Gal. v. 22, 23; 2 Pet. i. 5–8). Is it so?

Some may think me legal, and say this is legality, and what have we to do with good works? We have just got *this* to do with good works—if we have no good works found under our profession, we stand in danger of this terrible withering. There *will* be judgment, and " judgment " will " begin " where there is profession and promise—even " at the House of God." (1 Pet. iv. 17). But no mere leaves, in however rich profusion they may grow, can ever satisfy the thirsting and hungering. There must be *fruit.* Jesus Christ " was hungry," and this tree yielded Him " no meat."

Do you say, How shall I bear fruit? How shall I mortify this, and crucify that, and bring forth constantly " the fruits of the Spirit "? My answer is—by union with Jesus Christ—that living union which is by " faith " —and by abiding in Him. Then, when there is real faith and real abiding in Christ, there will be obedience, there will be holiness, there will be fruit,—yea, " much fruit." As in the case of miracles, faith ever lays hold of Omnipotence, even so does the believer humbly, but confidently, say—"I can do all things through Christ which strengtheneth me." (Phil. iv. 13).

XXV.

THE SECOND MIRACULOUS DRAUGHT OF FISHES.

CONCLUSION.

THE approach of spring and long evenings coincide with our consideration of the *last* Miracle, which is recorded to have been wrought on earth by our Blessed Lord and Master. Therefore, with this closing miracle of His, we close for the present our meetings here. Whether we shall be spared to meet again in this quiet way in this room, is a secret hidden with God. Whether He will give me health and strength to meet you again in this place, is a secret hidden with Him. These matter not. The question is,—Whether our souls have benefited, in the slightest degree, by the consideration of the wonders wrought by our Lord, and which we have been privileged to consider?

You will find this Last Miracle recorded in St. John xxi. 1—14 :—

"*After these things Jesus shewed himself again to the disciples at the sea of Tiberias; and on this wise shewed he himself. There*

were together Simon Peter, and Thomas called Didymus, and Nathanael of Cana in Galilee, and the sons of Zebedee, and two others of the disciples. Simon Peter saith unto them, I go a fishing. They say unto him, We also go with thee. They went forth, and entered into a ship immediately; and that night they caught nothing. But when the morning was now come, Jesus stood on the shore; but the disciples knew not that it was Jesus. Then Jesus saith unto them, Children, have ye any meat? They answered him, No. And he said unto them, Cast the net on the right side of the ship, and ye shall find. They cast therefore, and now they were not able to draw it for the multitude of fishes. Therefore that disciple whom Jesus loved saith unto Peter, It is the Lord. Now when Simon Peter heard that it was the Lord, he girt his fisher's coat unto him, (for he was naked,) and did cast himself into the sea. And the other disciples came in a little ship; (for they were not far from land, but as it were two hundred cubits,) dragging the net with fishes. As soon then as they were come to land, they saw a fire of coals there, and fish laid thereon, and bread. Jesus saith unto them, Bring of the fish which ye have now caught. Simon Peter went up, and drew the net to land full of great fishes, an hundred and fifty and three: and for all there were so many, yet was not the net broken. Jesus saith unto them, Come and dine. And none of the disciples durst ask him, Who art thou? knowing that it was the Lord. Jesus then cometh, and taketh bread, and giveth them, and fish likewise. This is now the third time that Jesus shewed himself unto his disciples, after that he was risen from the dead."
—St. John xxi. 1–14.

You will, at once, notice what is said in the 14th verse, —" This is now the *third* time that Jesus shewed Himself to His disciples, after that He was risen from the dead "—that is, the third time that He shewed Himself to any considerable number of disciples gathered together. There were other manifestations, as to Mary Magdalene; but this was " the third time that

Jesus shewed Himself to the disciples" *collectively*, "after that He was risen."

The exact point of time is not mentioned ; it was—

" After these things,"—

after He had appeared, and given them their great commission, some time previously.   You will, perhaps, call to mind that He had told His disciples before He suffered, that He would meet them in *Galilee.*   They were Galileans, and He told them, "After I am risen again, I will go before you into *Galilee."* (St. Matt. xxvi. 32).   And you know, that when He had risen from the dead, He sent also to them a message of similar purport. At the same time,—He had said, on the last occasion of His appearing before this—" Tarry ye in the city of Jerusalem, until ye be endued with power from on high." (St. Luke xxiv. 49).   What He meant, and what they truly understood, was this—after these appearances, (I have before had occasion to show you the geography of the Holy Land, therefore I need not stop to do so now), they were bidden to go from the south right up to the north,—just as if a man were bidden to go from London to Lancashire, or Yorkshire, in order there to meet his friend.   And then, *after* that meeting in Galilee, where there would be some special manifestation—which we know indeed there was—they were to come back to Jerusalem till He ascended ; and to " tarry " *after He had ascended,* till they had received the promised gift of the Holy Ghost, to fit them to fulfil the ministry which they had been commissioned to fulfil— proclaiming to all mankind the doctrine of the Forgiveness of Sins. " Receive ye the Holy Ghost,"—He had said to them—" Whose soever sins ye remit, they are remitted unto them ; and whose soever sins ye retain, they are retained." (St. John xx. 22, 23). That was to be their solemn commission, and for the due preparation for the exercise of it, they were to wait at Jerusalem.

Now, you perceive, they are *back again in Galilee,* back again in the old place ; just as, early in this course, we considered a miracle like this in many respects, though in many respects different,—when the people " pressed upon " Jesus " to hear the Word of God," and when He got into a boat, and taught them out of it. *Then* Jesus had said to His disciples, " Launch out into the deep, and let down your nets for a draught ;" and they let down their nets, having told Him first, " We have toiled all the night, and have taken nothing ; nevertheless at Thy word, we will let down the net." And then the net brake, and, of course, a great part of the fish in the net escaped,—the rest were saved, and filled both the ships. (St. Luke v.).

They are back again now in their old haunts, in the old places, where Jesus had first said to them, " Follow Me "—back in the old places with which they had been familiar all the days of their boyhood, and all the days of their manhood—back in the scenes and haunts, which were as familiar to them as anything could be. And they were back again there, *because* Jesus had said, " Go, tell My brethren that they go into *Galilee,* and there shall they see Me," (St. Matt. xxviii. 10), and there they were, waiting in Galilee. We find *seven* of them gathered together by the side of the lake,—by the side of the lake of Tiberias ; two of them are not named, and one thing is remarkable—it is said He "**shewed Himself.**" Those are very remarkable words.　If we think at all—as we ought to do—about the eternal state, about what is meant when it is said, He "shall change our vile body, that it may be fashioned like unto His glorious body, according to the working whereby He is able even to subdue all things unto Himself," (Phil. iii. 21),—these words will strike us.　It was not that they *saw* Him, but that He SHEWED Himself to them—not that they saw Him as they might see any other man or woman, or an accumulation of material atoms, or as they saw material nature,—things that they could not help seeing.　Any other man standing by the lake would have been seen at once ; but in the case of Jesus, when He had risen from the dead, it is said, "He *shewed* Himself"—made Himself visible to them.

So, the two returning from Emmaus told "how He was known of them in breaking of bread." (St. Luke xxiv. 35).　How could they help knowing Him? we might ask.　They had known His voice, they had seen His walk, they knew every motion, and action, and peculiarity of His human form ; yet He could walk beside them for miles, without their even *suspecting* WHO He was.

This teaches us great lessons.　Jesus can manifest Himself when the mortal eye cannot distinguish any object, any more than we should see, if an angel were to pass through this room, to-night.　He made Himself *visible.* It appears, as if the eyes of men are incapable —except by some gracious, miraculous agency—of distinguishing the world of spirits, or a glorified body. It was not merely that Jesus came to the lake-side, but that He gave the disciples the power of distinguishing Him *in His resurrection body.*

One night, seven of the disciples met. They had not agreed to go fishing—but, just as if you go to a sea-side place, you know, the natural resort of fishermen is to the place where the boats are,—so, in any other trade, it is natural for there to be a gathering together of those engaged in it, in the particular place where that trade is carried on,—so they gravitate, you would almost say, to the sea-side where the boats were. It appears to be by accident; though it was *not* by accident, but by Providence.

The old spot comes to be the natural place for them to resort to. It was bred with their very life, it was bred in their very bones; they had been fishermen from very children—it was natural for them to go fishing, they had lived in it, they had lived *by* it. It was as natural for them to be *on* the water, as for the fish to swim *in* the water. They go where the boats, and oars, and nets, of their relations if not their own, are.

"Simon Peter saith unto them, I go a fishing."

I do not know that there was anything wrong in this; there was no harm in his going a-fishing. It had been the trade he followed in his youth. Why shouldn't he go fishing? The result shows that it was in the Divine Providence, that the Divine glory might be manifested.

Peter was not willing to spend his time idly, he was waiting for the Lord,—Jesus had said, " Go, tell My brethren that they go into Galilee, and there shall they see Me ; " and Peter seems to say,—" We have been here so many hours, or so many days ; we are watching for Him, hoping for Him, longing for Him, but the wheels of His chariot are long in coming. · Why shouldn't we go fishing ? Let us spend this night, at least, on the deep, let us go back to our old habits ; we may gather something that may be a help to us, or that may help others."

There is a touch of nature—a striking touch of nature —in all this, and it teaches us a great deal. The mind cannot always be, simply and solely, engaged in spiritual expectation, in spiritual contemplation. Man is made for the fulfilment of a very great variety of duties, of a very great variety of occupations ; and only let the mind of man be absolutely, and entirely, and prolongedly rapt, as it were, into the third heavens of spiritual enjoyment, of spiritual expectation, or spiritual exercise only, and the mind reels under it, and cannot bear it. God gives to every one of us our regular occupation, and, if we do not *work*, we ought not to be allowed to *eat*. (2 Thess. iii. 10). God does not expect,—while we are to " continue *instant* in prayer," while our whole life is to be lived in prayer,—He does not expect, that the mind should be on strong tension for twenty-four hours at a time. One is to go to his plough, another to his anvil, another to his spade, another to his books, another is to go fishing,—one in one direction, and another, in another direction, following perhaps material occupations—whatever his business is, whatever his duty is. So Peter, ever since his denial of his Lord, had, no doubt, been in a state of spiritual tension,—every feeling and faculty of his soul had been on the stretch. He had been looking back *upon*, he had been looking *into* his sin; he had been remembering his denial of Jesus, he had been dwelling on the great events of the past, on his seeing the Lord after His resurrection,—and now, he is expecting Him. It is a great spiritual expectation, but the poor man cannot hold out in that continuously; he turns naturally to what he had been accustomed to do,—to some innocent, material occupation, in order that his mind may be somewhat at rest.

Now, do not misunderstand me. I am not *depreciating* any spiritual exercise. The danger, with most of us, is on the other side of the question. Some people have even gone out of their minds on some religious ground, because their mind has been investigating spiritual, and unseen, and eternal things, till the very constitution of the mind gives way, and yields under the strain. Peter, probably under the pressure, says, like a wise man—" I go a fishing."

"They say unto him, We also go with thee."
Peter was always accustomed very much to lead them—so they follow. They do not expect the Lord (strange to say)—though it was " in the fourth watch of the *night*" that " Jesus went unto them," when He walked upon the water, and stilled the tempest—they do not expect Him to come *in the night*, they do not

expect Him to come on the lake.   He could come to
them on the lake, as well as on the dry land.   But they
think the Lord will not come at night, and therefore it
would be well to be engaged in an honest trade.

Now, I daresay, that, while I am speaking, many of
you are thinking about the Thessalonians ; you know
they got hold of the expectation of the Lord's personal
coming as being so very near, that they misunderstood,
they misapprehended, the whole thing.   They gave up
everything, and said, " It is of no use building houses,
because the Lord is coming,—it is of no use sowing
seeds, because the Lord is coming,—it is of no use
working at a trade.   We have nothing to do but to
expect the Lord."   That was all *wrong.*   We *are* to
expect Him, but when He comes, He is to find His
servants *doing* the work He gave them, whether it be
ruling a kingdom, or scrubbing a floor, or exercising
any other occupation,—fishing on a lake, or working in
the fields.   When He comes, He expects to find us *at
our post*—not neglecting our work on the expectation
of " His coming."   " If any would not work, neither
should he eat," (2 Thess. iii. 10), says the Apostle afterwards.   So these men go and "*occupy* their business
in the great waters," (Ps. cvii. 23, P. B. V.,) "*till He
come*"—that they may do an honest piece of work,
though they *are* expecting the coming of the Lord.

It all appears, as I said before, to be accidental ; but
it was *not accidental ;* all was most accurately and particularly arranged, by the finger of the Divine Providence.
It was all arranged by the same Providence, that led

them to get into the ship ; and it was by the same Providence, that all the fishes of the sea were kept out of their net all night. They had to learn a lesson that night,—

"That night they caught nothing."

I wonder, as the dawn came on, and the net was still empty—I wonder, whether they thought of that other case, when, a while ago, they had gone forth and " toiled all night and caught nothing," and then had met the Lord next day ; it does not seem as if they did. *It does not seem as if they did*,—and, if they did not, I don't wonder ; yet we ought to mourn, because they were so " slow of heart " to remember when HE had appeared and done them good, and made Himself known as the God of all grace, in days past. Yes,—when new trials come, when new disappointments overtake us, how slow are we to remember another time, when we had great disappointments and great trouble, and yet, " in the morning," we found the Lord was there with the opening light, to take the bitterness out of the disappointment, and to remove the sting out of the trouble and sorrow. They might have remembered it, and if they *had* remembered it, they would have been comforted ; but they appear not to have thought of it.

They " toiled all the night," but they " caught *nothing*." And this is one lesson for us, to-night—they go toiling, all seven of them together,—they go with all their experience as long-experienced, crafty fishermen—they are on a lake abounding in fish, yet *" that night they caught nothing." " I go a-fishing," said Peter,—

"we also go with thee," said the others; but they catch *nothing.* What is the lesson for them and for us? Peter goes on his *own* motion,—they go at *his* suggestion. Something was wanting in order to success. It was *Peter*—"*I* go," and the others "*we* go;" but they catch nothing all the night. There were fishes enough, their nets were good, their ships were good, and they were good fishermen, but "that night they caught nothing." They take nothing by this movement,—they must learn entire dependence.

"But when the morning was now come, Jesus stood on the shore; but the disciples knew not that it was Jesus.

"Then Jesus saith unto them, Children, have ye any meat?"

In other words—"Good people, have you got anything in your ship for sale? Have you any provisions?" It is the voice of one, who seems to be transacting the business of a person going forth to the market—of one who traded on the shore, to get provisions to take to the market. "Good people, have you any provisions amongst you?"

How that must have gone to their heart! how they must have felt it—"Have ye any meat?" How ashamed, and disappointed, and mortified they must have been! and then the pain of having to say "*No.*"

"They answered Him, No."

They, the experienced fisherman of Galilee,—*they*, all seven gone out in one ship, with their sevenfold wisdom to cast the net on the right spot, where it was likely that the fish, at that particular season, would have congregated together—*they*, with all their experience of life, and their seamanship, and their skill—are obliged to answer—" No." " We have toiled all the night, and have taken *nothing*." Here are fishermen, fit to go fishing, well-qualified, thoroughly diligent, knowing the waters they were going on, and yet obliged to say that they have " caught nothing."

How often have we to say this! how often have we to feel this! and how often does our God send forth fishermen to teach them their nothingness—to ask them the same question—to bid them take stock. He asks them to look in their ship, and to examine their net—" Children, have ye any provision there? Have you caught anything? have you laboured and toiled to some purpose? or have you spent your strength for nought? *Who* sent you? on whose motion did you go? who went *with* you? whose strength had you? You went as fishermen of Galilee on your own lake, you have taken nothing where there is plenty; but you must be taught your own impotence, and your unwisdom. Your toil must come to nought, and you be forced to confess it. Have ye anything for the merchantman to carry to town to his fish-stall?"—" They answered Him, No."

"And He said unto them, Cast the net on the right side of the ship, and ye shall find."
Now there is the wanting element come in,—here is just what was wanting before. Peter thought he knew every inch of the sea, he thought he knew every wind from every fissure in the mountains; he knew how to

put the sail, and how to tie the sail, and how to let the sail be untied ; he knew how to steer the craft on the lake, as well as any man in Galilee. " I go a fishing— ' we also go with thee.' We may take something, I will guide you, and we will all go." Jesus has to teach them a great lesson, that was to go down into the hearts of every one of them. He had made them " fishers of men." (St. Mark i. 17). Peter says " *I* will go—*I* will steer the craft ; *you* throw the net where I tell you,"— but " that night they caught nothing."

But now *the Master comes*, Who alone is competent to trim the sails, to guide the ship, and to say where the net should be cast. One element had been want- ing before ; they had not *the command of their Master*, they had not the directions of their Master. *He* did not tell them to go, nor in which direction to go ; He did not promise them His blessing in it. They went on their own motion, and, going on their own motion, they " caught nothing." But now Jesus says, " Cast the net on the *right* side of the ship, and ye shall find." When- ever His word is to cast the net, it is sure to be with a *shall*—" cast the net on the right side of the ship, and ye *shall* find."

It does not appear that they knew, even then, Who He was. He had, perhaps, they thought, seen a move- ment in the waters, some blackening of the waters, or a shoal of fishes, and could point them in that direction, because He, from the shore, could see by a particular light of the sun resting on them. He tells them to " cast the net on the *right* side of the ship."

"**They cast therefore, and now they were not able to draw it for the multitude of fishes.**"

It does not appear, that, because He pointed them to a particular place, they suspected Who He was ; but, when they found that they could not drag the net up— when they find it *immediately* filled—when they found that it was fast, and that they could not draw it, they are obliged to have recourse to something beyond themselves. It is when a man is in difficulty—when he begins to find that he cannot do anything—when he is in anxiety of mind, that he is stirred up. Jesus says to these men, "Cast it *there*," and they think nothing of it; it is a good thought, and they *may* get something,— but, when they stick fast, when they are held, and bound, and tied, as it were, they are *obliged* to think— " Isn't there something more than ordinary in this ? "

"**Therefore that disciple whom Jesus loved saith unto Peter, It is the Lord.**"

We see here what it is that finds out the Lord,—it is the disciple of love, the disciple whose heart was full of love, who knew the love of Jesus, who rested in His bosom. Love has the sharpest sight in the world, and love sees the Lord *first*, and says,—

"**It is the Lord.**"

This is a new vision—the promise " I will go before you into Galilee," (St. Matt. xxvi. 32), is fulfilled ; and then, the old miracle is wrought over again, though with great variety. We see the Lord standing on the side of the lake ; and if we had the time, and if we had the power, to go into it, what a marvellous—*marvellous* sight it is!—Jesus standing on the shore of the lake. Why, what is this—this great sea bound round with just a rope of sand—but a great symbol of all the tribes and kingdoms and nations of all the world? Jesus is seen working *His last miracle*, standing on the brink of the sea, and the fish come out of the sea at His bidding. His disciples know that, without Him, they cannot catch fish, that, without His word, they cannot bring the great net to the shore where Jesus stands. This is a great symbol of what He would do—of the " great multitude " " of all nations, and kindreds, and people, and tongues," (Rev. vii. 9), who shall be brought to stand with Jesus at last.

"Now when Simon Peter heard that it was the Lord, he girt His fisher's coat unto him, (for he was naked),"—

They cannot draw the net, but *Peter*—headstrong Peter—ready, ever ready—with only the little vestment fishermen use when they are fishing, "girt his " outer " coat unto him ;"—as an old father has said, " unmindful of danger, but mindful of reverence," remembering into Whose presence he was coming.

"And did cast himself into the sea."

It was not far, or Peter would have sunk ; it was only about a hundred yards,—but he, at any rate, would be *first with* the Lord.

"And the other disciples came in a little ship; (for they were not far from land, but as it were two hundred cubits), dragging the net with fishes.

"As soon then as they were come to land," what

do they find? **"A fire of coals there, and fish laid thereon, and bread."**

Who had put them there? *Who* had made that provision? *Who* had provided a meal, on the side of the lake, for the toil-worn fishermen the moment they landed?· We think again of Elijah, who was "touched" by the angel, and reminded that "the journey" was "too great" for him, and there was the provision ready. And so it is here.

This points us on to the great Ingathering—to the time when the fishermen will be bidden to let down their nets on the right side, and bring the net to land with every single fish. And there is *one striking difference* between this and the other miracle; in the other miracle, you remember, "the net brake," and a great number must have escaped,—but *here*, they brought *all* safely to land, **"and for all there were so many, yet was not the net broken."**

In the one, we have a picture of the Church *visible*, which has good and bad all mixed together. There were multitudes *in* the net, but many came not to land; the field has "tares" as well as "wheat" in it,— some of the fish go at last into the dread abyss, but some fill the vessel, and are brought safely to shore.

But here, we have a picture of the *invisible*—of the *real* Church of the living God,—all together; those who have been baptized not only with water, but with the Holy Ghost—not those who are merely nominal, but all who are real, Christians.

"Simon Peter went up, and drew the net to land full of great fishes, an hundred and fifty and three."

"*An hundred and fifty and three.*" This is a most wonderful statement! It is one of the most puzzling things in the Gospel, *why* we should be told exactly the number of fishes. Why did they count them? Why did they stop to do that? and why is it of sufficient importance to be put in the Gospel history? I do not know of any explanation but one. Most expositors leave this alone,—but a great naturalist tells us that there are just so many known species of fishes—one hundred and fifty and three; and that, therefore, this was intended to represent the idea of *universality*. That is to say, every nation, every kindred, every tongue, every tribe, shall have its representative at last, and join in the great song—" Thou wast slain, and hast redeemed us to God by Thy Blood, out of EVERY kindred, and tongue, and people, and nation." (Rev. v. 9).

And so they stand on the shore there, with the promise realised; and the Lord says to the disciples,—

"Bring of the fish which ye have now caught."

There was " fish " there, cooked on the fire, there was " bread " already there; but Jesus says—" Bring of the fish which *ye* have caught." So, when they shall sit down to " the marriage supper of the Lamb," He will still say to His Peter, and to His John, and to every " fisher of men "—" Bring of the fish which *ye* have caught,"—to be a " crown of rejoicing " in that great day of glory.

"**Jesus then cometh, and taketh bread, and giveth
them, and fish likewise.**"

And so, when He shall have gathered His people
together at last, He—" the Lamb which is in the midst
of the throne shall feed them," (Rev. vii. 17), as He
promised when He said, " I appoint unto you a kingdom
as My Father hath appointed unto Me, that ye may eat
and drink at My table in My kingdom." (St. Luke xxii.
29, 30).

And now, in bringing these Lectures to a close—we
have been permitted to consider the more prominent of
the thirty-three Miracles,* recorded in the Gospel history
—the question for each one of us is, Have we *understood*
all these things ?   Have we had our spirit enlightened
to see what great lessons there are for us all, in them ?
Have we been brought as the poor leper—" Lord, if
Thou wilt, Thou canst make me clean ? "   Have we
come like ˙ the poor Syro-phœnician mother—" My
daughter is grievously vexed with a devil ? " ·Have we
come like the unbelieving believer—" Master, I have
brought unto *Thee* my son ? "   Have we been brought,
like the paralytic, to hear the word—" Son—Daughter,
—be of good cheer ; thy sins be forgiven thee ? "
Have we, as we have gone step by step through these
Miracles, had the word brought home, by the Holy

* For the Demoniac of Gadara, and for Bartimæus, see " Notes
of Open-Air Sermons," Nos. I. and III.

Spirit, to our consciences, and to our hearts? Have we found there the image of *ourselves*—and the image of our Blessed Master, ever ready to speak the word of salvation, to give sight to the blind, hearing to the deaf, life even to the dead?

Then we shall, like these, be brought *safe to land* in the great Day of Ingathering—even as that great multitude of fishes was, in the day that Jesus stood by the side of the Galilæan Lake.

THE END.

Sanson & Co., Printers, Edinburgh.

51